PENGUIN BOOKS

East of Croydon

East of Croydon

Travels through South East Asia

SUE PERKINS

PENGUIN BOOKS

PENGUIN BOOKS

UK | USA | Canada | Ireland | Australia
India | New Zealand | South Africa

Penguin Books is part of the Penguin Random House group of companies
whose addresses can be found at global.penguinrandomhouse.com

First published by Michael Joseph 2018
Published in Penguin Books 2019
001

Set in 12.01/14.33 pt Garamond MT Std
Typeset by Jouve (UK), Milton Keynes
Printed and bound in Great Britain by Clays Ltd, Elcograf S.p.A.

A CIP catalogue record for this book is available from the British Library

ISBN: 978–1–405–93814–3

The documentaries mentioned in this book are *The Mekong River with Sue Perkins*, and *Kolkata with Sue Perkins*, both produced by Indus Films, and *The Ganges with Sue Perkins*, produced by Folk Films. All broadcast by the BBC.

For Dad
in the deep heart's core

If you never did you should
these things are fun
and fun is good.

Dr Seuss

Contents

Laos

China

India

The Ganges

Introduction

I am deep within the forest, the raw heat of the day softened by the canopy above. The man in front of me is swaying, a gobbet of raw pig's liver hanging from his ear. Another man, to his left, has what looks like a piece of lung adorning his fringe. As I draw nearer, someone flicks a bit of kidney in my direction, which hits the white of my eye and bounces off again. Nearer still and the tribesmen rush to adorn my shoulders with offal, a ventricle here, a pancreas there. I think I can make out a spleen on my shirt collar, but am not sure. I was never any good at biology.

I am the only sober person in the forest.

Further offerings are made to the spirits, to the ancestors they believe inhabit this ancient land. A bubbling handful of intestines is respectfully arranged on a makeshift shrine. Men, and it is only men here, bob and bow – though I'm not sure whether this is down to reverence or simple intoxication.

The village elder is sitting next to a giant bottle, the glass stained with green fur. Inside is a strange liquid which smells like a holy trinity of gasoline, semen and Pimm's. For all I know, it may well contain all three.* One by one, the celebrants are invited to suck on the thick pipe that snakes from the murk. Some cough into the bottle as they drink. Some

* I am unaware of the global outreach of the Pimm's brand, but I am reliably informed the other two ingredients are readily available in South East Asia.

spit. Finally, the chief stares in my direction, his eyes glazed with grog. He beckons me over.

It is my turn.

The crew are some distance away, shooting on a long lens. I look towards them. It's the look of a woman who is about to cross every health and safety threshold she once held dear; a woman about to be exposed to the full spectrum of gastro-intestinal diseases known to man, and a few hitherto yet unidentified by medical science. It's a look that simply says, *Help me.*

I know that a choice is presenting itself. I can play the squeamish Westerner, protect the delicate flora of my intestinal tract and offend a bunch of festive animists. Or I can be another person, a different Susan – a fearless explorer, embracing with open hands and open heart a strange new world.

I know the sort of person I am. So I try to be the opposite.

I steel myself. It is simply a case of mind over matter. I accept the blessings of the forest. I accept the glistening unknown in the vat beneath. I accept it all. Then, as I bend towards the liquid, breathing in its oily reek, someone leans over and pops a chunk of pig bowel on the end of the straw.

And I drink.

1. Journeys Past

Historically, the Perkins tribe were neither explorers, nor adventurers. Dad, in a moment of genealogical fervour, traced his family tree back two hundred years and discovered that all the men had been either labourers or soldiers, and all the women charladies. None of my ancestors got the chance to leave the UK, unless, of course, it was to offer up a limb or two at Gallipoli. Dad broke the mould, venturing as far as Kingston, Jamaica, while on National Service – but he was so terrified by the flora and fauna he vowed never to leave the shores of Britannia again.

'The crabs, Susan! The crabs! They were the size of land-mines!' he'd recall hysterically – as if the crustaceans would prove the more dangerous factor in that equation.

Mum was a little more intrepid. She had travelled to Ibiza in her mid-twenties, but pronounced it 'not Spanish enough' and returned a week later, disappointed.*

Our parents didn't do 'foreign', and hated sleeping in 'strange beds', so we tended to holiday places where you could arrive and return on the same day. These trips were planned with military precision, like Navy SEALs – and felt more like tactical strikes than mini-breaks. Occasionally, we visited my grandparents in their 117th-floor flat in Torremolinos. It must have been just 'Spanish enough' for my mum because we

* Mum had never been to Spain before, so I'd be interested to know what she was comparing it with.

went twice. We'd get sunburn, drink Fanta, ride on a poor, beleaguered donkey in Mihas then fly home.

When I was fourteen I went to Jersey with the Children's Youth Theatre and got fingered on a ferry by a boy named Michael. At eighteen, I went to the east coast of America, got mugged and came straight home again. At twenty-one I went on a week's trip to Madeira and drank vodka in an underwhelming villa with sea views so distant they stretched the very bounds of trade description.

See, I told you – *not* adventurous.

I'd never been one for leaving the comforts of home. That person wasn't me, I didn't spent my formative years youth-hostelling round Rwanda, or climbing Everest in a tie-dye playsuit to raise awareness of something or other. After all, why visit the Bora Bora crater, when you can stay right where you are and enjoy Netflix and salt and vinegar crisps?

As an adult, the obsessive dynamics of self-employment meant it was impossible for me to take a break. What would happen if I disappeared for a week or two? I would be forgotten. For ever. A once-in-a-lifetime opportunity would, doubtless, present itself – and I would miss the chance to seize it. That six-part series on krumping? *Britain's Best Kettles*? *Eamonn Holmes Under the Hammer*? I'd never get those jobs if I went away. No. Best stay here, alert and primed at home in London, and wait.

And then something wonderful happened – work itself afforded me the chance to go away. Finally I got to leave my desk with a clear conscience.

In 2013, I was asked if I'd like to make a documentary about the Mekong river, following it for over four thousand kilometres from Vietnam all the way to the snowy peaks of

Tibet. It had been a dark, difficult year. Poor Dad had been sick with throat cancer, and our days were spent bombing up and down the A30, taking him to and from his daily radiotherapy sessions. He was now in remission, but the treatment seemed not only to have shrunk his tumour but his horizons. Now, he rarely left the house, content only to explore the already-explored, the safe, the pre-experienced – the familiar poles of armchair, bed and dining table. Occasionally his swollen legs would carry him as far as the biscuit tin and back. That would be a good day.

I agreed to the trip. Perhaps, deep down, I felt I would be travelling for him. And for Mum too – who has an adventurer's heart but a carer's role, glued to her partner through times, of late, more thin than thick, and certainly more in sickness than in health.

There was another reason. I have a voice inside me, a voice that drives me to darkness. It dims the lights, it drains the colour, it turns the sound down. It calls me in when I want to be out; it tells me to expect the worst, rather than hope for the best. To travel is to quieten that voice, to know that it cannot and will not control me.

I take after my dad: he feels too much and cannot cope.

I take after my mum – constantly fretful in times of safety but stoic in a crisis.

We're all contradictory souls at heart – a mix of intrepid and afraid, outgoing and solitary. The measure of your sanity, I guess, is where you draw the line between those poles. Perhaps this adventure would give me the chance for some much needed recalibration.

So, even though I was frightened, I said yes. I will always say yes. I will throw myself into every experience, I will accept every dare,* I will agree to maddening offers and crazy adventures.

Yes.

~~~

I've said I take after my mum. This seems like a good moment to introduce you to the nine-stone bag of true grit that is Ann Perkins.

I grew up, as is a matter of public record, in the charming hamlet of Croydon. If you've not been, and want to conjure the aesthetics of the place, imagine a long scream into oblivion that has been commemorated in concrete. Architecturally, it was a curious mix of brutalism and the worst excesses of 1980s office building – as you approach by train, it looks like the skyline has been designed by a pre-school competition winner.

But I was young: I didn't care for beauty. I craved the important things in life, like cheap cider, knock-off fags and newsagents with a lackadaisical approach to security. In that regard, Croydon gave me everything I needed, and it was a blissful childhood.

We lived in a house on a bank. The house was called High Bank. I admire the simple, honest pragmatism of that nomenclature. It's like calling the Houses of Parliament 'Swinging Dick Palace' or Trump Towers 'Look Upon My Gold Toilet And Weep, O Migrants'.

* Once, in Menorca, I got dared to jump off a vertical cliff face some thirty metres above the sea. I did. As the saying goes, how you fall doesn't matter. It's how you land. I hit the water at an odd angle and shattered my coccyx.
~~~

I digress. Because the bank was, indeed, high, it meant that mowing the lawn was hard – unless, that is, you're my mum. Ann Perkins is undeterred by petty inconveniences like gravity. For her, gravity is just another thing to be overcome – like stress incontinence and Dr Liam Fox.

Mum had pioneered a revolutionary system for trimming grass on a gradient. This involved tying a long loop of string around the handle of the Flymo, letting the machine trundle down the bank and then pulling on the string to haul it back up.

What could possibly go wrong?

It was a rainy day.

I could end the story there, couldn't I? I could simply let your imagination fill in the blanks and save us all the horror – but both literary form and the contractual necessity that this book is 90,000 words long mean I should now elaborate further on the scene.

It was a rainy day, and Mum decided that, what with the ground being sodden and extra slippy, this might, indeed, be the perfect day to go out and cut some grass. I watched her from my bedroom window, striding out into the mizzle. There was the sharp stink of two-stroke and a thin plume of black smoke as she fired up the Flymo. Then off she went.

The next thing I heard was a cry – hard and fast – the sort of cry that has gone before it arrives. The sort of cry that lets you know something is seriously, seriously wrong.

I found Mum slumped at the bottom of the bank in the mud holding her foot and muttering. I approached. It was then I noticed that the trainer on her right foot had been sliced off, and, by reason, her toes along with it.

'David!' I shouted. 'Call an ambulance!' thereby simultaneously sounding in charge while not having to actually do anything. This is what is known as Eldest Child Syndrome.

'David!' I shouted again. He was nowhere to be seen.

My sister, Michelle, appeared and took in the scene. Rather than moving to help, she felt the best contribution she could make was to scream into Mum's face.

MICHELLE: Oh, God!
ME: David!
MICHELLE: Oh, no!
ME: David!
MICHELLE: Shit! Fuck!

That's when I knew things were really bad. My mum hates swearing, and even now isn't averse to dragging me into the bathroom and anointing the inside of my mouth with the cleansing fire of Imperial Leather. The fact that she was getting a full four-letter fanning without batting an eyelid was of genuine concern.

The commotion had, by now, attracted a few local kids who had pulled up on their bikes. My sister responded by rushing down the steps and directing the abuse at them instead.

MICHELLE: No! Get lost! Go on! Piss off!

David had now arrived, and was sizing up the situation.

DAVID: FUCK!

It was an excellent summary.

MICHELLE: Yes, you! Go on, fuck off!
DAVID: FUUCK!

This carried on for several minutes, after which I decided it might be a good time to call the ambulance myself. It took nearly five minutes to explain to the bemused operator what had happened:

OPERATOR: She was mowing. In the rain. On a *bank*?

I returned with some advice.

ME: David, we need to find the toes.
DAVID: What?
ME: Find them! Find the toes!

That's a role nobody wants, isn't it? Chief toe-finder. Toefinder General.

I bellowed again.

ME: David! Pick up the toes!

I felt it was more of a boy job, something that someone with a Y-chromosome should take care of. I was young. I was yet to learn about the toxicity of gender roles. David picked his way gingerly through the grass.

DAVID: Is that a big toe? Is it? JESUS!

While we waited for the paramedics, Mum eased into one of her favourite emotional states – martyrdom: Saint Ann of the Bleeding Feet became calm, a preternatural serenity descending over her

MUM: I don't know what the fuss is all about. I am totally fine.
ME: Mum, there's blood pouring out of your foot.
MUM: Nonsense.
MICHELLE: It's like a fountain.

MUM: Don't worry about me, it's nothing that a bit of Savlon won't sort out.

ME: Since when did Savlon glue toes together?

DAVID: (*spotting something pink and shiny in the grass*) Oh, God! Oh, God. Fuck!

She hopped into the ambulance, aided by a pair of paramedics. They were about to learn that Mum is the John Lewis of chat. Even with a severed foot, she is never knowingly under-talked. Once seated inside, she chose to display her home-economics prowess by randomly listing everything lurking within our chest freezer. She loved that freezer and was the only person on earth who could identify the grey cellophane-wrapped rubble buried in the permafrost.

MUM: (*clutching what's left of her foot as her face turns green*) OK. Dinner tonight. There's mince. You could do that with boiled potatoes or some pasta.

PARAMEDIC: Ann . . .

MUM: And there's bound to be a Bernard Matthews turkey roll in there somewhere. Let me think . . .

(*Mum consults her Menu Mind Palace.*)

MUM: Yes. Left section, underneath the Crispy Pancakes.

ME: Is her face supposed to be that colour?

MUM: Or you could have prawns.

ME: It's really green . . .

MUM: And there's that kilo block of Cathedral Cheddar. Mature. But, remember, no broccoli or courgette.

ME: I know . . .

MUM: It messes with your father's bowel.

ME: I KNOW.

MUM: Viennetta for pudding. That's in the bottom compartment. Oh, and, Susan . . .

ME: Yes?

MUM: Don't, whatever you do, tell Dad where I am.

ME: What?

MUM: He's not to know.

ME: Well, what am I supposed to tell him? Where shall I say you are?

MUM: Knitting class.

PARAMEDIC: Ann, I'm sorry to interrupt, but I'm afraid you're going to be in hospital at least a week with an injury like this.

MUM: Right you are. OK, lace class then, that's more involved. Say I'm making an intricate bookmark.

ME: You've gone away for a fortnight, without notice – making an intricate bookmark?

MUM: Do you know, I think I might have some of that gas and air now . . .

And with that, the paramedic, who had been waiting patiently for Mum to pause for breath, popped a mask over her face and whisked her to Mayday Hospital.

2. What's It All About?

I've never been sure where holidays end and true travel begins. Perhaps the distinction lies in a deeper engagement with the local people, a lengthier, immersive stay in communities. Perhaps, more simply, it has something to do with the inherent difference between a rucksack and a suitcase. I don't know. All I know is that holidays weren't much my thing – I don't tan and I'm not built for staying still – but travel, well, that turned out to be something altogether different.

I know I look like a proper square; a total cube. But underneath that nerdish topcoat I am someone who eschews order for chaos. Routine is my nightmare, and the unexpected is my safe space. Nothing makes me happier than being thrown in at the deep end, and nothing excites me more than a journey where the destination is organic and unfixed. It turns out that what I'd been looking for all these years wasn't a mini-break, but a proper adventure.

There is a strange tendency among us TV presenters to pretend we know it all, adopting a mask of clear-cut professionalism and unquestionable authority. Of course, if that were really true, if we had any real authority, we'd have proper jobs and not be preening about on the goggle box. My travels taught me the most invaluable lesson of all: I'm a fool. So why not save time and be honest about it? To pretend otherwise borders on proper stupidity.

Instead of meeting a hostile tribe in a highland rainforest clearing and acting like it's all rather familiar, I want to own my ignorance. I want to learn everything, feel everything, acknowledge my fortunate, cushioned existence, in the face of those who struggle.

The most glorious and the most difficult thing about my job is that I get to observe. I get to watch some of the most exciting, breath-taking and curious things on the planet; I also get to watch some of the most cruel and heart-breaking things too.

I often think about war photographers, capturing that moment when the bullet pierces a skull, when the napalm ignites a village – and I have always wondered, 'Did you hang around just waiting for that moment? Why didn't you intervene? Why didn't you do something? Did commemorating that suffering for posterity, so that others might learn from it, ameliorate the fact you stood by and did nothing?'

I ask myself that question. Sometimes I have had to watch impossibly difficult and painful scenarios: death, abuse, cruelty, grinding poverty. Sometimes I, too, did nothing. Sometimes there was nothing to do. Other times the reality was that the only job I had, the only positive contribution I could make, was to observe, to hear the testimonies, to bear witness.

Some of the things I encountered were too traumatic for screening, too awful to show. There seemed no purpose to broadcasting suffering without context or solution. Equally, sometimes things were too silly and childish to warrant the edit. But even if television's lens can't encompass it all, if the frame only captures a corner of the experience, the human eye sees the full panorama. I saw everything.

Here it is.

3. It's Not All My Fault

In my head, television is made like this: I go to a place. I eat food, get drunk, have a dance – I share an intimate cultural moment with a stranger. I might even cry. Then, I go home.

Six months later, as if by magic, it appears on the telly.

I've since been told that there is an awful lot more to making a show than popping this old meat puppet in front of a camera. So, before we begin, let me introduce you to the team who really make it happen.

I haven't changed their names because they are *far* from innocent.

Steve. Steve is the boss. He is the Charlie to our Angels but 25 per cent more real. Steve and I have a lot in common. He despises television and all it stands for – and so do I. Steve is obsessed with television and all it stands for – and so am I.

Steve is a media Eeyore. He doesn't just worry that the sky is falling in, but that the sky is falling in and the industry is so rapidly deskilling he might not have a decent enough crew to make a six-part BAFTA-winning documentary series about it.

Steve loves surfing, his family and anything to do with Wales. He is super-clever. Like, *super*-clever. He has a particular interest in the intricacies of rural agribusiness, and films directed by him will invariably feature sequences devoted to nuanced farming techniques in the middle of nowhere. Steve cannot understand why I don't share his fascination for all things agricultural, and when he sighs on set

I know that he is dreaming of working with a proper presenter who asks about the complexities of irrigation in terrace systems and doesn't just make fart jokes in a forest.

Olly is our sound guy. He's a rarity in the business, as he actually listens to every word that's recorded. I know that for a fact, because, after a twenty-minute piece to camera about religion in Angkor Wat, Cambodia, he turned to me and said, 'What the fuck was all that about?' You see? All ears.

Olly has seen things a human being should never see – namely the contents of my trousers. His job is, essentially, to stick wires where the sun don't shine. As a result, he is very familiar with all my catchphrases, such as 'Remember I always go commando' and 'Sorry, I forgot to shave again.'

Olly has an anecdote for all occasions, which comes in handy when you're spending every waking hour with someone for weeks on end. Sometimes I love his stories so much, I'll make him repeat them again and again – like the time he went for a run in Tokyo and got lost for thirteen hours. Or the time he detonated a BBC controller's conservatory in a rather over-zealous fireworks display.

Olly's superpower is his packing capacity. He brings everything, and I mean everything. I once saw him casually bring out a NutriBullet in the Sunderbans (the low-lying islands on the border of India and Bangladesh), attach it to the loose plug socket and pull, from a waterproof pouch, some diced melon, a punnet of raspberries and a handful of chia seeds.

Matt, our cameraman, is a cherubic Bristolian with a dazzling array of neckerchiefs. I have never heard him swear. Ever. Once, he was filming some monkeys playing on a bridge in Rishikesh. One had nicked an Hermès scarf from a passing tourist, and was trying to put it on. Matt laughed so hard that the monkey dropped the scarf and ran towards him, baring his teeth in full attack mode. Still, no swearing.

Matt makes the world look beautiful. However shocking and saddening the environment, he will always find a way to bring out the dignity of people or the richness of the landscape.

He's also amazing at walking backwards – trusting that the assistant guiding him by his belt loops will keep him from harm, warn him when a step is approaching, and steer him past the inevitable piles of dog, pig and cow shit. Eighty-seven per cent of the time his trust is well placed. In the 13 per cent likelihood that he will end up tumbling into cack, he always has a spare pair of trainers at the ready.

Matt's superpower is that he is able to find spaghetti bolognese wherever he is in the world, be it remote hill tribe or floating village. Also, he is very good at making sure the colour saturation settings on his camera minimize my jowls. And for that, if nothing else, he is family to me.

Vicky is super-model tall and, quite simply, the best producer in the world. Vicky lives her life according to her own special lexicon, where the word 'No' doesn't exist. The phrases 'I'm really tired', 'Should we really be eating that?' and 'I'm not sure that's entirely safe' are also, seemingly, not recognized.

You can go to Vicky in the middle of the night and she will have whatever you need to fix stuff. She'll put up a mosquito net in the pitch dark, she'll diagnose and treat minor ailments – she'll even accompany you for a wee at 2 a.m. in the middle of a Tibetan plain to make sure the wild dogs don't eat you.

Vicky's superpower is that she is never fazed. Not even

when you make her come round to your room at three in the morning saying you can't sleep because of the noise of the electricity pylons. Not even when she has to break it to you that the noise is merely cicadas and that we are in a rural hamlet hundreds of miles from an electricity substation.

Steve and Vicky were aided by a team of brilliant assistant producers and researchers whose job was twofold:

First, they had to lie to me – 24/7.

1. If the walk is long, tell me it's short.
2. If I see a snake, tell me it's not a snake but a piece of rope with diamond markings on its back that is moving in the breeze.
3. If I ask how long the day is going to be, tell me it's nearly done.
4. If I ask why the hotel has no running water or electricity, tell me it's an off-grid paradise where I can truly commune with nature.

Then, when all these things turn out to be untrue and I start grumbling, the second phase of their job kicks in.

Feed me. Just feed me.

Then, and only then, will I shut up.

This book is for them, the production team and crew, and for all the local guides, fixers, drivers, porters and helpers who made life better for us during our travels.

Thank you.

Vietnam

4. That Noo-dle That You Do So Well

I landed at Ho Chi Minh City, wheeling a suitcase so large it looked like I was using it to perform a magic trick.

'Ladies and gentlemen, as you can see, my assistant is now locked inside the Samsonite, and if you walk around you will see there is no way for her to get in or out. Now let's see whether she can survive the baggage-handling.'

I was the furthest east I'd ever been, if you exclude the time I took mushrooms and thought I was one of Kubla Khan's handmaidens.

I was the furthest in *any* direction I'd ever been.

A gaggle of can-do Vietnamese lads were there to meet me outside the airport terminal, but even they struggled to load my outsized luggage onto the van. I am willing to admit that I had somewhat over-packed, and that the industrial waders, oxygen tent and satellite tracking system may have been a bridge too far.

I got into the back of their jeep and we drove around for what felt like hours. Ten miles or so into the journey, it struck me that I had no idea where I was going, who these people were and whether, indeed, I'd even got into the right car. Still, I wasn't fazed, thanks to the diazepam I'd necked some thirty-nine thousand feet above Ukraine. I am terrified of flying, you see – but I do it nonetheless (screw you, scared, sad voice within).

That night I lay on a lumpy hostel mattress for six hours and pretended to sleep, my senses struggling to adjust to the thick, hot air and the frenzied airborne traffic of insects and birds. This continent was going to be my home for the next three thousand miles: I'd better start getting used to it.

The next morning we headed to Can Tho, where I transferred onto a wooden boat with a precarious motor dangling from its rear like an industrial haemorrhoid. It was time to start filming.

Up to that point, my combined seafaring experiences had been:

- Getting on the Woolwich Ferry with my nan, *c.* 1976.
- Crossing the Irish Sea.
- Taking a pedalo out in Málaga.

Looking back at that footage, I can remember how out of my depth I felt. I couldn't get my bearings. I couldn't put words to the sensory bombardment. I was so bewildered and excited you can barely make out what I'm saying amid the gabble.

On the delta's edge was some of the most precarious real estate I'd ever seen – rows of wooden shacks perched on bamboo stilts, the walls and roofs clad with a patchwork of tarpaulin, rice bags and corrugated metal. Not one single element of their construction had been fashioned in a straight line. In fact, the houses all looked like they'd fallen from the sky and crumpled on impact with the river bed.

Our vessel nudged the edge of one of the dwellings, and came to an abrupt halt. I made a rather ungainly leap from the boat onto the rickety stairs leading to the main platform, which seemed to have been constructed at a near-forty-five-degree angle. The whole structure creaked and wobbled as I entered.

'Hi, I'm Sue,' I said, in execrable Vietnamese.

A woman roared with laughter, her mouth widening to reveal a somewhat sparse assembly of teeth.

'Di Hei,' she replied, and hugged me.

How lovely, I thought, as I melted into her. Someone who is as tactile as I am. I love her already.

Arm in arm, we wandered further into the house. Her entire extended family were there to greet me.

I could have headed home that day and, in that snapshot, had a microcosm of everything I would witness in Asia over the next few years. The wife, bent double over the fire, her face burnished by a lifetime of wood-smoke. The silent, sick husband, looking out over the water with that thousand-yard stare. The whip-thin kids, running everywhere, the backs of their heads routinely slapped by a legion of aunties, uncles and grandparents. A million shiny black pupils trained on you, looking at the vastness of you, the wealth of you. Looking at what you were and what you had. At everything you had.

I looked down at my new shoes, purchased online for their robust waterproof capability. Everyone around me was barefoot, their toenails eroded to nothing by the acidity of the river water. I watched the kids, deft and graceful, sprint across the narrow wooden beams that connected the houses. I looked down at my bloated belly, courtesy of a defunct pituitary and unwise dietary decisions. I felt embarrassed about a lifetime of softness, of ease. I felt like a pappy, white giant.

I said my hellos to the assembled clan and launched, unbidden, into a hi-energy game of pat-a-cake with the youngest grandchild, who was so cute she was in danger of detonating my ovaries.

The room contained several makeshift sleeping platforms, all of which appeared to be adjustable. This proved to be essential, as during the monsoon the river levels are so high, the water flows right through the house.

'The more it comes up, the higher we make our bed,' said Di Hei, pragmatically.

She pointed to the tidemarks on the bedposts where the river had come and gone.

ME: Do you notice the climate changing?

I was desperate to impress upon Steve that his new presenter was capable of sticking to the environmental message of the film, and not just there to hug random children.

DI HEI: It's the highest it has ever been this year.

She pointed to a line some four feet above the mattress.

ME: But that line's almost at the ceiling! What if the water keeps on rising? Where do you sleep?

She gestured towards the roof and laughed. She started miming swimming. Then she did an impression of someone drowning. It was starting to feel like a rather twisted, climate-change edition of *Give Us A Clue*.

And then, before the atmosphere gave way to darkness, she laughed that toothless laugh again, and reached over to hug me.

We returned the next morning at the edge of first light, the moon and sun still fighting over the sky. All was silent, except for the sound of our oars cutting through the water. By the time we reached the opposite bank, the moon had conceded and a thin band of yellow light on the horizon had begun to illuminate the way ahead.

My first thought as I ventured inside was *Jesus, this building's on fire* – black smoke billowed through the tarpaulin roof and the cracks in the timber. *There can't be any survivors in this heat and smoke. No one could survive this conflagration.* I gestured down to Steve, but he seemed unconcerned and waved me onwards.

A familiar face materialized through the acrid plumes.

'*Xin chao!*' I bellowed at it. '*Xin chao!*'

'*Xin chao!*' muttered the face, vignetted in carbon. Then a bony hand appeared, grabbed my wrist and dragged me forwards into the murk.

My eyes tickled as they adjusted to the culinary inferno raging around me.

It was four thirty in the morning. Di Hei had already been up, cooking, for at least two hours. On the floor, vast iron pots of pungent grey broth sat bubbling over the open flames. There was a selection of boiled meats, grey, beige, yellow, and more grey. There were buckets of white noodles and a dazzling array of condiments. The smoke was burning the inside of my nostrils and I was starting to fight for breath. Through the gaps in the floorboards, I could dimly make out the acrid water lapping just centimetres beneath. I guess this was as close to a fire safety measure as we were going to get.

The little girl approached. I wanted to play with her again, but it became clear from Di Hei's percussive tuts that there was no time for chat. We had work to do.

The Di Hei I met that morning was a different woman altogether. Gone were the easy laughs and constant hugging. This Di Hei was thrillingly strict. She was there for one thing, and one thing only – business.

The cooking seemed to be finished. She slapped my arms briskly and bellowed into my face, her eyes sparkling like embers.

The translation came back.

DI HEI: OK! You! Time to sell!

I gulped nervously.

~

I am useless at selling. Always have been. That may come as a surprise to you, since I'm a trappy little bastard – but, in truth, I lack the killer instinct and retain a distinct cynicism about the eternal quest for material wealth. I have had minimal sales experience, but what I have had, I have loathed with every fibre of my being.

The moment I finished my A levels, I wanted to work. I wanted to get as far away from a desk and a book as possible. Being young and naive, it hadn't really occurred to me that there might possibly be a disconnect between *wanting* to do something and *being capable* of doing something.

I answered a rather shady ad in the *Croydon Advertiser*, which promised MAXIMUM WAGES! and MINIMUM TRAINING! As a diehard fan of both of those concepts, especially in conjunction with one another, I rang the number provided, and was connected to a man named Gary, in deepest Addiscombe.

Throughout our conversation Gary sounded like he was running a marathon. Angrily. He said something about turning up the next morning to his house for a briefing, before putting the phone down mid-wheeze.

The next morning my mate Neil dropped me off at the estate. There was a gaggle of weedy-looking blokes outside Gary's house, waiting. As I walked up to join them, I noticed the car in the driveway was on bricks. After a few minutes,

Gary wandered out, like a prize-fighter greeting his adoring crowd, and sat atop the bonnet, his expansive belly quivering before him.

'Right,' he said, his gelatinous gut finally juddering to a halt over the waistband of his jeans.

GARY: Good mornin', one and all. You don't know it yet, but you lot is my crack team.

Are we? I thought. Really? But I don't know them. And I don't know you. And you still sound angry, even though you are technically smiling.

GARY: I was standing where you is now. I didn't have nothing. Not a sausage. Now, I can do whatever I want. I'm me own boss. Isn't that right?
ALL: Yes, Gary.

We just came out with it. All of us. In unison. Christ, this is how cults get started. One minute you're in an estate in south London agreeing with a stranger, next you're in a poly-amorous commune making potato prints of your beloved leader.

Gary started up again.

GARY: What's the secret of selling?

Nobody responded. I suspect we all knew that a reply was superfluous since Gary was inevitably going to tell us.

GARY: Get in their house. Get. In. Their. House. Got it?
US: Get. In. Their. House.
GARY: Once you're in the house – you done it.
US: OK, Gary.
GARY: I ain't finished. You get in, you give 'em a quote, get their details, and get out sharpish. Once you done

that, old Gary here gets on the blower to 'em and works his magic.

As he sat there, perched on the bonnet, legs akimbo, it struck me that I still had no idea what the job entailed. Or what Gary's 'magic' involved.

GARY: Here's your script.

Excellent. Now we're in business. I know where I am with a script.

GARY: Don't mug me off by just learning it. You 'ave to be it. Be it!

He smashed the palm of his hand against his chest. I watched his moobs vibrating. He really was mesmerizing.

He handed us a sheet of paper. I looked down at it.

Nu-Again Carpet Cleaner. Make YOUR carpets Nu-Again.

OK, I thought. It's not *Hamlet* but I can do this.

Gary sparked up a Benson's and embarked on the three-minute monologue that was to encompass our training.

GARY: Right, time to get into the technical details. I'm gonna show you how to measure up and do the quote once you got in the house . . . Cos what you gotta do?

ALL: Get. In. Their. House.

GARY: That's more like it.

I arrived back the next morning in a howling gale. Gary was already outside, in a Metallica singlet, marshalling the troops. Three of the lads were no-shows, making eight of us in total.

GARY: OK. You all good?

ALL: Yes, Gary.

GARY: Yous ready to go?

ALL: Yes, Gary.

GARY: Course you are, you fucking legends.

Out of nowhere, a Transit van burst into view. It clipped the kerb as it came round the bend and screeched to a halt in front of us.

Gary flushed with excitement.

GARY: What you waiting for? Geddin!

We pulled the rusty door to the side and climbed in. We were the household-solvent branch of Special Forces. We were ready.

'Have you learnt this?' said a pale bloke to the left of me.

'Yes,' I said, almost entirely smugly. I have a photographic memory, so I'm lucky in that department.

'I don't know it,' said a guy at the back.

'Me neither,' said another. 'You're not supposed to – remember?'

There were assorted grunts from behind.

Gary turned around from the passenger seat and addressed the crew. As motivational speeches go, it fell some way short of the full Henry on St Crispin's Day.

GARY: You know what you gotta do, don't ya, lads?

US: Get in.

GARY: Yeah. You get it. Every house you get in, you get a quid.

Finally, the salary details!

GARY: You get the most quids, you get on Gary's leader board.

He pulled out a small whiteboard, on which seemed to be

scrawled the remnants of a shopping list. Someone in the family really liked Crispy Pancakes.

Great, I thought. I've got this. I've memorized the speech. I'm way ahead of the curve. I'll be in twenty houses by lunch, that's twenty quid, that's seven packs of Marlboro Lights.*

After ten minutes or so the van came to a sudden halt and we all piled out.

GARY: See you later, you killers! Look at ya! You're gonna smash it! We'll pick you up at five.

A puff of black exhaust smoke and he was gone.

I looked around me. I was in another estate, much larger than the first. It struck me that I had no clue where I actually was.

The group fractured. The most eager got the houses nearby, the more sluggish, like me, had to wander a few roads down to avoid covering the same patch. Think door-to-door sales version of *The Hunger Games* and you'll get the general gist.

I walked up the path to my first house, steadied myself, then rang the doorbell. I heard footsteps from within. I took a deep breath as the door opened, and began, in my crispest RP:

ME: Hi there, I just happen to be in the area today . . .

There was a gust of air as the door slammed in my face.

OK, I thought, undeterred. Of course some people are going to be a little resistant to this stuff – we're at the cutting edge of shagpile rehabilitation after all. I tried the next house along.

ME: Hi there!

MAN: NO, thank you.

* At this point in my life I measured everything in packets of Marlboro Lights.

Slam.

And the next house

ME: Hi . . .
WOMAN: Who are you?
ME: I just happen to be in the area . . .

Slam.

And so it went on. All. Day.

Like Liam Neeson in *Taken*, I have a unique set of skills. Sadly, the vast majority of them are not transferrable to practical situations. No one ever got lost and asked for the person who does stumpwork embroidery of butterflies. No air stewardess ever shouted on a plane 'Is there someone onboard who can play Beethoven sonatas?' I was useless. Utterly useless.

To compound the misery, around about 1 p.m. I discovered that I'd forgotten to bring any lunch, so I wandered around from house to house all afternoon with my stomach an angry and acidic mess.

At half past four, tired from the endless wandering and sick with hunger, I rang on yet another doorbell. A dog barked. The sort of bark that little dogs make when they want to sound bigger and more frightening. The door opened and a Cavalier King Charles Spaniel reared up and started licking my kneecaps.

WOMAN: Oh, she likes you.
ME: Aah, she's very sweet.
WOMAN: How can I help?

I cleared my throat.

ME: Hi, I just happen to be in the area and wondered do you happen to have carpets?

This was the first time anyone had let me get my first full

sentence out without slamming the door. I could now see what a ridiculous opening gambit it was.

WOMAN: Well, yes – we do.

I thought of the next line in my script: *Did you know that there's a cleaner that can restore your carpets to Day One freshness – for just a fraction of the cost of buying new. For just £29.99 we can clean your entire house – but, remember, we're only here for today and tomorrow, so you'll need to act fast.*

I thought of that line, and I looked at that sweet lady with her sweet dog and thought, *I can't do this.*

She seemed to sense the existential crisis raging within me.

WOMAN: Are you OK? Can I help at all?

I responded suddenly, without thinking.

ME: Yes! You can let me in your house. Just for a minute. I know that sounds mad, but I'm not a nutter, I promise. I'm supposed to be selling carpet cleaner and if you let me into your house I can earn a pound and it'll be the first pound I've earned all day and I'm so incredibly hungry.

WOMAN: Sure.

And, to my utter surprise, she ushered me in.

WOMAN: Would you like a biscuit?

ME: Yes, please.

I felt like crying.

She showed me through into her living room. *Gosh, these carpets DO need a clean*, I thought. I immediately recoiled. That wasn't the sort of thing I would ever think. Gary was getting to me. He was already in my head.

WOMAN: So, what do you need to get your pound?

ME: Well, I need to assess the space and give you a quote.

I had amended the script and put in the word 'assess' as I thought that sounded more professional.

ME: I'll take your number, if that's OK, and a man called Gary will call you to see if you want to take it any further.

WOMAN: OK. But I don't have to take it any further?

ME: No.

Although I would – that deep pile is filthy. SHUT UP, GARY, SHUT UP.

WOMAN: Great. Now I'll get you that biscuit – I can hear your tummy from here.

ME: Thank you. I'll get cracking on the quote.

My mind flashed back to Gary's training.

GARY: Right, time to get into the technical details. I'm gonna show you how to measure up and provide the quote once you got in the house . . .

I got ready to follow his instructions to the letter.

GARY: Go to the corner of the room. Put one foot in front of the other until you get to the opposite wall.

I walked along the wall, one foot in front of the other.

GARY: Then do the next wall along.

I turned, and did the next wall.

GARY: Times those two numbers together.

I did the mental arithmetic.

GARY: And whatever number you get, it's fifty quid.

The lady reappeared, brandishing a Rich Tea.

WOMAN: So what does that come to?
ME: It's . . . it's fifty quid. But I'm sure Gary would do you a deal. What's your number?

The woman started scribbling her number on my photocopied sheet. I bit into the biscuit. A cascade of crumbs fell to the floor.

WOMAN: There you go!

In my mind's eye I saw Gary waving his leader's whiteboard. I saw my name at the top, just above a faint mark saying 'Viennetta'. I thought about the satisfaction of beating the boys. And then I thought about this sweet lady, and her sweet dog, who was currently licking biscuit crumbs off the carpet.

ME: Thank you. Thank you so much. We'll be in touch.

I smiled, and walked out of the door. I carried on walking until I reached the edge of the estate, until I'd found a bin to put my Nu-Again script in, along with the sweet lady's number. I walked until I found a phone box – whereupon I rang my mate Neil and asked him to come and get me.

~~~

One thing was for sure, there was no Neil in the Mekong Delta. No one was coming to get me.
~~~

Di Hei slapped my arms and bellowed into my face.

The translation came back.

DI HEI: OK! You! Time to sell!

I gulped nervously as she led me from the gloom of the house and into a brand new world.

The Mekong I'd floated in on was the stuff of romantic fairy tales – a still and silvery waterway lit by a retreating moon. Now, in the sunlight, I could see it was slicked with diesel and dotted with plastic bags that bobbed in the brown foam. Hundreds of boats jostled for space, laden with dragon fruit, coconuts and sugar cane. Dogs stood proudly on the bows, barking at the horizon. The air bristled with the shouts of traders hawking their wares.

My reverie was interrupted by a sharp poke to the ribs. 'Move! Now! You move!' barked Di Hei, gesturing towards her boat, a rickety wooden craft, its oars lashed together with twine. It wobbled as I got on. I wobbled as I got on. Di Hei ran inside, then re-emerged from the smoke carrying two cauldrons, suspended either side of a wooden pole around her neck. I offered to help. I say that – I proffered a lone palm in her direction. She snorted in derision, the mucus from her sinuses discharging into her mouth, then spat. I made a note not to eat anything from the pot on her right. Or the pot on her left. Or, indeed, anything, ever again.

Di Hei dumped one of the cauldrons between my legs, the hot broth soaking the hems of my trousers. Into the cavity of the bow, she placed towers of plastic plates and metal forks, corroded by years of being washed in river water. Then came chopsticks, a vat of stringy local greens named morning glory, and a pile of miscellaneous grey meat cosseted in thick white fat.

I had hoped for a gentle training period, an apprenticeship, during which I would be instructed in the ancient art of *pho*-making. Di Hei would take time to explain its history, before taking me, stage by stage, through the rich tapestry of flavours, the diversity of textures and the layers of aromatic, mouth-watering *umami* that made this national dish so very, very special.

Nope. Never going to happen.

There was a reason that Di Hei had the nickname Queen of the Noodle. There was a reason she sold more bowls of soup than anyone else in Can Tho. And that reason was that she had developed a failsafe way of attracting the tourist dollar. Not for Di Hei the lengthy sales pitch, the trust-building conversations, *The Art of the Deal*. No. Di Hei had no time for that. Di Hei had a much more direct approach.

'*Di di nào!*' she shouted again, this time to the driver. Come on, let's go!

There was a splutter as the outboard motor fought for life, and with that we lurched forward through the water. I noticed the gobbets of pork sliding perilously close to my groin.

DI HEI: *Di di nào! Di di nào!*

We were now building up quite a head of steam. We headed out towards the other vendors, identifiable by the wares hanging from their masts. The greengrocers had cabbages, and the butchers had pigs' heads swinging in the breeze. It was useful, not least because it made it easier to work out exactly who we were about to crash into.

Di Hei started cackling as she caught sight of a pleasure cruiser.

DI HEI: Ha, ha, ha! Yes! There! Now!
ME: Di! DI!

She pointed frantically at the tourists on board, urging the driver onwards.

ME: Di! We're getting very close to that boat!

I noticed her left eye was starting to close in piratical fervour as she started to get within range.

ME: Di, honestly, we're getting really close. We're going to crash! We're going to . . . Trung! TRUNG! What's Vietnamese for 'help'?

Trung was our fabulous fixer, cook, translator and go-to guy on the ground. When I turned round to get his answer, I noticed he and the rest of the crew had their hands covering their eyes. Our first day on the Mekong and already we were only one Risk Assessment Form short of a calamity.

So, this was Di's sales technique. She would pick a tourist boat, set a course for it at full speed, ram it head-on, then barrack its passengers into submission. She simply frightened customers into buying from her. You had to admire her verve.

I braced myself. There was a sharp bump as we smashed into the side of the target vessel. On impact, the pork made its final hop onto my groin where it began its slow and greasy leak through my trouser fabric.

I was now less than a metre from a gang of wealthy Chinese ladies, wearing bonnets and holding parasols, all of whom seemed to be a tad shocked at being broadsided by a floating soup kitchen.

'Hello!' I said, with an unintentional hint of Leslie Phillips. 'Lovely to see you all.'

Having traumatized them with the crash, Di wasted no time in getting stuck into her sales pitch, shouting what appeared to be a menu at the top of her lungs. One of the tourists responded, '*YES! YES!*', more out of panic than interest, I suspect, whereupon Di Hei dug me in the ribs.

I took this as a cue to bung (culinary technical term) the entire contents of the boat into a single bowl; vast tangles of noodles, ladles of broth and a precarious heap of spring onions and pork.

I handed it over to Di Hei, who appeared horrified. She turned her back on the customers, and deftly flung two of the larger bits of meat back onto my lap.

She muttered something in Vietnamese, which, although I'm far from fluent, I understood to mean something along the lines of 'Stop fucking with my profit margins, you hooning doofus.'

~

That night, I dreamt of the council estate in Addiscombe. I felt the dread as I approached a stranger's door and rang on the bell. I felt the familiar lurch of disappointment as the homeowner asked what I wanted and I duly launched into my spiel. I felt the draught as the door slammed in my face.

'*Di di nào!*' screamed a voice from behind me, a voice somewhat incongruous in 1980s south London. Out of nowhere came Di Hei, flying through the air. She smashed right through the door, her bare feet ripping through timber, and came to a halt in the hallway. I stepped through the wreckage to join her.

DI HEI: You! Look here! Your carpets are filthy. Filthy!
You must clean them. You will buy this carpet cleaner.
Yes? YES? Good. Yes, you will. We call you tomorrow.

And with that, we marched through the remains of the door and were gone.

At six o'clock, the van screeched to a halt at the pick-up point. My dispirited co-sellers trooped into the back. I joined them, beaming.

ME: Gary.
GARY: Yeah . . .
ME: You know that sales chart you've got?
GARY: Yeah . . .
DI HEI: You gonna need a bigger whiteboard.

5. I Want to Be You

The next day we headed to Vinh Thuan, a rural district of Kien Giang province in the Delta where we planned to hook up with a pair of rice farmers called Tuk and Huong. It's almost impossible to overstate the importance of rice, or 'white gold', to Vietnam, and this area in particular. The Mekong delta produces around half of Vietnam's rice and Vietnam exports around $4 billion of the stuff, around a fifth of the world's total.

Steve, the director, was on fine form that morning. He'd been looking forward to this particular story since the programme had first been commissioned, some six months earlier. Steve loves a sequence on agrarian reform; give him an involved discussion on evapotranspiration, amylopectins and transgenic cropping and he's in clover. Sure, he'll endure the endless scenes of me monkeying around with children, he'll tolerate the incessant punning, but inside he's just counting the hours and days until we can get back to a meaty chinwag about the real issues – like the role of monoculturism in contemporary agribusiness.

We puttered along narrow canals, framed by willows bowing like leafy supplicants to the water's edge. On either side, a peppering of houses – some rickety and wooden, others concrete-stiff and painted in bright yellows and pinks. It feels timeless here, but there's nothing ancient about this place. It's been fashioned by man through hard labour and the horrors of war. This tranquil spot, where the birds sang and the trees waved in the mist of early morning, this was one of the most bombed places in the world. Just decades earlier, military transport planes rained down death from the skies, leaving vast swathes of forest drenched in the cancerous pall of Agent Orange.

We left the boat and hopped onto mopeds, chugging into the interior. Clusters of farm workers were bent double in the emerald green sheen of the paddy fields, the soft sky silhouetting their broad, conical hats. What a beautiful photo that would make, I thought. I must grab a snap later. I wouldn't even need a filter, which was great – because I have no idea how filters work. The last time I used one I put it on the sepia setting and everyone ended up looking like they were part of a Victorian post-mortem daguerreotype.

Now, of course, after all these miles, after everything I've seen, I can't imagine ever thinking that. I can't imagine ever looking at men, women and children labouring in the blistering heat and my first thought being how best to capture it on an iPhone. But that's the beauty of hindsight.

How pretty poverty looks when you don't have to live it.

Tuk and Huong had invited me for lunch before I began my probationary period as a rice farmer. The Vietnamese are generous and hospitable hosts, so I was treated to a towering banquet of river fish, prawns and rice. The food was delicious, if a little earthy. Everything seemed to have a slight back-note of dredged river-bed – a kind of Mekong Gravy.

Grandma sat at the head of the table. She didn't speak, not once – she didn't need to. That was because Grandma seemed to have developed a very effective non-verbal way of communicating her feelings to the family.

If Grandma was interested in the conversation, she would

quietly go about her own business, eating her rice, chopsticks darting back and forth in the bowl. However, if Grandma became bored, she'd lean over, grab a crab's leg and suck the meat from it with a noise akin to an airlock on a submarine giving way. She'd finish this scene-stealing move by spitting the extraneous shell across the table. Let me tell you, as party pieces go, it was certainly memorable.

Tuk handed me a tumbler of pale yellow liquid. I downed it. I always like to drain a glass before I know what's in it. It's a Croydon thing.

He laughed, which worried me, and poured me another.

Huong, it transpired, was a somewhat harder nut to crack. She spent most of the meal staring at me, scrutinizing my every move. We kept on drinking. As I reached over to grab a little chilli sauce, she took my hand, turning it in hers, examining the soft white pads and pink rounded fingernails, before dismissively tossing it aside like an old slipper.

HUONG: Farming – it's hard work.
ME: Yes. I can imagine. I'm ready for that.

Huong looked me up and down.

HUONG: You can't do it.

Huong had many great qualities, but it's fair to say that motivational speaking wasn't one of them. Put it this way: you wouldn't want her as group leader on your team-building river-rafting weekend in Lee Valley.

HUONG: You can't. It's very hard.

I laughed at her bluntness. She had only just met me, yet she'd sized me up perfectly. I vowed to prove her wrong.

Steve had spent the entire meal, behind camera, waving his arms in the air trying to get my attention. Thirty minutes and approximately two hundred units of ethanol later, I finally glanced in his direction.

STEVE: (*whispering over*) Sue!
ME: Yes!
STEVE: Ask them about salinization and aquaculture!
ME: What?
STEVE: Salinization and aquaculture!
ME: What?
STEVE: Salt and prawns! Salt and prawns!
ME: Oh, yes. Yes. Of course, Steve. Give me a second.

Damn, I thought. Why didn't I ask the question about alternative cropping systems before I had the litre of spirits? Schoolgirl error. My head was swimming. *Think, Susan. THINK.* Come on – you can do it. Ask a proper question, something about climate change and food security.

Tuk poured me another drink.

ME: Cheers!

This was going to be quite the gear change.

ME: So Tuk, Huong . . .

I felt an acidic burp bubbling up through my oesophagus.

ME: With sea-water levels rising, are you finding you have to invest more in shrimp farming than rice farming?

There was a noise like an air-gun. A shard of crab shell bounced off my glasses. Grandma had just fired another crustacean cannon into the centre of the table.

I loved Grandma. She had excellent taste in dinner-party conversation.

~~~

The rice paddy was accessible by boat, a narrow craft that hugged the banks on either side.

Huong beckoned me to join her. The moment I stepped onto the plot, the thick clay pulled at my ankles until I was six inches deep and utterly stuck.

I didn't know the word for 'help', so just stuck with the vocabulary I was familiar with.

ME: *Xin Chao! Xin Chao! XIN CHAO!*

Huong shot me a withering look – as I would, if a tourist was repeatedly screaming HELLO into my face while I was trying to work.

I strained to lift my left foot, the mud sucking at my skin. Finally I wrestled free and lurched forward. Again the thick goo dragged me down. I heard something that sounded like tittering, but when I looked up Huong appeared blank-faced, staring in my direction.

It's a good thing that cameras now use a digital format, because it took me around ten minutes to get to Huong. In the old days, that would have been on tape. It would have had physical form, spool upon spool of dyspraxic fumblings that would have cost money – licence-fee payer's money – to cut away and reassemble in an edit suit. Thankfully now, with modern technology, my Munster-esque lurchings were mere gigabytes of data that could vanish with the touch of a button.
~~~

It struck me, as I finally reached Huong, that I had no idea what a rice plant looked like. None whatsoever. I eat rice, on average, twice a week, yet couldn't have told you how on earth it was harvested. I guess I was about to find out.

ME: Right, Huong, I'm ready to be a farmer!

Three minutes later I was ready to stop being a farmer.

The temperature had settled around the 40-degrees mark, but that wasn't the kicker. It's the humidity that fells you. Within moments, every pore of your body brims with moisture. Your bones feel wet and heavy. To harvest the rice plants (think green, green grass with tiny beige tassels at the end), you grab a sheaf with one hand and scythe it with the other, a few inches from the ground. Then, when you have a decent bunch, you tie it with plant twine and leave it to collect later. You are bent double. You are done in. You wheeze with the effort; you feel the blood thumping in your temples.

Tuk and Huong do it for eight hours a day. Every day.

Huong started up with a little more of her high-energy confidence building:

HUONG: No. You are very bad.

Yep, Mrs Feel-Good was at it again.

I plunged and pulled, plunged and pulled my legs until I finally reached the edge of the field, whereupon I clambered up the bank. From there we walked to the dirt-track road where a man was standing next to a turquoise threshing machine, which seemed more rust than metal. It spluttered into life with a black gaseous wheeze and began separating the rice from the stalks. This is the only part of the farming process that is mechanized. The rest of it, it's all done by hand. All of it. By hand.

Hours of labour between us, and the threshing machine reduced our endeavours to a small bag of grain in a matter of minutes.

I returned to Huong for the final verdict. It was as glowingly positive as I'd come to expect:

HUONG: I am a farmer. She is not. Absolutely not.

And with that rubber-stamp of approval, I left the paddy field for good.

I would like to take every climate-change denier in the world to Vinh Thuan (and to the Sunderbans, but more of that later). The district is low-lying, and the sea is rising, meaning the paddy fields are becoming salinized and borderline infertile.

Perhaps you're one of the few for whom the jury is out, who believe we are simply in an anomalous weather period, that the Arctic ice-melt is part of a natural cycle – that the modelling is unreliable, or that there is no real scientific consensus.

Then come here. See how precarious life is. Imagine your food, the mainstay of your diet, comes from a plant that grows a fraction above sea level. A plant that can't thrive if flooded with seawater. A plant that feeds fifty million people in this region alone, that is threatened by even a centimetre's swell in the ocean.

We imagine life and death situations to be immediate. Dramatic. A *Titanic* Hollywood disaster movie with Dolby surround sound and in glorious technicolour.

The lesson here is that life and death can also be monochromatic, slow and unremarkable – right up to the point of no return. Then it's game over.

We headed back for another seafood banquet.

Grandma had already embarked on her crustacean spit-athon – the table littered with pink shells. Huong brought out a plate of prawns but, I'll be honest, I didn't enjoy them as much as the ones I'd had for lunch. There was a reason. Steve had collared me on the way back and told me about the intense research he'd done on prawn fisheries in South East Asia.

STEVE: There are twenty prawns in every square metre of water.

ME: Right . . .

STEVE: And the water is foul, endlessly recycled. It's basically a Petri dish of chemicals, fertilizer and feed.

ME: OK . . .

I could hear the sounds of Grandma's crab shell whizzing through the air. Hell, if I'd had a crab leg to hand, I would have done the same.

STEVE: It's toxic. Really dangerous. It's been proven. Those chemicals harm the workers, the environment and possibly the consumers.

I picked at my shellfish all night. On the plus side, I finally got to learn the recipe for that delicious gravy: two parts tetracycline to one part phenicol and fluoroquinolone.

We spent the evening drinking a brand-new liquid, slightly less yellow in colour – but equally hostile on the gullet. I assume it was a distant, boozy cousin of the rice plant. After one shot, it made your tongue go numb, then your jaw. After the second, your eyes stopped working.

Tuk was an extremely magnanimous host. Every couple of minutes he'd head off to the kitchen, walking across the bare, red-earthed floor, and emerge with yet another bucket of shrimp and crab. He'd mix up a quick sauce of tamarind and chillis in a cracked glass cup, pour it over the seafood and cook them on a tiny rack above a dish of hot coals. We drank and ate shrimp, drank and ate shrimp in a loop for a couple of hours until my mouth was sour with river-water and weird booze. Their dog came and begged for scraps. I cuddled him. We chatted and laughed; the lucky ones smoked. God, I miss smoking. God, I miss my dog.

My entire journey was studded with nights like this, where families with nothing to call their own opened their arms and their doors and fed and watered me. The generosity of the have-nots is a constant, shocking source of wonderment – though the term 'have-nots' is something of a misnomer, since Tuk and Huong seemed to have more of the things that mattered than I ever will.

Dusk was falling. Outside, a squadron of mosquitoes was amassing, ready for their nocturnal sortie. Everyone was busy applying Deet, Olly positively glistening with the stuff. I seem to remember my mum telling me that it dissolved your watch.* Or your arms. Or both. I can't remember. Anyway. I declined.

Instead, I opted for something a little more me. A cold-pressed Amazonian tincture, strained through a shaman's sleeve and only available in the remotest corners of the internet. That was bound to keep the mozzies at bay.

Word had got out that strangers were in town, so the entire neighbourhood popped over that evening to have a good gawp. They were all hammered. One of the older

* My mum possesses 1950s America levels of paranoia. Kim Jong-un levels of paranoia. She lives in an almost permanent high-tensile state of red alert. In the winter just gone, there was an article about raisin shortages. She went to Morrisons and bought SEVEN KILOS of them. Why? Because her friend Margaret likes to make fruit cakes. Go figure.

women, in her seventies, took a real shine to me. Yep – I still got it. She started off winking and pinching my boobs. Text-book flirtation. In the end she simply plonked herself on my lap. For nearly an hour. Let me tell you from experience, that's an awfully long time to have a drunk pensioner sitting on you.

That night, Vicky and I slept in the living room, on Tuk and Huong's dining table, which we'd decked with mosquito nets.

I thought about the conversation we'd had earlier. I'd asked Tuk what he would like if he could have anything in the world. He'd replied, 'A tractor.' I imagined him atop a shiny red, state-of-the-art machine. The ultimate Communist's wet dream.

I'd asked Huong the same question. She'd answered without hesitation.

HUONG: I want to be you. I want to be rich so that I can do the same as you and travel everywhere.

I was becoming acutely aware of how much stuff I'd brought with me. Some of it was essential, of course – after all, my Western body wasn't used to this climate or its pathogens. But, increasingly, most of my possessions felt like insulation, part of a pointless safety net. It was all junk, really, but I'd fashioned it with meaning, valorized it with the false narrative of need.

– *I have to have that, else I can't sleep.*
– *I need that, it's my favourite.*
– *I can't be without it, it's my lucky . . .*

I was new to sleeping like this but, over time, I developed a pretty neat system for in-house camping. First, I'd hang my net from a lamp or hook on the wall. I'd arrange the end fronds around the mattress and weigh them down with bits and bobs from my suitcase – books, iPad, water bottles. That way, there was no gap through which an airborne incursion could occur. When darkness descended, I'd slip in, reseal the area, switch on my head torch and get out my puzzle book. It felt like being a child again, under the covers, secretly reading after lights out. If I shone the light upwards, out into the room, I'd be able to make out the rolling clouds of bugs hurling themselves against the mesh in a desperate effort to make dinner of me. Most nights my unconscious would rouse me, bothered by an unfamiliar noise – rustling, croaks, buzzes – all indistinguishable in the gloom. *You're safe!* I'd remind myself. *You're all tucked in. Nothing can get to you.*

Trung wasn't so lucky. He was stationed outside, sleeping in what could only be described as an outsized dog crate. Each side was covered in netting, with a small door at one end so he could let himself in and out. Once in, he was sealed in a bug-resistant cube, designed to fit snugly around a mattress, that could withstand a night in the open air without him becoming Nature's very own pincushion.

So far, so good. The problem was, Trung, like the rest of us, was absolutely battered – which made him a little cavalier as regards insect vigilance.

ME: Trung, it's dusk, mate. You need to set up your bed.
TRUNG: (*slurring*) Don't worry! They never get me. Never!

He started erecting the cage. It took a little longer than expected – and there was a lot of falling over and swearing.

TRUNG: See?

He pointed to his bare arms and legs.

TRUNG: No mosquito. They don't like my smell.

ME: What do you mean?

TRUNG: They only like sweet blood. Like tourists. You have sweet blood!

ME: Do I?

TRUNG: Yeah. Visitors have sweet blood.

I vowed to return home and start work on making my blood more savoury. There was bound to be a naturopathic website I could subscribe to which would specialize in exactly that.

For some reason, and I suspect that reason was alcohol, Trung then took his newly built cage to the ideal spot – directly under the porch light. This meant his bed was now a homing beacon for anything and everything airborne within a five-mile radius.

Once inside, Trung settled down to sleep. It was ten minutes before his bladder reached peak capacity. Out he stumbled, desperate for a piss. What he didn't do, as he left the cage, was close the door. From where I lay, I could see myriad insects colonizing the inside of the netting and the top of his mattress, waiting to pick him off when he returned.

My last image of the night was Trung staggering back inside, zipping the cage shut, and thus imprisoning himself in a black cloud of a billion mega-bugs.

I was under my net, head throbbing. The grog was now starting to work through my system. My kidneys were aching and I, too, was desperate for a piss, but I was too frightened to leave the safety of the table. In the end I resorted to slicing open an empty water bottle with a penknife and weeing in it. I placed the sample at the corner of my mattress and tried to get some shut-eye.

Within minutes, something started clawing at me through the netting. I was so scared I daren't move, so spent the night stock-still with a hairy dead-weight on my leg. Outside, I could hear Trung snoring, shouting, then slapping himself in a loop. His blood was obviously a little sweeter than he'd thought.

I woke at dawn to find a skinny ginger cat licking its arse on my calf. In the midst of its frantic rimming, it had knocked over the severed water bottle, sending my piss across the mattress. I won't lie: it was a new personal low.

Trung was already up, and busy cooking.

'Hello!' he said cheerily, turning to greet me. His face looked like a Connect 4 board.

Something smelt incredible.

ME: What's this, Trung? This is amazing!

I couldn't believe it. I was in the middle of nowhere, and Trung was making chocolate pancakes. CHOCOLATE PANCAKES. There was an open fire with a large iron wok sitting atop it, a thick patina of scorched fat lacquering the insides. There was the sound of eggs cracking against a metal rim, and the rich sweet stink of burnt sugar. Gosh, I thought, he must really love working with us. We must be his favourite crew. Ever.

Six months later, as Vicky and I were pissing against a wall in the middle of the Tibetan plateau, she confessed that she and Trung had fallen madly in love with each other. They'd been dating since filming began. They are now married. As am I, according to local custom, to the septuagenarian who used me as an armchair for an hour that night.

The pancakes weren't about me at all. Or the crew. They

were a love letter, wrought in batter, for a woman forced to spend the night with another woman who appeared to have pissed in her bed.

So my pancakes were really love by proxy. But, boy, they tasted sweet.

6. I Don't Like Mondays

I'm passionate about many things – conservation, home-made scones, the music of Kate Bush – but I'd never given prawns much thought before. The people of rural South East Asia, however, seem to think of nothing else.

For the lucky ones here in Vietnam, prawns have made them and their neighbours relatively rich. Houses have televisions, shiny mopeds sit outside. School enrolment rates have soared. If you're lucky, there's gold in them there shells.

That morning, I accompanied Dam, Tuk and Huong's youngest son, to school. The playground was deserted, thick weeds displacing the paving stones, the odd rusty bike waiting in vain for its next outing. From inside, I could hear singing and the occasional peal of laughter. It was a far cry from my own schooldays: the high note of hormones, girls screaming, the odd casual fist-fight.

The schoolroom itself was essentially one largish room, with old-fashioned desks and chairs stationed in neat rows.

There was a shocked intake of breath as I stepped inside. *What?* I thought, *What's wrong? Have I forgotten to observe some important custom? Have I made a cultural* faux pas? *Oh, Christ. Did I forget to put my trousers on again?*

The truth is, these children had never seen a Westerner before. They'd never seen this jumble of white flesh, round eyes and strange utterances – let alone the fact I'd walked in with a camera crew in tow. They were cute as buttons, dressed impeccably in their uniforms, with not an untucked shirt in sight.

KIDS: *Xin chao!*

'Hello. Welcome. Would you like to take class?' said the teacher, as I walked in.

What? Oh, God. No. Don't ask me that. I was a useless teacher in my own country, in my own language. Useless. Here, I'll be ten thousand kilometres worse than useless.

'Miss Perkins,' he said again, interrupting forty-eight years of cumulative self-loathing, 'I asked you – would you like to take class?'

But I didn't answer. In my head, I was somewhere else entirely.

~~~

It was 1993. I had graduated, and was spending my time 'being creative'. In this context 'being creative' meant sitting around with my mates talking about what I might write one day, if I could be arsed to pick up that biro.

I spent the autumn as part of a sketch troupe (think *League of Gentlemen*'s Legz Akimbo minus the irony) travelling round schools in a play designed to encourage kids to apply for further education. Among the many roles I brought to life, I was most proud of UCAS. You may not be familiar with UCAS. Sounds like a Marvel superhero, doesn't he? A strong-jawed, tights-wearing fellow. But, no. UCAS is a far harder character to portray than anything in that canon. UCAS is the Universities and Colleges Admissions Service. Yes, you heard. Doubt no longer my thespian versatility. The venerable Dame Judi Dench is our greatest luminary of stage and screen but even she cannot claim to have made
~~~

flesh an organization responsible for undergraduate application procedures.

Note: for those wishing to recreate my character of UCAS, I used a Geordie accent.

Shortly after the tour, my mate Sally asked if I wanted to help teach some drama courses at the local all-girls comprehensive. Sure, I said. Why not?*

The class was brimful of tall, sassy teenagers called Kelly, Shane and LaTisha, most of whom wore gold-hooped earrings so large you could have developed a Crufts' agility course around them. Mere moments into the lesson it became obvious they already had more street-smarts than I ever would.

These kids weren't interested in anything outside of the nail bar on the Harrow Road. A quick poll during our careers chat revealed a 100 per cent class tendency towards hairdressing. From very early on, it became clear I'd be playing second fiddle to a teaser comb.

Undeterred, Sally and I ploughed ahead with our ambitious project, which was to bring Caryl Churchill's feminist masterpiece *Top Girls* to north London. The school didn't have a theatre space, so we made do with a gym.

At least it meant that giving stage directions was easy:

ME: Shanice! Move there for your monologue. Yes, there, in the penalty box.

SALLY: Jazmine! Can you do your birthing scene by the pommel horse? Great. Thank you.

* I am not qualified:

1. I am a child myself.
2. I have no qualities that would inspire or motivate a young person.
3. I have attention issues, which means my mind is even more likely to wander during a lesson than my pupils' . . .

None of the kids had ever acted before, which was fine since we'd never directed before. What I loved about the students was their refreshing uninterest in playing ball – although, ironically, had they wanted to play ball we would have had the perfect space for them.

ME: Guys, you need to learn your lines.
SHANICE: Why, Miss?
ME: (*wisely*) Because that is acting. You read the lines, you learn the lines, you say the lines. Acting.
SHANICE: That's a waste of energy.
ME: How come?
SHANICE: You can just read them from the book. Saves time. Don't need to learn them.
ME: How many people do you know who go around reading things out loud from a book? We're trying to be real here.
SHANICE: (*pause*) Miss, I feel sorry for you. This play is about a dinner party with a Japanese slag and a woman who lives in Hell. That ain't real. You don't make sense.

The performance (and, thankfully, there was only one) culminated in me walking backstage (a curtain hung just to the left of the crash mats) to find the kid playing Pope Joan smoking a six-paper spliff. The resinous fug was moving perilously close to the headmistress's nostrils, but by this point I was beyond caring. Rather than waste breath bollocking her, I simply joined in. It remains, to this day, my only blunt-share with a member of the papacy.

It was with this, rather limited, experience in education that I walked into Dam's schoolroom in Vietnam, woefully unprepared to teach a class in English.

KIDS: *XIN CHAO!*

They welcomed me in. The kids here greet elders with their arms crossed, palms resting on the opposite elbow. Think Cossack dancing. It's their sign of respect, of deference to those with more wrinkles and life experience. It's bloody wonderful to behold. I used to greet my teachers with a nicotine-stained grin and a middle finger. Different worlds.

'*XIN CHAO!*' I hollered back breezily. I really must learn some more Vietnamese.

Imagine sitting in class, minding your own business, when a jolly, slightly tubby lady comes bowling in. She screams HELLO at you, in an awkward inflection, then spends the next half an hour babbling in a language you're entirely unfamiliar with.

That, of course, is the key to being a successful foreign-language teacher. Knowing *both* languages, rather than just the one the kids are struggling to learn.

So there I am, on a raised dais, by a whiteboard, teachers and pupils looking on expectantly, the camera rolling and trained on my sweaty face.

Come on. You need to think of something. Now!

I had to think quickly. Grammar? Didn't know any. Vocabulary? Limited to swearwords and adjectives about baked goods and dogs.

I know, I thought. A song! Yes! Brilliant! You can't go wrong with a song. Unless, of course, you're Honey G – in which case you can't go right with it.

I'd need something educational, something that would be

both fun and instrumental in expanding their Anglo-Saxon lexicon. My mind flashed with possibilities, each of which was discarded in a moment.

1. 'My Heart Will Go On'. The theme from *Titanic* as sung by Céline Dion. Mmm. Limited vocabulary, plus it raises unrealistic expectations about immortality. There are no situations in which your heart will go on (see drowning).
2. 'Kung Fu Fighting'. Possible undercurrents of racism, or at least racial ignorance as *kung fu* was not developed in Vietnam, but, reportedly, in the semi-mythical Xia Dynasty around 2000 BC.
3. 'Do They Know It's Christmas?' Yes, of course they do: they're an emergent global powerhouse with 10 per cent of their population identifying as Christian. Stop patronizing them.
4. 'I Kissed A Girl' – STOP IT, SUE. THEY'RE JUST KIDS.

I decided it would be much safer picking a nursery rhyme.

Out of nowhere, my brain conjured the classic ditty 'Heads and Shoulders'. Perfect! It's a cross between a workout and an anatomy lesson. Easy to remember, plus they'll learn the English for all the body parts they'll ever want to know and more.

I was ready to face my class.

'*XIN CHAO!*' I bellowed again, aware that the lengthy period of time taken wrestling with my internal monologue might have, indeed, lost the room.

ME: OK, kids, let's sing a song!

Silence. I carried on, undeterred, pointing to the relevant bits of me while shouting:

ME: Right, here we go! Head!

I gestured frantically towards my bonce. They joined in, pointing along with me.

KIDS: Hezz!
ME: That's right! Shoulders!
KIDS: Shoo-ders!
ME: Knees!

The kids bent down to touch their kneecaps.

KIDS: Neez!
ME: Toes!

And down they went to touch their toes.

KIDS: Tuzz!
ME: Great!

I went through the entire song, getting more confident and more animated as I went along. This is great, I thought. We're really connecting. This is a fabulous lesson.

I carried on, through eyes and ears and mouth and nose, before enjoying once more the sight of the kids bending, like obedient hairpins, for the knees and toes section.

I was about to start on 'feet and tummies, arms and chins' when I noticed Steve and Vicky in the corner, shaking their heads. If I didn't know better, I would have suspected they were about to make an intervention. No, I thought. I must be mistaken. They can't want to stop this because we are all having SO MUCH FUN. I started again.

ME: Heads!
KIDS: HEZZ!

I looked over again. Steve and Vicky were now looking positively concerned. Olly and Matt appeared to be giggling. It was all extremely distracting. How dare you? I thought. How dare you interrupt this incredible moment I am sharing with these children? They are LEARNING here. I am teaching them valuable words – words which they will be able to use to describe their extremities should they be called upon to do so when visiting the UK.

I carried on regardless:

ME: Shoulders!
KIDS: SHOO-DERS!
ME: Knees!
KIDS: NEEZ!

Steve starts motioning towards Matt to move the camera away. What is going on? I refuse to back down.

ME: Toes!
KIDS: TUZZ.

The infants jackknife once more.

And that's when I notice it. Out of the corner of my eye, I see the teacher heading towards a tiny little boy at the back of class. I watch as he sings along: 'Hezz, shoo-ders, neez and . . .'

And every time he bends down to touch his toes, he smacks his forehead – BAM – on the lip of the desk. Every single time. But because this is Vietnam, he says nothing. He does nothing. He does not cry out in pain every time his little forehead slams against the hard wood. He endures.

This stoic, beautiful kid, who will for ever remember the time the white lady came and gave him a headache. If indeed the concussion will allow him to remember anything at all.

We mourn the loss of respect in our country, we look upon this unquestioning obedience as the model that our children should aspire to. But honestly, kids – take it from me – sometimes you do just know better.

~

As we drove away, I saw a roadside shack with a makeshift sign proclaiming that '4G was coming'. Those kids were on the cusp of change. 4G was indeed coming. Roaming. High-speed internet. Social media, Instagram, SnapChat, and all those shiny lozenge-shaped apps lined up on their phone inviting the scrutiny, the peer pressure, the keeping up with the Nguyens. In a click they would be able to see the panorama of piss-awful humanity, everything, good and bad, all at once. Pandora's box open for ever. The information formerly wrought through trust and time – where you live, who you live with, your family, where you work, what kind of breakfast you like – now accessible in a click.

And even though one of those kids left the class with the worst headache of their lives, it felt good to do something silly, and simple, before the full horror of the world hit their inboxes.

As I got back on the river, heading towards the Cambodian border, I started to feel ill – truly, madly, deeply ill. My bones ached, and I felt hot and restless. I started to worry that the paraben-free Shamanic Bug Deterrent might have been a waste of six months' wages. As it turned out, nothing could have saved me from the one thing I hadn't banked on: *aedes aegypti*, the *daytime*-biting mosquito, the *Lorraine Kelly* of mosquitoes. I don't know exactly when I got nipped, but it was the start of a rather interesting month-long descent into the realms of the unwell.

The border crossing was on the river, a floating passport control policed by some rather intensely costumed men. The job seemed simple; a check of your papers, a cursory discussion about travel plans and a 'thank you very much'. Yet they were all dressed like Prince Philip at a ceremonial banquet.

It's by design, of course.

Bureaucracy is the same the world over. It smells the same, it looks the same, it makes time drag the same. But they don't want you to think that this is just another humdrum routine affair. They don't want you to feel safe in the knowledge that this is merely procedural. They want to make their paperwork special, threatening, even, with the addition of medals and epaulettes and shiny boots.

There is a tense moment as a heavily decorated man in an enormous hat looks at my documentation. For a second, I wonder if I'm in trouble. And then, with the flourish of an ink pen, and a lingering stare towards my jugs, I am officially admitted to the Kingdom of Cambodia.

Cambodia

7. Kampong Phluk

As we rowed in, along the mangrove forests on the margins of Tonle Sap, I felt a hundred eyes trained on our crew. Yes, folks, it's us, another boatload of tourists on a float-by gawp, come to take pictures of subsistence living with our expensive cameras.

We entered a narrow thoroughfare, akin to an underwater high street, with a jumble of houses either side, all on six-metre-high stilts to accommodate the ebb and flow of water. The roofs were frayed and patched with plastic sheeting, the houses themselves Heath Robinson-esqe piles of reclaimed wood. Wonky masts held loops of electrical cable above the water. Just.

The surface of the river was littered with foliage. At first glance it looked like river-weed – but it transpired that the greenery was the tops of trees in this submerged forest.

Cheeky kids with red eyes and swollen bellies bounced on jetties made from chicken wire. In the pens beneath, a bask of young crocodiles thrashed and rolled. They are farmed here for their meat and their skins. The children laughed at us and back-flipped into the water, seemingly unconcerned they were mere centimetres away from the snapping jaws. Teenagers emerged from the houses wearing faded football shirts and dead snakes round their necks, like scarves.

To my right, there was a monastery perched on a tiny island; to the left, my attention was caught by a group of rowdy women bashing tiny fish from their husbands' nets using what looked like tennis rackets.

We got to the end of the village and the boat butted a house, a bright concrete monstrosity towering above the water. We climbed the stairs and entered what would be our home for the next few days. There were three rooms: the main room, where the boys would sleep, a back room with a toilet plumbed in just for us, and a side room, where I got to kip. There were luminous pink mattresses littering the floor. Black mould sat on the wall, like a shadow, and liquorice-loops of electric cabling hung from the ceiling. All day and all night, we were accompanied by the incessant flashing of camera battery packs recharging.

'What do you want to do?' said Steve. 'Where do you fancy going?'

I didn't hesitate. My curiosity had been piqued. 'I want to talk to the tennis ladies,' I said.

~

Now might be a good time to discuss one of the great perils of filming abroad: the translation. There are two problems that tend to occur.

First, the varying speed of the translation, and what you do while waiting for it.

Second, the quality of the translation itself and the sensitivity of the translator in question.

Waiting for a translation is the curse of the travel documentary. You ask a question, and the interviewee answers it. While they are answering it, you nod – because that is the televisual law. The shots are even referred to in the trade as 'noddies'. There's a problem, however. Noddies capture you looking like a toy dog in the back of the car, head moving up and down – which can sometimes feel gloriously out of step with whatever your interviewee is saying. Let me give an example.

ME: What's it like living here?

The contributor starts talking in an animated, passionate way. I smile, nod – even laugh a little. Then the translation comes back.

TRANSLATOR: She is saying she hates it here. Life is unbearable. This existence is a vale of tears and I cannot wait for it to end.

See? I look like an idiot. I quickly wipe the smile off my face and look horrified. She carries on talking. I tilt my head in listening pose, occasionally shaking it in disbelief, tutting and generally looking sad. This should cover all the bases of her tragic story. Finally, the next burst of translation is forthcoming.

TRANSLATOR: Or at least that is what the West assumes. Actually, life here is fabulous, she says. She feels happy and blessed. She loves this life. She loves this life!!

I quickly remove the pained expression from my face, and relax into a grin.

In translation situations, you are always behind the beat, emotionally syncopated, your responses out of step and at odds with the content.

If they are describing a traumatic attack by a mountain lion, you are roaring with laughter.

If they are telling you about a transcendent spiritual experience, you are shaking your head in disbelief.

You cannot ever win.

The other problem with translation, of course, is that every translator is different. Some can perform the job almost simultaneously. Others take their time. Some are formal, others more colloquial. Some are even kind enough to spare my blushes, so I have absolutely no idea when I'm being slagged off. It's only in the edit that I find out that the monk in rural Mondulkiri, with whom I'd thought I had an intense soul-connection, actually went on record to say he thought I was a monumental dickhead.

In Kampong Phluk, Om, our Cambodian translator, showed no such kindness. Om* had been a Buddhist monk in a previous life† and, as such, valued honesty above all else.

I approached the women, who were still busy serving forehands into the dense netting, and asked them what they were doing.

ME: Hi! Nice to see you! What are you up to?

Om translated. There was a burst of laughter and much chit-chat. The response came back.

OM: They say you are an idiot. What does it look like we are doing?

ME: Well, you look like you're bashing fish with a tennis racket.

Back went my response. More laughter. I noticed even the translator was laughing with them now. He turns to me.

OM: They say, 'We *are* bashing fish with a tennis racket.'

* I know, this is the perfect name for a monk, right? With a name like Om he was never going to be anything else.

† Not literally. I meant in his earlier life. In his previous life, he was a goose.

Further peals of laughter.

ME: Great. Well, that's that sorted, then.
OM: The ladies want to ask *you* something . . .

Things had moved on swiftly. Now I was being interviewed.

The ladies didn't wait for confirmation, they just went ahead and asked. It was the very first time this question was posed on my travels – but it went on to dog me throughout.

OM: They want to know – are you married?
ME: No. I'm not.

Om stared at me with a mixture of disbelief and pity.

ME: Om. You can tell them. No.

He relayed the news. There was a collective gasp, followed by lots of fervent muttering.

OM: They are asking, 'Why not?'
ME: Well . . .

I racked my brains as to how to explain my situation.

I obviously took too long, because Om decided to start answering on my behalf, embarking on a lengthy monologue that included mimicry of my glasses and lots of sad faces.

There was more laughing and eye-rolling. They were now looking very intently at me. I thought about how on earth to get out of this. Some more muttering. I was on tenterhooks to see what insult might come my way next. All the while, on film, I'm still grinning that shit-eating grin.

OM: This lady here, she is asking if there is something wrong with you.

And . . .

And I laugh. The thing is, I don't feel offended. Not in the slightest. I feel exhilarated because we have stopped that one-sided formal interview and are now having a proper conversation.

We talked and laughed all afternoon, swapping stories. Theirs had common threads: poverty, a love of family, hardship. There were tales of violent abuse at the hands of those tasked with protecting them, fathers, husbands, sons – all delivered casually, like gossip, like it was nothing.

Throughout the afternoon, I tried helping them bat fish from the nets, but the angle of my racket was a little off. One misplaced backhand sent the catch back into the river. A rogue lob hurled it towards a lady's face. At the end of the day, I even found a kilo of soggy fry in my left bra cup.

This set the template for my stay. I was deemed an innocuous buffoon, a curiosity, and, as such, men and women would row up to the house to make our acquaintance. I started getting invites to community activities, the most prestigious being a chance to compete in their annual boat-race festival, Bon Om Touk. The offer of high-octane watersports? With super-fit strangers? I felt frightened. Anxious. So I said . . .

Yes.

~

We didn't sleep that night. Not one of us.

It transpired that one of the Cambodian crew, stationed in the back room, was an Olympic snorer. Every few minutes, he would let out a thick, gurgling rasp, and the house would vibrate to the sound of his rattling sinuses.

All night, an animal whimpered, its cries carried across the silent water. I would pace the balcony every hour trying to work out which direction the sound was coming from, but as soon as I thought I'd located it, it would switch source and I'd have to search all over again. Every night, that noise would find me and up I'd get, until I was half asleep all day and half awake all night.

The locals were up at first light, hawking their phlegm into the river and lighting the fires for breakfast. There was *pho*, rice and fried fish (Mekong Gravy optional).

We got up just as the sun hit the rooftops and got our waterproofed equipment together. We rowed to the opposite bank in good time to take part in the main event.

No one was there to meet us. The place was utterly deserted. Then, out of nowhere, a commotion. Things happen hard and fast out there; the fragile peace is shattered, and then, in a heartbeat, things fold back to silence once more. A boat emerged from the morning mist, with a dozen priests holding a man, as if he were their hostage. They dragged him from the boat, forced him to kneel in front of the temple and proceeded to slap and beat him with their hands and fists. Let me tell you, there is nothing more surreal than the sight of a group of monks in orange robes beating the shit out of a defenceless guy in a loincloth.

Later, we were told that this was a familiar ritual. An old man in the village was very sick, and not expected to last the day. The man getting beaten was a soothsayer who had been in touch with the patient. He had offered himself as a proxy: he accepted the beatings on the dying man's behalf so that the evil spirits could be driven away, clearing his ascent into heaven.

What a thankless job, I thought. You spend your life

getting walloped by a gang of Buddhists. Having said that, I'd still take it over telesales.

The Dragon Boat Race was a write-off, so we filled the day with a fishing trip with the village elder, Mr Lee. This cheered Steve hugely, because he might finally get the chance to talk about the dismantling of foreign-owned industrial trawling corporations in the early 2000s.

We headed out of Kampong Phluk towards the Tonle Sap – a freshwater lake and natural phenomenon. At the end of the wet season, something remarkable happens here. The volume of water flowing down the Mekong is so great that the entire delta turns into a giant floodplain. The Tonle Sap can't then drain away, so for a short period, the river *reverses* its flow and the water floods back into the vast lake. It expands to four times its normal size and, in doing so, the flooded forests become one gigantic fish nursery. The billions of fish that spawn here provide Cambodia with three-quarters of its annual protein. That's one hell of an important lake.

At least, that's what is supposed to happen. When we arrived in mid-November, the dry season hadn't yet made an appearance. The waters were unnaturally high, and flash floods hit us most days. Here, by the riverbank, you could see how the slightest changes in global temperature would dramatically affect the livelihood of farmers and fishermen.

Rather than me tell you all the many wonderful things Mr Lee was, let me tell you the one thing he wasn't: chatty. In fact, even when heavily prompted, it was hard to get more than a sentence or two out of him. Per hour.

He sat, facing forward on the bow, staring directly at the sun and thus directly away from me. Essentially, he'd rather get solar retinopathy than look at my face. We puttered further into the tangle of the mangroves, where he dragged up one of his nets for inspection.

And found nothing. Not one single fish – in the biggest inland fishery in the whole world.

We had been filming for hours and had nothing usable in the can. We desperately needed a sequence here. We changed tack, opting to tell another story; snakes. Because of the over-fishing in the lake, the fishermen had started killing snakes. And now the snake population was declining.

Mr Lee rowed out to the snake traps.

And found nothing.

That night, we had a team pow-wow. There was a feeling of gloom in the air – we were having an interesting time meeting the community, but none of the encounters were gelling into anything that could coherently tell the story of the place.

But we hadn't counted on Vicky.

As dusk fell, I watched her put on her head torch, commandeer a boat and row across the lake. I lay on my mattress and watched the bugs dancing on the wall. My eyes closed. My breathing steadied. I started to drift. And then, on the breeze, that sound: an animal in distress.

I have no idea what Vicky did that night, but it was certainly effective. As we left the next morning, I could see the opposite bank heaving with competitors.

Approaching the monastery, it became clear that the men had really embraced the majesty of the occasion. Half of them were wearing dresses and sporting vivid scarlet lipstick, which, if I'm being entirely honest, was not a shade that worked for all of them. The women sat around in heavy woollens, rolling their eyes, as if to say, 'Bloody show-offs'.

There was lots of shouting and play-fighting, with a little spitting and cat-calling thrown in for good measure. I couldn't help thinking the Oxford–Cambridge boat-race would benefit hugely from some of this drag-queen glamour.

I wobbled onto our vessel, the tennis ladies laughing at me. A woman took her place to my right, others in front and behind. I was handed an oar, damp and suspiciously small, almost half the size of my fellow rowers'. The opposition's boat manoeuvred alongside us in preparation for the start, and a boy in rather fetching fake lashes blew me a kiss.

Steve and the crew, meanwhile, had boarded a separate boat, which would run in parallel to the action and get all the necessary shots. 'We'll use the first race as a rehearsal pass,' he said, 'just to get our bearings.'

Great, I thought. We can take it easy, plod along just to give a sense of the course. Sadly, Steve forgot to tell the locals his plan. As far as they were concerned, this race was the real deal.

There was no starter pistol, or referee's whistle. Instead, without warning, the head monk gave a violent nod of his head and the two boats lurched forward. Suddenly the air was filled with the breathless shrieks and grunts of the competitors.

'*Moy!*' went the team, as the thick wooden oars hit the water

'*Moy!*' went the team as they brought them out again.

I lost my stroke within seconds, my tiny oar scudding against the water's surface and sending droplets splashing onto my face. This was my worst fear realized. The water. From the moment I'd arrived, I'd been terrified that even so much as an atom would make contact with my skin. It wasn't so much the colour, foaming and brown, as having seen, over the last few days, every local void their bowels in its shallows.

Within a few metres my teammate sitting behind was rhythmically twatting me on the back of the head with her massive oar. The pain was sharp, but at least this violent metronome helped me keep my stroke in time. We powered through, low in the water, the prow inching forward, falling back, inching forward again.

'*Moy!*' went the team, as we pulled in front. My heart was fit to burst with the strain. The camera boat picked up speed, racing towards us to get a shot of us in action. As it drew near, the wash built and the foul water started to spill over the right side of the boat, until my lap was soaked.

'NOOOOO,' I screamed, with the ardour of one who knows she is perilously close to typhus.

Suddenly it was over. The race was done. We had won, by a whisker. I was panting with exhaustion, my eyes burning from where little spits of river water had hit my face. But it was worth it. My first ever win! My first ever sporting triumph! Screw you, mega-jocks of my youth – I just did sport!

What I'd failed to realize was that this was just a trial run and that we needed another pass for the cameras. I had peaked too early. So Little Miss Shattered got back on her wet bench, tiny oar in hand and waited for the rhythmic concussion to begin again.

I collared Steve as we made our way back to the start of the course.

ME: Listen – please don't come that close again. We were taking in water and I thought we were going to capsize back there.

STEVE: I'm sorry, Sue.

ME: Honestly, it was really, really close.

STEVE: I know – I'm really sorry. We won't do it again. I promise.

ME: That's OK, just be careful.

My grump subsided. In truth, I can never be angry with a Welshie. They're my weakness – along with Mary Berry and all batter-based foodstuffs.

I was now exhausted, my pulse hammering in my ears. My fellow competitors, however, seemed to find the practice lap a mere cardiovascular *amuse-bouche.* I stared down at my groin. The splashes from the boat were now receding in the baking heat, leaving a yellowy watermark at the margins and a distinctly acidic whiff.

I had survived my first Mekong spattering. I had briefed the camera boat. All good. What I hadn't factored in was the competitive zeal of the rival boat in our second race. As soon as we were underway they drew next to us so that our oars were clashing. Their massive oars, my tiny one. They drew so close it felt like we were more sword fighting than rowing, as the wooden poles clicked and clacked against one another. A shout went up from behind, and I saw some of the kids try to push the boats apart. But it was too late. We started listing, taking in gallons of water that quickly filled the hollows of the boat. At that point, cheroot in gob and crinkly grin on face, the driver of the camera boat careered along the other side of us and I knew we were done for.

ME: Steve! Steve!

Steve had his head down, refusing to meet my gaze. We both knew I was doomed.

With boats now flanking us, the water poured in from both

sides, up to my knees, then up to my waist. My teammates began diving left and right, in perfect synchronicity, like something out of a Busby Berkeley movie. I, on the other hand, sat stunned and motionless, like a confused pudding in an explorer's hat, unaware until the very last minute that we were going down. I'd like to say that my remaining on the boat till the last was a matter of honour – a captain refusing to leave her stricken vessel – but in truth I was in shock and desperate to postpone the inevitable.

When the time came, I didn't jump. I didn't have the energy to jump. I simply leant to one side and capitulated to the foaming deep. I felt the water saturate my clothes and fill my shoes, whereupon I was surrounded by the womenfolk, who formed a protective circle around me, grabbing under my arms and attempting to bear me aloft.

They think I can't swim, I thought. *I'm so weak, they think I can't even swim.*

As I descend, I see Steve, head in hands. I see Vicky, failing to hide her delight that we finally have a sequence. And the last face I see is that of Olly, shaking his head ruefully as his entire collection of radio mics is submerged in the gloop.

On a lone positive note, I can say that I've not only been on the Mekong but in it.

The women surrounding me seemed very excited, shouting at me in a tone I felt was broadly encouraging. I shouted along with them, but ended up swallowing about a litre of Cambodian poo-water mid roar.

Later, having seen the footage translated, I understand that what they were actually saying, in deafening unison, was 'Keep your mouth shut! Don't open your mouth! Keep your mouth shut!'

I was pulled back onto the boat again, alternately coughing and gipping. There was a thick brown tide-mark around my neck and an unmistakable stench of toilet overflow around my shoulders.

It was then they broke the news: the villagers had requested it was the best of three.

I don't remember much of that final race. Perhaps the constant battering from my teammate's massive oar had had an effect on my brain capacity. I don't know. All I could think of was getting back to our little hut and washing the Mekong juice off my body.

Once ashore, the real race began. The race to get clean. My eyes were on fire, and there was a pungent stink coming from my clothes as they started to weld to my skin in the scorching heat.

I rushed to the back room, where we'd had the rudimentary plumbing rigged. There was a small toilet, next to which was an open grate with a plastic wand fixed above it for showering. I turned the tap on, to find the water pressure somewhere between non-existent and pensioner-with-prostate-issues. I peeled off my kit and stood on the grubby tiles as thick black rivulets of river muck ran down my leg. After a minute, the jet spluttered, then thinned, then stopped altogether. Oh, God. No. Not now. I waddled, butt-naked, into my room, grabbed two large bottles of water and some hand sanitizer, and returned. I began sluicing myself, rubbing the liquid alcohol against my skin to try to minimize the risk of infection.

I'd laid out my clean clothes ready. Once dry, I popped my pants and combats on, then reached for my bra. As I did so, I discovered two cockroaches, one in each cup, whirling round the edge of the under-wiring in perfect synchronicity.

Welcome to Asia.

That night we ate packet noodles and drank some rather suspect whisky. Olly sat apart from the group, packing his sodden radio mics in dry rice, in an attempt to bring them back to life. I tried to join in with the general chat, but my internal, hypochondriac monologue drowned out everything else.

My skin is itching. That's a sub-dermal parasite. That's probably bilharzia.

STEVE: Good day's work today, Sue.

Is that the one where you get snails in your bloodstream? Yes. Oh, God, I've got snails in my veins . . .

STEVE: Sue?
ME: Oh, yes. Cheers, Steve.

My head hurts. That'll be bacterial meningitis. Or, worse, a rare, local strain of viral encephalitis.

STEVE: Has Vicky told you what we're doing tomorrow?

There's a weird taste in my mouth. It's obviously some kind of mouth fly. It burrows into your tongue and makes everything taste of metal. I'm not going to be here tomorrow, Steve – don't you understand?

ME: Tell me tomorrow. I'm off to bed, guys.
ALL: Sleep tight!

Goodbye for ever. Tell my family I love them. Tell my parents they were right never to do 'foreign'.

And yet against all the odds, I survived. Later that night, as I wandered out onto the porch again and stared out across the lake, desperate to find the location of that suffering animal, I noticed Olly, still hunched over his mics, screwdriver aloft, tweezering grains of rice into a receiver cavity.

He looked up at me. 'It's the hope that kills you, Sue,' he said. 'It's the hope that kills you.'

8. Piggy In the Middle

I left the main branch of the river and headed to the homeland of the Bunong people, one of twelve remaining hill tribes in the highland forests of Mondulkiri on the far-eastern edge of the vast Mekong basin. This area is the second most bio-diverse place on earth after the Amazon – although the threat of deforestation looms large. In the last forty years, almost 40 per cent of Cambodia's trees have been felled for timber or agriculture.

I was led deep into one of its most sacred areas, the Spirit Forest, by a guide with more than a passing resemblance to Gangnam Style's Psy. As we wandered, he told me about the animists who have a profound connection with the natural world and believe their ancestors' souls inhabit this place.

The Bunong are a deeply superstitious people. They believe if you cut down a tree, something wicked will happen: someone will get sick, suffer an accident, or even die. This must be an increasingly stressful belief to hold on to, living, as they do in the shadow of logging and mass-deforestation.

On certain feast days and festivals, the Bunong congregate in the forest by the river, and make an animal sacrifice to the ancestral spirits to appease them. We were lucky enough to be invited. After much discussion between the tribal elders and the production team, it was decided that the pig would be killed before I arrived. I am not particularly squeamish, but I do get intolerably sad at suffering, and, since the animal was not, obviously, going to be stunned before death, there would be a degree of awfulness involved. I was delighted this was one scene I wouldn't have to witness.

I sat in a clearing nearby waiting for the signal for action. Finally, it came. I wandered down through the trees to where I could see the tribe had gathered. There was a huddle of frantic activity and chatter, so I headed towards its epicentre. There, in front of me as I walked into the group, was a pig, trussed by its hands and feet, its snout bound tightly with twine, very much alive and very, very frightened. So I burst into tears. I'm helpful like that.

'Sorry,' said Claire.* 'There's been a bit of a mix-up.'

While everyone set up their pots and pans, took out their incense sticks and offerings, and lit the fires, I sat down next to the pig and stroked it for a while, in an effort to calm it. I knew that my sensitive Western feelings were incongruous and irrelevant here, but I wanted to be true to myself, so I retired into the forest until the sacrifice had been carried out and the pig was beyond suffering.

I returned a few minutes later, by which time the pig had been gutted, its innards floating downstream like a bloody cobweb. The cavity was bathed in river water and the carcass dragged back to the bank and placed on a mat of banana leaves. I don't eat much meat, but I have always been, strangely, fascinated by butchery. When done well, it's a compelling skill to behold. Two men set about the pig with cleavers, deftly removing every single piece of flesh. Each family in turn took receipt of chunks of meat, which they tipped into large metal pots, bubbling with river water and vegetables. Finally, once

* Claire was the brilliant director on this second shoot. She is super bright and super cool. She once told me that she had never seen someone attack a buffet with as much vigour as I did. I took that as a compliment.

every last bit of the animal had been distributed, the cooking (and, more importantly, the drinking) began in earnest.

The village elder, Tom Yam, was stripping bamboo with a blade into delicate fronds. These he daubed with pig's blood and placed either side of an ancestral shrine, which resembled a small dog kennel on stilts. Inside the shrine, a handful of incense sticks were burning in a rusty can. From the label, I could see it had been a tin of tomatoes in a previous life. Several men stood alongside him, chanting.

The atmosphere was fast changing from hushed reverence to open-air rave festival. Out came plastic jerry-cans full of homemade hooch and the celebrations began in earnest.

That's when I first notice it. Hanging off the side of the shrine is a tangle of veins connected to what looks like a pig kidney. How strange, I think. It must have fallen in there by accident.

Then, as I look around, I notice that everything seems to have a chunk of raw pig on it – the rocks, the trees, even the kids. People are drunkenly embracing friends, then hanging bits of intestine over their ears as they pull away. Uncooked piggy is obviously a sign of good luck for the Bunong.

The man in front of me is swaying, a gobbet of raw pig's liver hanging from his ear. Another man, to his left, has what looks like a piece of lung adorning his fringe. As I draw nearer, someone flicks a bit of kidney in my direction, which hits the white of my eye and bounces off again. Nearer still, and the tribesmen rush to adorn my shoulders with offal, a ventricle here, a pancreas there. I think I can make out a spleen on my shirt collar, but am not sure. I was never any good at biology.

A young man approaches me, holding out something that looks like a sliver of heart. 'I wouldn't have said that was hygienic!' I mutter anxiously, as he grabs me in a headlock and starts grinding it into my quiff.

CLAIRE: Sue!

She is loitering behind the camera, safely out of range.

CLAIRE: Look! Go over there! There! They're calling you over!

She points to Tom Yam and a gaggle of elders hunched over a vat with a clear hosepipe sticking out of the top – the sort of pipe you'd use to siphon petrol out of a car. Those who had already had a drink were red in the face and clutching their foreheads, like they'd just done a shit ton of poppers.

Tom Yam sucks on the hosepipe. He swallows, then coughs violently into the bottle. He beckons me over.

ME: (*whispering desperately towards the crew*) Shit! Where's the Sanex?
CLAIRE: What do you mean? Sue, you can't use Sanex – it's a tribal ceremony!
ME: That's raw pig on there. RAW PIG.
CLAIRE: It'll be disrespectful. It's rude!
ME: Do you KNOW what RAW PIG can do to you?

I have a sudden flashback to a YouTube video I'd seen of a Korean man in surgery, trichinella worms cascading out of his arse. What a wonderful resource the internet is.

It becomes clear that I have no choice. I need to step up. I need to embrace the Bunong's unique hospitality, even if it kills me. And it might.

The crew are some distance away, shooting on a long lens. I look towards them. It is the look of a woman who is about to cross every health and safety threshold she once held dear, a woman about to be exposed to the full spectrum of gastro-intestinal diseases known to man, and a few hitherto unidentified by medical science. It is a look that simply says, *Help me.*

I steel myself. It is simply a case of mind over matter. I accept the blessings of the forest. I accept the glistening unknown in the vat beneath. I accept it all. Then, as I bend towards the liquid, breathing in its oily reek, someone leans over and pops a chunk of pig bowel on the end of the straw.

A few sips in, all my fears vanish. In fact everything vanishes. The world goes dark. The last thing I remember thinking is that nothing – *nothing*, no parasite or bacteria – could ever survive in the presence of that much ethanol. So I raise my eyes to the heavens, toast the ancestral spirits and drink again with impunity.

9. Please Release Me

The next day we drove for five hours through clouds of red dust, jolted by the endless potholes and bombarded by car horns.

We were heading west, that was all I knew. It wasn't safe for me to know any more than that. I was due to meet a man called Dean from the Wildlife Rapid Response Rescue Team – Cambodia's most alliterative animal welfare unit – to witness a raid on a restaurant suspected of selling illegal bush meat.

Eventually we pulled up at a large roadside restaurant, packed with locals – the air thick with the smell of fried pork and garlic.

The guys went in, as they always did, to put a mic on the contributors and set up shots. I waited outside, my stiff bones warming in the midday heat.

There was a row of motorbikes parked outside the entrance, and as I walked past, I noticed a duck hanging upside down from one of the seats, its head dangling by the exhaust. We eat our meat, skinless and boneless, from a sealed plastic tray. Here, things are different. More often than not, you transport your dinner live and kicking home with you. Once, in rural Vietnam, I saw a man riding a push-bike with a pig on his lap. It might well be the cultural norm in South East Asia, but it never ceases to distress me. It was already nearly 40 degrees and the little thing was starting to pant, its chest heaving.

I knew what the boys would say: *You have to get used to it. You have to look away. You can't try to save everything, Sue. You'll go mad.*

And sometimes it felt like that. Like I was going mad. I'm too porous, that's my problem. I start to inhabit someone's or something's reality so much that I can hear their thoughts running through my head – their skin becomes my skin. I can feel their pain and, before long, my body will start mimicking their physical symptoms.

Sometimes I think that's the route to madness. Not knowing your own limits, the boundaries of your own flesh. Not putting out some line of defence between you and the world. If depression is the price you pay for seeing everything, then perhaps this anxiety is the price you pay for feeling it.

For me, empathy is a magnet whose polarity I can't control. Everything, every sensation, flies at me. And it sticks. By God, it sticks.

I took out my water bottle and started gently splashing the duck to cool it down. And then, the strangest thing happened: I said a prayer.

I am not a religious person. I don't go to church. I don't pray. It's a reflex – a buried, automated response. It's always been like this. I used to bury everything when I was a kid – bluebottles, worms, earwigs. Every single dead creature I came across had a woodland burial complete with lollipop-stick cross and full Catholic rites. I was so busy with insect requiems, I barely had time for important kid stuff like snorting Tippex and practising kissing on the inside crook of your arm.

So here I am, a woman in her forties, in a dustbowl dead-end town in Cambodia, praying over an upside-down duck on a motorbike. If there was ever a sentence that better described me, I haven't come across it yet.

The boys were heading back. I got up, quickly, so they wouldn't see what I'd been doing. As I walked away, I gently brushed the bird's wing and said sorry. I am sorry. I'm sorry for all of it. Then I tried to push it from my mind.*

Matt adjusted the lens. I pushed my hair from my face.

MATT: Camera speed . . .

That's telly-speak for 'The Camera is about to record your babble.'

I side-stepped a pregnant mutt, snuffling in the dust, and walked into the restaurant. The place was bustling, vast wooden tables and benches populated by chattering families, arguing over vast pots of noodles and rice.

'Have you seen Dean?' I asked random strangers. 'Have you seen Dean?' They stared at me as if I was mad. 'Do you know a bloke called Dean?'

I don't know why I was surprised at the lack of response. Imagine being in your local greasy spoon, when a Cambodian television crew bursts in. The presenter starts shouting in Khmer at the top of her lungs. You'd set your grandma on them, wouldn't you?

Minutes went by – still no sign of anyone resembling a Dean. I noticed that the restaurant curved round to the side, to a makeshift lean-to with dirt floors. I walked through. There, in the middle of a group of uniformed men, sat a white guy with a chiselled face. The sort of face that said, *See these lines on my brow? Each one represents a dhole, a langur, a pangolin that I've saved. So many animals . . . Sure, it came at a cost . . . friends, lovers, all gone. I live alone now. It's for the best. I can concentrate on my work.*

* I managed this until the end of the day, then spent the whole evening thinking about it.

'Excuse me. Are you Dean?' The guys around him stiffened, drawing themselves up to their full height. Dean didn't answer immediately: he simply sat there, sizing me up as I stood there, hanging.

That's the measure of Dean. After a full briefing, an hour-long pre-interview with the researcher and countless emails listing in detail what the filming would entail, Dean was *still* suspicious of us. I was enthralled by him. I had a real-life Bryan Mills right here, a man whose trust had been broken by the countless horrors he had seen, a hard man, a man of steel, who guards his broken heart . . .

My wandering imagination was thankfully cut short by a response: 'Yep, I'm Dean,' he replied, in a gruff Aussie burr. He extended his hand. It was heavy and dry, like a baseball mitt, worn from all the years of handling those pangolins, I guess. Those critters have scales that can *really* exfoliate.

He introduced me to the rest of the group, to Saro, from the Forestry Commission, and to some silent heavies from the Military Police, who were there to provide the muscle. It began to dawn on me how serious this all was.

Dean drained his cup, and motioned to the others to leave. As we got up, I noticed Saro covering his uniform with a denim shirt.

DEAN: It's so we don't get spotted along the way. Everyone's looking out for us, so we need to stay as anonymous as possible.

We drove, in convoy, for well over an hour, until the roads petered into tracks, and the tracks to paths. We came to a halt at the edge of dense woodland, next to a restaurant with a gaudy blue corrugated fascia. I would have thought it deserted, were it not for a teenager, newborn baby in her arms, sat outside on the porch, drinking soda and staring at us from her hammock. Saro got out of the car, removed his denim shirt to reveal his official uniform in all of its gold-threaded glory, and in they all rushed.

The girl didn't so much as flinch as we swept on through – she just kept on staring. The guards knocked on doors, checked the kitchens. Nothing. The place had the feeling of an Asian *Mary Celeste*. The raised floorboards creaked in the wind, the rows of burnished metal pans chiming as they knocked against one another. There were no adults about so they questioned the girl, but still she remained silent, slurping through her straw and staring. If I had known better I'd have pegged that look as stone-cold hatred.

We headed to the rear of the restaurant. Often, those who sell illegal meat will keep it stored off-premises, so if it is discovered, the contraband can't be pinned on them directly. The place backed onto a hill, dense with shrubs and trees. I followed the guards as they climbed the embankment, scrambling over rocks and thick tufts of grass. I wasn't sure what I was looking for, but I wanted to be of use. A cry went up. We went to investigate. One of the guards had found a large plastic cooler box buried in the ground. Inside were packets of bloody bush meat, mouse deer, monkeys, all hacked into quarters and wrapped in plastic.

Another cry went up. And another. More meat. More contraband. More death.

It was then it struck me. The wood was silent. Other than the men in uniform, cutting through the bush, there was no sign of life. No birdsong. No rustle of undergrowth as a douc or bamboo rat got spooked. Nothing. Nothing was living in that place – it was all gone, portioned up and stored in makeshift fridges. The forest had been asset-stripped. All that remained were the empty trees, waiting in vain to be colonized once more.

The economics are compelling: a Cambodian farmer can earn 250 times his monthly salary on the sale of a single dead tiger. Ivory from an elephant's tusks can fetch upward of $15,000 on the black market. With incentives like these, it's hard to think of an attractive alternative that would allow them to leave the wildlife alone. These people – the restaurant owners, the poachers – they aren't the real villains. The real villains are the men hundreds of miles away, sitting at their banqueting tables demanding tiger penis so they can feel like the Big Dude.

An hour later and we were still finding hidden stores – under clumps of earth, in gaps between boulders, tucked underneath tree roots. Piles and piles of the stuff.

We finished up and wandered out front. The girl hadn't moved. She didn't even acknowledge us as we emerged, the guards laden with contraband.

'What happens now?' I asked.

Bureaucracy: that was what happened now. Forms were filled out. Ancient scales were produced and the carcasses weighed and measured. There were photographs taken, details logged – all accompanied by intermittent head-shaking and low-level conversation. Then, when the procedural stuff had been completed, the meat was lugged on a tarpaulin to the centre of the village and a path between two rows of makeshift houses.

The guards took shovels out of their jeep and began digging a trench. Once it was around two feet deep, they tossed the animal parts into the dirt and poured petrol over them.

ME: What are you doing? What are you doing? No, don't do that! DON'T!

A match was tossed into the gully, and the whole lot erupted into blue flames. I stood there, over a mass grave, on fire. Acrid smoke curled around the houses and crept in through the windows.

'It's a message,' said one of the guards.

'It is the law,' said another.

Claire motioned to Matt. I knew she wanted me to talk about how I felt. *Trust me, you don't want to know how I feel*, I thought. *How I feel isn't going to wash at 9 p.m. on BBC2.* I kicked a wall. Then I kicked it again, harder. Then one more time, so I could really feel the pain in my toes. Fuck this. Fuck all of this.

'Speed,' said Matt.

'Sound speed,' said Olly.

It's Pavlovian, with me. When I hear those words I start talking. I can't help myself.

It's the end of a long day, and what do we have to show for it? Nothing. We're just choking in the smoke of a funeral pyre. What a waste. No one benefits from this. All this struggle and death and no one benefits. The animals aren't running free in the forest. The children don't have full bellies. There are only victims here. The animals died for nothing. The hunters killed them for nothing. All that fear and endeavour and loss – and it ends up here, in a smoking pile of ash and bone and the stink of gasoline.

It's impossibly hard for the human brain to comprehend the lack of a solution state. We are not wired to accept grey. We want the hard and fast absolutes of black and white. But this, this is all grey.

All I want to do is help. But there's no help to give. That's the truth of it. There's no remedy here. There's nothing I can do, or put my name to, there's no one I can agitate on behalf of, or donate to. This is fucked, pure and simple. This is all fucked.

There was a silence, bar the crackle and spit of burning fat.

'Do you have anything positive to say?' asked Claire.

I had forgotten I was being filmed.

'No,' I said. I was aware I was being petulant and difficult. 'No, I don't.'

And I turned and kicked the wall again, just so I could feel the pain in my body.

We wandered back to the car. I noticed that in one of the jeeps, to the rear of the convoy, there were three large wooden crates, partially covered by tarpaulin. An armed officer leant against the door, guarding its contents.

We set off.

ME: Where are we going, Dean?
DEAN: You'll see. Best that no one knows too much.

An hour later, we pulled up next to yet more jeeps.

DEAN: Come on, let's move.

We all transferred to the new vehicles. I noticed in my rear-view mirror that the crates were being moved too.

We set off again. The roads were getting narrower, the villages smaller. As we entered one, I noticed a man making a call on a mobile phone.

DEAN: That's right, you little shit, you ring it in.
ME: What do you mean? What's he doing?
DEAN: He's spotted us. He's an informer. He'll be paid by the traffickers to keep an eye out for us and let them know where we are.
ME: Really?
DEAN: Really. That's why we change cars. To try and stay one step ahead.

This was as close to *The Bourne Identity* as I'd ever got, and I'd be lying if I said it was anything other than thrilling.

I didn't know what was in those crates – but they were getting more precious by the second.

Finally, we took a left turn and the track faded into grass. At the end was a river and a small jetty with a boat waiting for us.

The guards looked around, checking we'd not been followed. The coast was clear. We got on.

As we puttered down the river, I started chatting to Dean. It turns out he'd previously worked in child-protection services, identifying and rescuing trafficked kids. You'd think, after years' working with the very worst examples of humanity, that Dean's next job would have been something gentle and easy – working in an ice-cream parlour in Hobart, or a dog-grooming salon in Cairns. But, no, Dean went straight from abused children into threatened wildlife.

He looked away as he talked about his previous life. It must have taken chunks out of him. That's the mark of the man: that he could have seen the lowest mankind could stoop to and was still carrying on, trying to make a difference, day after painful day.

ME: So, are we going to release soon? Somewhere round here?

I was desperate to get back onto dry land. I'd eaten something fried and grey back at the restaurant and it was starting to clamour in my colon.

DEAN: Here? You must be joking. Anything we release here will get captured again immediately by the villagers. We need to go deep into the forest.
ME: How deep?
DEAN: You'll see.

Eventually, the river narrowed, and I saw signs ahead.

We were entering a protected area. An armed sentry, stationed on a jetty, nodded as we came through. Onwards we went, as the water wound through the cool calm of the primary forest.

Then, finally, the engine cut out and we drifted to the bank. We were here. After five and a half hours of travelling, it was time to unwrap our cargo.

DEAN: OK, you ready? We've got some belters for you.

Dean cracked open the first crate. Inside was a large wet bag – like an outsized mail sack.

DEAN: Right. Let's start with these.

What can it be? I thought. *Silver langur? Yellow-cheeked gibbons? A fishing cat?*

DEAN: Check these out!

And with that he pulled out the LARGEST SNAKE I HAVE EVER SEEN.

~~~

I am a little frightened of snakes. It wasn't always thus. Back in the old days, I'd have been more than happy to hold a corn, or grass snake – but that was before I'd met Jake the Snake.

Mel and I used to host a weekend show on BBC London. Those who tuned in will remember that the programme mainly consisted of three sounds:

1. The entire back catalogue of Dutch prog-rock band, Focus.
~~~

2. Us wheezing with laughter as we played the entire back catalogue of Dutch prog-rock band, Focus.
3. The sound of Mel scoffing endless blocks of cheese. She was pregnant at the time, and had a craving for all things dairy. Barely a minute would go by without another Babybel, Dairylea or family pack of Cathedral City getting popped into her mush.

We enjoyed a wide variety of guests, but the most memorable, perhaps, was the professional wrestler, Jake 'the Snake' Roberts. He arrived with an enormous US mail sack, which he deposited on the studio floor.

'Guess what's in that?' he asked.

I figured if he wanted to be more enigmatic, he shouldn't have added 'the Snake' to his showbiz moniker.

JAKE: You scared of snakes?

'I am,' said Mel, mainlining a large cube of Red Leicester – thus shutting down any possibility she might be the one to handle the reptile.

That left me. Before I had a chance to reply, Jake had opened the sack, reached inside and plonked the huge snake around my neck, where it hung like a fifty-kilo dry scarf. My legs buckled under the weight.

JAKE: There you go, that's Damian.
ME: Damian? You called your snake Damian?

As if recognizing its name, the snake's head came round to face mine, its tongue flicking against my glasses. I could feel beads of sweat pricking my forehead.

MEL: (*starting on a mini Gouda*) Looks good on you.
ME: Is it OK?

JAKE: Sure.
ME: Will you tell me if it's not OK. If it's going to . . .
JAKE: Oh, you'll know if he's annoyed.
ME: (*tremulously*) How's that?
JAKE: He'll get you.

Gulp.

ME: Get me?
JAKE: Yep. Little squeeze to the neck. Here. (*He points to his own jugular.*) Knock you clean out. Fucker did that to me once. Was showing him in the ring, got a little cocky and, boy, did I get payback. Next thing I know, I put him round my neck and BOOM – I wake up twenty minutes later. Anyhow, we gonna do this goddamn interview or what?

Dean drew from the bag a water python, approximately two metres in length, and handed it to me. I had a matter of seconds to overcome my fear, as the last thing I wanted was for Dean to think I was a wuss. I extended my hands and received the snake, gripping onto it for dear life. Instantly I realized this was a mistake. Suddenly, this powerful length of muscle was thrashing and splashing in my arms – a creature who had come from God knows where and suffered God knows what – fighting with every ounce of her strength to get back to the river. With one final push she wrestled free from my grip and hurled herself into the water. She did it. She was finally home.

The others were easier. I didn't try to hold them. I merely acted as a conduit, letting them slide over me and into the deep.

We moored the boat and headed into the forest. Just two boxes left. I walked across the forest floor, the crunch of pine under my feet. I looked up and felt awed by the towering verticals of trees and shrubs. My ears retuned. No more white noise, no hiss – no technological backdrop. The natural world began to fill my senses, like a balm. I felt truly at peace.

Dean gestured to the guards who brought forward one of the boxes.

DEAN: Right, let's do this. Do you want the honour?

ME: Yes, I'd love to.

DEAN: OK. Now you gotta be quick to see these fellas. They are going to sprint up those trees.

I positioned myself to the side of the crate, and gently lifted the sliding wooden door at its front. For a second, just for a second, I saw them. Two macaques, cowed and frightened, blinking into the sudden sunlight. I saw their pupils adjust, recalibrate, saw them recognize their surroundings and then, with one giant bound, spring forward at lightning pace towards freedom. Out they ran, and straight up a tree. They were lost from sight in a heartbeat. We smiled, applauded and hugged one another.

The final crate remained. In the canopy above we could hear the monkeys, calling to each other.

DEAN: This one's for you, Sue. This one's special. And it's nearly dusk, so this is the perfect time for release.

I wondered what it could be.

The wooden door slid open and, for a second, I didn't know what I was looking at. At first glance it looked like a Mogwai – and I worried that in the low evening light it might go full gremlin on us.

We backed away. One of the guards started videoing the scene. Slowly it emerged. So very slowly. In fact, there would have been a trade description issue if this gorgeous creature was anything other than slow – for this was none other than a slow loris.

It began to climb the tree, stopping and turning its head every minute to check all was OK. It finally reached head height, and only then, when it felt out of our reach, did it get into second gear and climb higher and faster. I could feel my heart beating fast with the exhilaration. We did it. We saved them. We did it.

Five and a half hours. Six cars. Several dummy turns. A dozen guards as escorts. For three water pythons, two macaques and a slow loris.

And guess what – they're worth it.

Today, just as I'm finishing writing this chapter, I flick to the news. The lead story is that the last ever Northern White Rhino has died in Kenya. Another species eradicated, in what is the most troubling mass-extinction event the planet has ever seen. The Holocene Extinction, as it's known. The cause? Humans. This is why the macaques matter, and the loris, and even those scary pythons. Someone has to be the custodian – amid the consumption and the carelessness. Someone needs to take account of what we are doing. How poor we have become in seeking riches. How denuded and monochrome our world will be if nothing is done.

I went to bed that night cheered by the release of those beautiful animals. A good deed in a shitty world. And just as I drifted off to sleep, as the electrical activity in my brain slowed and my breathing steadied, I thought of that poor duck, upside down, panting, on that motorbike.

I told you: I'm a magnet.

10. Holy Moly

The drive to Kampong Cham is an easy two hours, once you've navigated your way through the hell of Phnom Penh traffic.

The roads here are pocked with holes, some so large they almost earn the title of craters: giant scoops in the gravel created by collapsed soil and badly patch-worked aggregate. Worst still is the dust, the endless toxic dust, clouds of thick red particles that tumble in the air, covering everything in their wake. It's like a dystopian Tatooine in the early days of capitalism.

Tides of traffic fight to be the first through the narrow arterial roads, sleek Lexus SUVs jostling side by side with tuk-tuks and pushbikes. There are scooters whose passengers, often kids, are coming home from hospital, holding saline drip bags attached to bamboo poles. Dazed pedestrians weave in and out of the oncoming traffic, coated in filth, staggering like terracotta zombies. Beggars and amputees line the streets, choking in the gloom.

Your eyes can't take it all in. It's too much. You're tired just witnessing it all, let alone trying to think and feel about the place. It's a version of Hell quite unlike any other I've seen, and I was very, very glad to be leaving it behind.

From Kampong Cham we took a boat to Hermit Hill (the second cousin twice removed of Henman Hill). The river was dark and acidic, leaching its stink in the heat. For miles, all I could see was the soul-deadening order of rubber plants.

Finally some twenty kilometres upstream, Mother Nature reclaimed the landscape and a haphazard explosion of greenery filled the horizon. We had reached the forest.

All I knew was that I'd come to the Preah Kuk to meet a holy man, a hermit, who had lived in splendid isolation for over thirty years. My knowledge of hermits was a little limited, I'll admit, but I was fairly sure that one of the cornerstones of hermitry was an eschewing of humanity and all it represented. Not for this hermit, however. With this hermit, anyone and everyone was welcome. He was an access-all-areas hermit.

And he'd invited me for tea.

There are many words I'd associate with a hermit – loner, recluse, ascetic, solitary. Sociable, however, wouldn't be one of them. This gentleman was a walking oxymoron – like a benign serial killer or a trustworthy estate agent.

I climbed what felt like a never-ending set of steps, which wound upwards into the forest canopy. Monkeys hung from the branches, eyeing me, calculating if I had anything worth stealing. One of them looked briefly enthralled by my nylon quick-dry shirt from Mountain Warehouse, but decided against it at the last minute and returned instead to the firm cupping of his voluminous ball-sack.

Halfway up, I paused to catch my breath. A woman passed me, making her descent. I assumed she was the hermit's 11 a.m. tea appointment. Busy, busy, busy . . .

I was a wet, wheezy mess when I reached the top and turned the corner towards his house. There he was, waiting for me, straight out of Central Casting, my first ever hermit. He was gaunt, swaddled in robes and sporting an impressive, lengthy beard that waved in the breeze.

There was an awkward pause, that moment of stasis when

you first meet someone: when the canvas is still blank and all's to play for.

He walked towards me. I walked towards him. I placed my hands together in prayer, as did he. I bowed and, at the exact same moment, he did the same. Our foreheads smashed together in one mother of an intergenerational head-butt.

Two worlds colliding. Literally. My first ever holy man, and I'd given him concussion.

The hermit shows no signs of moving. So I stay there, stock still. Time passes – so much time, in fact, that I wonder whether he's OK, or whether he has sustained some form of brain injury in the collision.

The minutes tick by, and still we are welded together.

Finally, there is movement. He reaches out and grabs my shoulders. I flinch for a second, but soon relax. He starts muttering something under his breath, which I strongly suspect is some form of Buddhist incantation. How wonderful, I think. This is how the Ancients must have welcomed each other. So I ignore my embarrassment and the sound of the crew sniggering and choose to commit fully to the experience. After another minute or so, I even start to approach something close to relaxation.

His grip intensifies.

God, I am so fortunate right now, I think. *I'm being blessed by a holy man* – a man who has turned his back on the empty trinkets and hollow promises of this world that he might live simply, among his ancestors, in this lush tropical forest.

His grip loosens on my shoulders and I relax, imagining the blessing to be over. To my surprise, however, he regrips – this time lower down, at my elbows.

Gosh. This is incredible! I can't get over it! How many people get to experience this kind of intimate spiritual exchange? I imagine this is how the sangharaja greeted each other after a long rain retreat. Magical!

Come on now, Sue. Accept the blessing. You're SO uptight. Just relax into it.

The arms move again.

This must be a local ritual. Strange, because no one mentioned it – it definitely wasn't in the notes. It doesn't matter: I'm just lucky to be here. For God's sake, don't move. The last thing you want to be right now is culturally insensitive.

His hands were on my arse.

Relax, will you? It's just a way of saying hello, Sue. For God's sake. Can't you stop sexualizing everything? You are such a pervert. You are in the presence of a deeply spiritual being – you should be ashamed of yourself for even thinking that.

Finally, the hermit drew himself upright. I did the same. I can't be sure, but that's when I think I saw him wink.

Cheeky fucker.

I learned a valuable lesson that day: that there's a fine line between a traditional Cambodian greeting and an old geezer using the cultural barrier between us as an opportunity for a grope.

He took both my hands and led me into his home, a single-storey box built from concrete. Inside there was one small window, the rest of the space illuminated by a large candle. I could dimly make out shrines, deities, and dried floral garlands, which littered the floor around us.

On the wall I noticed a strange scrawl in thick charcoal. I couldn't make out the script in the gloom, but from the dense curlicues I figured it was either ancient Cham or Khmer. How *authentic*, I trilled, still trying to normalize the madness around me. *How bloody authentic.*

Once inside, our bristling sexual intensity simmered to a

level of camaraderie – albeit he was still rather tactile. We bowed to each other once more, hugged a little, then let silence take the room.

The peace and quiet didn't last; from under a brass offertory bowl, came the unmistakable ring tone of a Nokia 3310.

'Is that your phone?' I asked, somewhat incredulously.

He nodded and let it ring out.

Silence enveloped us again.

The idea of the Hermit Sequence was to illustrate the painful lot of the holy man during Pol Pot's reign of terror. I expected him to tell me about the years spent on the run, how his spiritual belief kept him going in the face of persecution – but no. This is the Hermit. He doesn't play by the rules of television.

Instead he grabs a photo and holds it up to the light. In it I see a group of Cambodians posing with an Elvis impersonator. I have no idea what this has to do with running from the Khmer Rouge but, nevertheless, I nod encouragingly at the image. Then he points at Elvis. A lot. It slowly dawns on me that Mr Vegas '67 Comeback Special is actually the hermit – in disguise.

He senses my bewilderment.

'I had to act like that in order to survive,' he says, by way of an explanation.

This answer only serves to throw up more questions. You want to avoid detection as a holy man so you dress as ELVIS? Surely there were more anonymous outfits he could have opted for. Surely a simple peasant costume would have done the trick? But what do I know? Maybe the forest was full of holy men in fancy dress, with monks dressed as Neil Sedaka, David Cassidy and Creedence Clearwater Revival.

Then, out of nowhere, he reaches across me and brings

something into the light. At first glance it looks like a stuffed sable guinea pig. Then he raises it up to his head so I can see it properly.

The wig.

What I particularly enjoyed was that it wasn't a full wig; it was merely a resplendent nylon hairpiece at the front, with a metal band to attach it round the back of his head. Essentially, it was a tiara with a quiff on it.

He pops it on. Ludicrous. I laugh out loud.

I try it on. It looks exactly like my own hair. No difference whatsoever.

I'm not laughing any more.

His phone rings again. I wonder if it's his mum, asking where the hell he's been for the last thirty years.

In the brief window between rings and pings, I ask him about the forest.

HERMIT: I love the forest, it is our parent.

His voice is gentle and sweet. Mild groping notwithstanding, I do really love him.

As I leave, I ask him to read my fortune. He is known for his power of prophecy in these parts. I'm not sure of the technique he uses, whether it be palms, tea leaves, cards. I half wonder if he'll grab my buttocks again to divine my destiny. Instead he just looks at me and says:

HERMIT: I feel you are in a good place.

Even for a cold reading that's one hell of a bland, generic start.

I wander outside. Our wonderful assistant producer, Kate, is standing there with a large bolt of fabric.

ME: What's that for?

KATE: We asked him if there was anything he wanted – you know, to say thank you. He wanted a donation for the monastery, and a new robe.

ME: But it's a leopard print . . .

KATE: Yeah, that's what he wanted. A leopard-print robe . . .

The Hermit appears, giving the thumbs up. I bow, taking care to keep my distance this time, and hand him the fabric. His eyes mist with tears.

'Call me,' he motions, making the internationally accepted thumb-and-little-finger phone gesture. He then starts pointing at something inside.

'OK,' I say, bewildered as to what he is gesturing towards. And then I notice, as the candles change direction in the breeze, that the scrawl on the wall isn't Khmer or Cham. It is plain, old-fashioned digits. It's the Hermit's phone number.

The Hermit widens his eyes and gives me the thumbs-up. I briefly consider adding him to my contacts list, but I know deep down that would merely open the door to a whole world of holy-man sexting.

As I walked back down the hill, I turned and saw the Hermit winding the leopard-print cloth round him. We'd bought way too much – ten metres, to be precise. He kept winding and winding, like a Buddhist bobbin. In the end, he resembled a mummified Bet Lynch silhouetted against the lush forest.

I looked at him and laughed. I was sad to leave. And as I wandered off, I couldn't help thinking, *D'you know what? He's right. I* am *in a good place.*

11. The Pig of Kratie

I woke the following morning with a bag of nails in my throat. It was hard to swallow, and what was left of my voice floated up through my engorged tonsils, like mist through a pothole. I was, to quote freely from *Withnail and I*, drifting into the arena of the unwell.

Getting up was worse, my legs heavy and my brain fogged. I don't think I've ever felt as rough in my entire life – and that comes from a fully paid-up member of the Hypochondriacs Club. By the way, if you're thinking about joining the Hypochondriacs Club, most of the meetings get cancelled, so don't knock yourself out if you're too ill to attend.

The filming schedule was as tight as a jazz musician's snare drum, so there was no hope of staying in bed and resting up. I rolled into the car, moaning. Rather annoyingly, no one noticed the difference between Well Susan and Ill Susan. It transpires that both of them are whingers. Thankfully, it was a short trip to our next location. As we parked up, I completed my make-up routine in record time. It was hard to hold the brush to my face – it felt like I was carrying a ten-kilo hammer. I rubbed make-up round my eyes and ran some coconut oil through my quiff. I'm camera ready, baby.

Sod's Law dictated that this was not to be an easy morning. There was no dancing in a rainforest with a shaman, or learning the recipe for barbecued rat. No. That morning, I was tasked with conducting a serious interview with a gentleman whose life's work had been championing the preservation of the endangered Irrawaddy Dolphin. Yes, I needed to know and elicit *facts*. Mr X (I didn't catch his name as I was semi-delirious during the briefing) was responsible for changing local fishing techniques so that these beautiful creatures didn't get caught as collateral damage. I was looking forward to it – I mean, what's not to like about a conservationist?

I got out of the car to say hello to him.

'Who is this?' said Mr X, pointing, but not looking, at me.

'This is Sue, our presenter,' said Claire – somewhat confused by his manner.

'Oh.' He paused, still determinedly not looking at me. 'I thought presenters were blonde and beautiful.'

There was an awkward, shocked silence – made worse by him delivering a mime to illustrate his point. His hands traced the outline of a curvy Barbie-doll figure with unfeasibly large breasts.

Oh, I thought. *You want an albino Jessica Rabbit. Well, I'm afraid she's busy running our current-affairs department, so you're stuck with me.*

As conversational ice-breakers go, this kept us still firmly at the 32°F mark. I had rolled out of bed, bundled my aching limbs into a car and smeared eye-shadow round my face and this was my reward. Part of me laughed at his stupidity and bare-faced rudeness, but a little part of me – the part deep inside – bristled with a familiar shame.

Personal affront notwithstanding, the interview had to be done. I'm not a stormer-outer, I'm more of a grit-your-teeth-and-get-on-with-it kind of a girl, so I resolved to carry on.

'Hi,' I said, 'I'm Sue,' extending my hand for him to shake, partly out of politeness, but mainly in the hope that whatever virus had gripped hold of me was contagious through skin contact.

He took my hand. He still didn't look at me.

We climbed onto the fishing boat. I wasn't sure if it was swaying or I was. Once onboard, things took a further turn for the worse. It turned out that the only thing Mr X liked more than insulting strangers was the sound of his own voice. Who would have thought that 'misogynist' and 'bore' would share some of the same space in a Venn diagram?

The interview ran like this: I'd ask a simple question, and fifteen minutes later he'd pause for breath. The sun was up, and the water was millpond still. What a waste of a beautiful day.

The babble continued. Listen, I thought, you might know a lot about the river dolphin, mister, but you don't know anything about television. An hour's diatribe about your personal journey through the rank and file of the Cambodian civil service isn't going to zing its way into the edit. To be honest, mate, we just want a couple of soundbites about the real star of the show here: the Irrawaddy Dolphin.

I was now in full fever, and losing a grip on my surroundings. Fortunately, Mr X was so emotionally invested in his own brilliance he had failed to notice that the entirely non-glamorous TV presenter opposite him was slumping heavily to one side, eyes closed. I don't know about you, but such signals have always proved enough of an indicator that I am boring the tits off someone for me to stop. Each to their own.

His monologue hit me in waves as I faded in and out of consciousness.

MR X: I was a remarkable child . . . They said they had never seen someone with that level of skill before . . . The board gasped in amazement at my ingenious suggestions . . . Then I was honoured with the highest prize in all the land . . .

I made my peace with the fact I was never going to make it off that boat alive. I was going to die there, in the heat, with the sound of a braying bureaucrat in my ears. This is how it ends. Not with a bang, but with a lecture in Khmer on departmental restructuring.

And then, something extraordinary happened. At the end of a particularly long ramble about his distinguished academic career (trailblazing intellect, staggering insight), I saw a sleek grey head poke from the river's surface behind him and blow water into the air. The impossibly rare Irrawaddy Dolphin. Mr X turned round, but by now it had submerged, out of sight.

I smiled to myself and carried on. I acted as if nothing had happened as, in truth, I wanted this dolphin all for myself. I teed up another info-dump:

ME: So, Mr X, tell me about the changes to fishing in this area.

MR X: Well, I was commended many times by officials for my great work, so it was no surprise to me that I was given this task. After all, every job I take on I complete perfectly. I was the natural choice. I have always been excellent as a leader . . .

Again the dolphin emerged behind him and fired a shower of droplets into the air.

MR X: . . . And if you ask anyone, they will tell you I am the best choice for this project because of my impeccable pedigree . . .

Another glorious marine fart erupted, just behind his head.

Three or four times that happened – each time Mr X embarked on a monologue, the cheeky dolphin would appear and spew water into the air, then disappear when he turned to look for it. It was as if the dolphin was making a point. In my febrile state, I imagined it talking to me. For some reason, it talked in a broad Brummie accent. Don't ask. I was off my face.

DOLPHIN: Hey, Sue, how's it going?

I smiled, my dry eyes rolling in my head.

DOLPHIN: This guy's banging on, isn't he?

MR X: I could have been a world beater at anything. Anything. But someone of my abilities is best placed to save an entire species, which is what I am doing.

DOLPHIN: I'm gonna let you into a secret. This guy is an absolute joke. Me and the lads take the piss out of him constantly.

MR X: I expect, after this project, that many nations will be interested in my work and I will probably be called into high office elsewhere.

DOLPHIN: I mean, I know that life isn't fair – but surely the wrong species is facing extinction here. Surely this wild bore should be eradicated from the planet – not me.

And with that, the dolphin, that strange, exotic beast, dived into the water for the final time. Gone. I never saw it again.

Soon, none of us will ever see it again.

I became so sick, that finally it was decided I should get seen at a hospital in Phnom Penh. I am not good with hospitals, following a psychologically scarring trip to A&E I was forced to make in the early nineties.

I was at Cambridge studying* at the time. My particular college was a hotbed of political activity, and we'd spend long nights discussing how we'd take down Thatcher and Pinochet, just as soon as we'd put on our pants and finished that pint of snakebite and black. Demonstrations were a constant feature of student life – you name it, we'd make a banner about it. The best thing about a march, of course, was that they invariably happened in London, on a Saturday, so you could hop on a free bus first thing in the morning and be in the capital for the day.

Mel was all about the free bus ride to London – after all, politics was one thing, but an all-expenses-paid trip to Oxford Circus and back was another. She joined a demonstration about education and managed to hold her placard upside down, all the while chanting, 'Loans not grants! Loans not grants! Loans not grants!' before someone kindly corrected her. Minutes later, she surreptitiously peeled off to the King's Road to look for a pair of acid-pink Dr Martens.

There was also a tantalizing employment opportunity waiting for a handful of students. The boss? MI5: the national security service tasked with keeping the UK safe. It's pretty good at it, too, from what I've read: scoring a total of 4.1 out of 5 on Google Reviews – meaning we're *mainly safe*.

Cambridge was not only a recruitment hotspot for MI5,

* A breakdown of this 'study' reveals 10 per cent Renaissance Literature, 10 per cent Greek Tragedy, 40 per cent gossip, 35 per cent scones, 5 per cent marijuana.

but M16, the Secret Intelligence Service. Since the days of Philby, Burgess, Blunt and Co., the rumour was that undergraduates were being monitored and covertly enlisted, with a Fellow in every college tasked with identifying potential candidates. Word got out that our mate Jez had been approached on a park bench. Quite what he had been approached for is beyond me, but the gossip spread that he was being tipped for a job as an international spy.

I wanted to be an international spy. I was already competent in most of the major disciplines – I liked martinis, I enjoyed a good game of poker, and pretty much every woman I'd ever slept with was dead. Or at least they must have been, because every time I called them I got no dial tone.

Sadly, my turn on the park bench never came. There was no whispering in corridors. No clandestine meetings in Whitehall. No 'for your four-eyes only' documents placed down in front of me. On reflection, I think the reason might lie in M16's motto: *semper occultus*. Always secret. Let's face it, I would have told Mel within thirty seconds of being recruited. And thirty seconds after that she would have told half of Lithuania. So it was probably for the best.

I digress. Outside of shouting and marching, I spent the rest of my time at college trying to make jokes in the comedy club. Every year, the Cambridge Footlights put on a pantomime. It was fashioned as a wry sideways look at the genre, and much more politically correct than its traditional antecedents. The audience responses were less 'He's behind you!' and more 'He's behind you, but that shouldn't unduly concern you unless you're a latent homophobe.'

I was playing the part of Head Nun. I thought I'd given a rich resonance to the role, but I seem to remember a rather unkind reviewer saying he wished I had been in silent orders.

We were coming to the end of the week-long run, and I won't lie, I had had a few – but there are no laws, after all, about being drunk in charge of a habit. There is no 'Thou shalt not drink own-brand vodka while in a wimple' in the Ten Commandments, although there might well have been if God and Moses hadn't got so caught up in Ox Coveting.

Anyway, there was a dance routine at the end of the first half, during which I managed to get my feet caught up in my outfit. In the ensuing kerfuffle, my friend Nick (dressed as a jester) accidentally punched me in the face. I crashed downwards in spectacular fashion, cracking my head against the floor. I got up, and immediately saw stars, but tried to work my dizziness into some kind of extemporaneous jazz dance routine. By the time the interval came, I felt sick and very, very sleepy.

I won't lie, the speed at which I was replaced was galling. It really was as simple as pushing one of the props guys onstage. They didn't even put the outfit on him. It was one of many ego-levelling moments in my professional lifetime.

The theatre management decided that I was to go to Addenbrooke's Hospital, where I lay waiting on a bed for several hours, still dressed as Mother Superior, listening to some toff-shaped turd called Rupert getting his stomach pumped in the neighbouring bed.

I was so concussed I couldn't speak – so at first the nursing staff took it at face value that I was a bona-fide member of the religious community. After all, why else would I be in a habit, wimple and twelve-inch crucifix? Staff would come by and say, 'Are you all right, Sister?' and I would give them a woozy thumbs-up. One visitor even genuflected and crossed herself as she passed by my bed.

It was only when they asked how I had sustained the head injury – 'Well, Doctor, it was the Act One finale and I was a bit pissed, a jester punched me in the head and I tripped over my habit' – that it became clear I was some way short of the full Bride of Christ.

This new information prompted not only a change of tone but a sudden downturn in my treatment plan. Now, I was just another drunken student. Now, I was just like Rupert next door.

DOCTOR: So, you've been drinking, yes?
ME: Yesh, jush a little. My teeth are furry. Ish that a sign of something?

He signed in resignation.

DOCTOR: Do you have a headache?
ME: Yesh. I can shee two of you. Are you twins?

Another doctor appeared.

DOCTOR 2: Oh, God, not another one. Does she need her stomach pumping too?

I closed my eyes and desperately tried to remember the patron saint of sobriety.

That ignominious scene was at the forefront of my mind as I entered the hospital in Phnom Penh. Admittedly, this time I was dressed as a bargain-basement Indiana Jones, rather than a holy woman – but I still expected the worst. A gaggle of men shouted at me in Khmer and my bloods were taken. After a cursory check over, they seemed satisfied all was fine and I wobbled out. But I didn't get any better.

It became apparent that, for insurance purposes and in the name of good practice, I should get myself seen by the doctors at the Hospital for Tropical Diseases on my return home. By that point, I'd given up on finding a diagnosis, and instead resigned myself to feeling a bit below par for the foreseeable future.

I love the staff at the HTD. They are gleeful. They cannot contain their glee. Their glee is unbridled. A quick scout through my travel itinerary and their eyes were positively bulging with excitement. So much possibility! So many pathogens! Such diverse disease vectors!

It was here I learned the word 'zoonotic' – as in 'I'm afraid I can't come to work today, as I have acquired a zoonotic disease.' It was a perfect new addition to my hypochondriac's arsenal.

I proffered my right arm, and four phials of blood were taken, labelled and put into the centrifugal machine. I've never had so much blood taken. After a thorough examination, I was diagnosed with chikungunya, a nasty little mozzie-borne disease, and suspected typhoid. Yes, typhoid.

DOCTOR: Oh, one more thing, Sue – when you got seen in Phnom Penh and they did the blood test . . .

ME: Yes?

DOCTOR: . . . did you check they used a clean needle? I mean, did you see it come out of the packet?*

My silence was all he needed to start afresh with an HIV test on my right arm.

* Thank God for Steve and co. Of course they had checked on my behalf, and all was well.

12. The Pig of Kratie 2

The village of Kampi is essentially a dirt track, bordered by wonky wooden shacks, that runs parallel to the Mekong. Knackered fishermen lie on hammocks, smoking, out of reach of the fierce midday sun. Kids play with sticks in the dust. The women squint into the distance with intense thousand-mile stares – looking for the Bigger Picture.

The road is lined with makeshift stalls, all selling carvings of the Irrawaddy Dolphin. I'd like you to get a real sense of this scene so, at this point, I'd politely ask that you turn to your preferred search engine and call up a picture of that magnificent beast. The Irrawaddy Dolphin. When the image pops up, do any similarities spring to mind? Yes! You got it! It's a little bit, well – penisy, isn't it? Let me tell you, it's even more penisy-looking when it's been hastily rendered in wood for the tourist market. Imagine thousands of them, big and small, thick and thin, lined up on never-ending trestles. When we arrived, it looked like there'd been an explosion in a rural Ann Summers factory.

It turned out that Dildo Alley was neither photogenic nor appropriate for your average BBC2 viewer, so we headed down to the water once again, to place the Mekong geographically and emotionally at the heart of the story. As we snaked behind one of the larger huts, we came across the usual South East Asian visuals – mounds of plastic bottles, trees heavy with bronze dust, a scattering of chickens and dogs – but then we came across something we'd never encountered before.

A MEGA PIG.

Matt and I both started laughing uncontrollably – trying to comprehend what we were seeing. Because when I say MEGA PIG, I mean a

MEGA PIG.

I am a fan of pigs. I had the opportunity to raise a couple during the filming of *The Good Life* – a series in which Giles Coren and I attempted to be self-sufficient in the style of Tom and Barbara from the legendary TV series. During this period of intense husbandry, I learned several things about our porcine chums, namely that they are (a) not as clever as dogs (for some reason they don't want to say *sausages*, however intensively you train them) and (b) they reach sexual maturity an awful lot sooner than you'd expect. Or, indeed, want.

The show featured many handy practical tips on home thrift, such as how to render your pet cow into candles and how to make nettle cheese through a pair of tights. Useful, see? But I'd be lying if I said that the programme wasn't somewhat challenging to make. The pigs were great, don't get me wrong, as were the goats and the chickens (the odd flare-up of anal mites notwithstanding). It was the location of the shoot that presented the main issue. In the sitcom, Tom and Barbara escape the rat race by transforming their surburban semi into a make-do-and-mend paradise. Up pop their nouveau-riche neighbours, Margo and Jerry, and the odd bit of well-meaning capitalist versus off-grid badinage occurs.

Britain, of course, has changed hugely since 1975. So, instead of Margo and Jerry as neighbours we had an observant Jewish couple on one side and a devout Muslim family on the other. Both were a delight. Neither, however, was a fan of pigs.

So, rather than being a meditation on the joys of 'getting away from it all', we spent months negotiating a religious and cultural tightrope, while trying to stop the male pig getting his curly cock up something he shouldn't.

And they say the licence fee is wasted.

Anyway, back to

MEGA PIG.

Imagine a Shetland pony. Then imagine it pink and hairless. Then imagine it with a gut that could sweep the floor as it moved – like a puce wall made entirely of fat. That was Mega Pig – and, Mekong be damned, I *had* to stroke her. She was tethered, with a loose rope, to a pole at the base of the house. As I came within petting distance I saw that her head actually came level with my belly button.

A smiling lady with blackened teeth emerged from the shadows. She seemed to be Mega Pig's right-hand woman.

ME: Wow! She is amazing!

The woman nodded. I suspect she was used to this reaction to her pet pork-ship.

ME: What did you do to get a pig this big?

Om translated. There followed much discussion and laughter.

LADY: Nothing! We were very lucky. We are very blessed!

You bloody liars, I thought. You've been busy genetically engineering this pig under your house. You've been mating a Middle White with an Asian Elephant. Sod Dolly the Sheep, this is a Pork Colossus.

'Is she friendly?' I asked, even though I was already running my hands along her ears. They resembled the flaps of a marquee.

A couple of minutes' chat, and then a two-word translation came back.

LADY: *Too* friendly!

More laughter.

Too friendly. My imagination ran riot. What would an over-friendly pig be like? Where do you draw the line? At what point does friendly pig tip over into *over*-friendly pig?

LADY: This is not our biggest pig. The biggest pig was even *more* friendly. It was a problem. She used to wander around the village and say hello to everyone.

I couldn't conceive of an even bigger pig. My mind conjured the image of a vast bacon fortress with whiskers. Saying hello. I bet it was a problem, I thought. I bet there was a real frisson when the locals were down at the riverbank, washing their smalls in the water, and a two-tonne hog bore down on them desperate to make their acquaintance.

I didn't ask what had happened to over-friendly Megamega Pig. I imagine she had gone on to be an over-friendly ham that had fed the entire population of the Mekong delta.

Om beckoned me over.

OM: This lady has a question for you. Are you married?

Oh, God, not again.

It's fair to say that Pig Lady was starting to take a real shine to me. For the next hour she walked around glued to my hip, as if we were part of a Cambodian three-legged-race.

Finally, Claire interceded: 'C'mon, Sue!' She had the patience of a saint, but even she had grown weary of my need to stroke every animal I came across. 'Stop petting the pig. We need to go next door and make cakes.'

I said my goodbyes, and left. Mega Pig's parting gesture was to back up onto the post and rub her buttocks against the rough wood. Now *that's* a pork scratching. I watched on, in awe, as the whole house vibrated in time to her anus.

Our next encounter, with a group of cake-makers in the village, was meant to illustrate how the womenfolk of Kampi supplemented the income of their family. Everywhere we went, fish stocks were down and life was hard for the beleaguered fishermen so it fell to the wives and daughters to diversify and find alternative sources of cash. I came into our contributor's house, took off my shoes, and fired out another round of excruciatingly pronounced hellos. I sat down next to the mother, who was squatting by a small fire with her kids around her. She was silently making 'cakes', local specialities that took on a number of forms. One was a confection made of warm rice, wrapped round a hard cone of sugar, and another, a greasy rice batter cooked on the fire until it browned into a cross between a pancake and a waffle. These would then be sold at the local market bringing in a few much-needed *riel*.

I had just started watching the woman make these cakes when Pig Lady re-emerged. I don't know what she had been doing, but by now her hands were almost completely black. She waved at me and I clocked her gunk-coated palms. I waved back nervously. She chatted to the other women, and suddenly they all started shouting at one another. I had no idea what was going on, but tempers were distinctly frayed.

Pig Lady came over and unceremoniously plonked herself down next to me. There was a sudden and strong whiff of farmyard billowing from her skirts. The other ladies moved away from me as she took her seat, seemingly afraid.

It was then I understood what the argument had been about. Pig Lady had laid claim to me. I was now her property. Her bitch, and hers alone. It had all got rather *Orange Is the New Black*.

Worse was to come. Pig Lady was so keen to impress me with her culinary skills that she leant across the mother and grabbed a ball of sticky rice from the pan. Her fingernails oozed dark liquid as she pressed the rice round the sugar, and the grains took on a slightly grey colour from where she had manhandled them. Then, just to make sure that everyone in the room knew I was under her protection, she offered the completed confection to me.

Oh, God. Oh, God, no. Not again.

It was time to walk that tightrope once more – the delicate balancing act between accepting hospitality from your hosts and preserving the sanctity of your intestines.

I put it into my mouth.

Genuinely, if I had licked Mega Pig from snout to tail and back again, it would have tasted less barnyard than that cake. In the phraseology of *Masterchef*'s Gregg Wallace, 'First you get mud, then sweet, sweet sugar, then comes that strong back-note of Babe.'

Thank you, Kampi. That's one mouthful I'll never forget.

13. Banlung

Making a film with an environmental message is hard, not least because there is no happy ending. Not one in sight, at least. I felt we'd done as much as we could on the ground, and that now it was time to get a different perspective. It became clear the only way we could truly and meaningfully show the devastation of the landscape was to film it from above, so we managed to charter a chopper to take us to our next destination, Ratanakiri.

The airstrip was a makeshift affair, a wide boulevard of red dust on which sat a spanking white helicopter, ready to go. As we approached, a crowd gathered – the kids begging, the adults staring at us with hatred in their eyes. I felt like an interloper. Like I was part of the problem. In a journey that had so far made me feel deeply connected to the people, this felt decidedly Them and Us.

Annie was our pilot for the day, a ballsy South African in mirror shades, with one hell of a health and safety speech:

ANNIE: Right. Before you get in my chopper, you zip up everything that's got a zip. Your flies, your pockets, your hoods. You lock everything down. You tie up your shoelaces, you secure your sunglasses, you fasten your hats. Do you hear me? You make sure that everything on your person stays on your person. One thing comes loose, one *tiny* thing comes loose, this bird is going down.

I was half terrified, half excited. She had actually referred to the helicopter as 'this bird'. It was all so magnificently *Top Gun.*

Her speech proved highly motivating. We started panic-checking our belongings, every pencil, pen and notebook buttoned in and patted down.

Matt was filming out of the side of the chopper, so was bound to his seat with reinforced ropes and carabiners. Then the camera was bound to him in the same way. The rest of us double-buckled, then buckled again, rammed earphones over the top of our caps and kept our fingers crossed. We took off, hovering shakily like a may bug, creating wide circles in the ochre dust below. The kids watched for a moment, then ran for cover as the dirt tore into them.

And we were off.

For the first ten minutes all I could hear was the sound of Claire, heavy breathing down the intercom in raw panic. Occasionally we'd shout out to each other, 'Are you OK? Are your pockets secure? Are all your zips zipped?'

It reminded me of the first time I'd ever been in a helicopter. I flew in an open-door army chopper for an episode of Armando Iannucci's topical comedy show, *Saturday Night Armistice.* The sketch was a protest against French nuclear testing in the South Pacific. The deal was, I had to fly over the Palace of Versailles and let out 40 kilos of mushrooms, thereby creating our very own mushroom cloud. What I didn't know was that Steve Bendelack, one of comedy's most brilliant directors, was frightened of flying – so I did the whole thing, hanging out of one side of a military copter with him screaming, 'SHIT! SHIT! SHIT!' in a frenzied loop. It made for a fairly stressful, high-stakes three minutes of comedy.

Annie flew us over acres of pristine forest and, for a while,

I felt like nothing could possibly be wrong with the world. Then, after we'd been airborne for fifteen minutes or so, we saw it – the great scars in the landscape ahead, the ground razed to dust, trees smoking.

We looked on in silence. I don't think there is anything more awful than the sight of a forest on fire.

Once we'd landed in Ratanakiri, we trooped to the hotel. Dusk was falling and we were shattered and caked in grime.

'Best get the Deet on,' said Kate. 'This is a really malarial area.'

You'll know by now I'm not a fan of Deet. For those of you unfamiliar with it, it's like Agent Orange, but rather than destroying acres of foliage, it destroys your arms and legs.* On the plus side, your arms and legs are rendered so toxic that mosquitoes don't fancy landing on them – so it's swings and roundabouts.

I think it's truly horrid stuff. It's a solvent – because that's what your skin has been crying out for: solvent. It burns through plastic and eats at your clothes. I don't want to think about what it does to your innards. The internet tells me it is 'mainly safe', which, for a hypochondriac and serial catastrophizer, simply isn't safe enough.

KATE: Oh, and Sue, have you remembered your Malarone?

ME: Yes. Of course! YES!

I was seething inside. Why must you all treat me like a child? How dare you imply I've forgotten to take my

* I am aware that this view is entirely my mother's and is not backed up by either personal experience or medical science.

anti-malarials? But, most importantly, how DARE you be RIGHT?

Malarone was our prophylactic drug of choice. You're supposed to take it days before you enter a high-risk area. Oops. I wondered if I could pop a few extra and protect myself that way.* I guess that would be like having unprotected sex, getting pregnant, and next time you sleep together, wearing five condoms.

I didn't want malaria. I was just starting to feel better, and the last thing I needed was to be laid low again.

Claire emerged from the gloom, her face glazed a vivid yellow with the spray.

CLAIRE: Sue, you got the Deet on, love?
ME: YES! Well, no. I'm getting it on. I'm getting it on now.

It's hard to know which came first: everyone having to look after me, or me being totally unable to look after myself.

The air filled with the stink of solvent as the crew started applying the spray. I didn't touch it. I had other plans. I had been mis-sold natural remedies before, but this time I was confident. I took out my alkalizing ayurvedic mosquito repellent, then spritzed it around my midriff and the back of my neck.

I headed to my room. Once inside, I plonked my suitcase on the bed, noticing that the management had left a handful of citronella coils on the table. I set about placing them around the bed and lighting them. All of them. On reflection, I might have overdone it, as, ten minutes later, the

* Once again, I display the worst traits of Ann and Bert. I am both cavalier and lacking in self-care. What a winning combination.

whole hotel smelt like an arson attack on an aromatherapy clinic.

I turned on the ceiling fan, which pirouetted drunkenly on a loose, exposed electrical cable. Then I fanned out my mosquito net, weighing it down on the inside, as I always did, with the things I might need in the night – books, snacks, water, a hundred photos of my dogs and more snacks. Sorted.

Next, I grabbed a hand towel, and began checking every square inch of the walls and ceiling, swiping at everything that looked faintly insect-like that landed on the white emulsion. All clear.

Finally, when I was satisfied that the room was mosquito-free, I opened the door to the bathroom and walked in.

The overhead light didn't seem to be working, but no matter: the room was faintly lit by the light of the full moon. In the gloom, I could just make out a makeshift bath to the right, and to the left, set against the wall, a shower-head. Luxury. I went over, turned it on and got undressed.

I had been under the water for a few minutes when I began to appreciate how truly bright the moon was. I looked up and there it was, right above my head. *That's so cool*, I thought. A glass ceiling. How wonderful to be able to have a shower and see the heavens above you. I carried on lathering my hair and body in as much soap as possible. My skin started to prickle, so I turned the heat down. It still prickled, so I turned it off completely.

It was then I felt the breeze.

That's strange, I thought. There must be a crack in the wall, some tiny fissure through which a draught is blowing. I waited there a while – and, sure enough, the breeze came again, this time more forcefully, whipping around my naked body. They should fix that, I thought. Get some Cambodian polyfilla on it – that'll sort it out.

It was then I heard the rustle. The noise of several animals snuffling in some undergrowth that felt mere feet away from me.

That's *really* strange, I thought. They can't have put any insulation in this bathroom, because the sound pollution is quite frankly terrible.

Then another gust, and some more rustling – followed by a grunt. I was starting to panic a little. I fumbled for my head-torch, popped it on, and looked up.

It was at precisely that moment I discovered there was no glass ceiling. In fact, there was no ceiling at all. The beam of light firing from my forehead met the endless black of the night sky and surrendered, petering out just a few metres later. I was basically showering outdoors, save for four rudimentary walls, roughly six foot high, covering my modesty. Essentially I was in a stall. In a jungle.

The head-torch also revealed that the bathroom walls were black. How bizarre. What an odd colour choice. You'd think they'd paint them white to match the rest of the room. It took a little time for my eyes to adjust, to work out that the walls weren't painted black: they were simply teeming with bugs – every genus of creepy-crawly lavishly represented in an en-suite panorama.

They had been waiting there for me. It was only the running water that had kept them at bay. Now, naked, dry, with a head-torch guiding them, like a runway light, I presented myself as a fat pink buffet for every airborne blood-sucker to come and get me. I began to feel pinpricks on my ankle and the small of my back. Something was making inroads into my upper thigh. One had mounted a sortie on my left tit and was now mid-munch. I ran as fast as I could into the bedroom and slammed the door.

I didn't wake the next morning. That would imply I had slept. Instead, I was up all night, listening to that high-pitched whine, intermittently scratching and slapping.

Cambodia would be the death of me. It was determined, determined to be the death of me.

14. Seebagh and the Kreung

The Kreung hill tribe live deep in the forests of Ratanakiri without running water or electricity. They rise with the sun, and spend their days foraging and harvesting. Their homes are makeshift huts, rebuilt each and every year once the monsoon has done its work, ravaging joints, rotting wood and soaking everything in its wake.

We parked up in the forest clearing. The village kids were playing cricket in the red dust: an old two-litre water bottle stamped on to fashion a bat, a smooth stone for a ball. Around them milled a large family of pigs, the thick skirt of their bellies creating waves in the fine dirt. Their behaviour had become so familiar: low-level grunting, an accidental collision, followed by all hell breaking loose. There'd be a short burst of hysterical, high-pitched squealing, then the porky brouhaha would die away as quickly as it had begun. Pigs – they're such bloody drama queens.

Olly, as always, was the advance party. He set off towards the huts to introduce himself in the traditional soundman way: a wave, a hello and a judicious hand down the shirt. Matt and I took advantage of the downtime and decided to have a wander around the place. In the shade of one of the huts we found a strange creature that was, on closer inspection, an emaciated brindled pig. It was so thin that it barely looked like a pig at all. This little runt had obviously been bullied off every single scrap of food in the village, and had all but given up.

Matt and I didn't need to say anything. We just headed back

to the truck and opened the boot. We knew the drill. Wherever we went there were always animals wretched with hunger and in distress, and we would empty whatever we had by way of snacks onto the ground for them. We always tried to be species-appropriate in our offerings (nuts, seeds, apples and the like) but in some areas it just wasn't possible. I won't lie, there was the odd dog baffled by our gift of a Khmer sponge cake or a bag of luminescent Chinese knock-off Doritos.

On this occasion, the boot yielded fruit. Literally. Our fixer had loaded it with a billion bananas from the market – stubby little things, like jaundiced fingers. We grabbed handfuls and headed back to the pig.

He didn't even acknowledge us as we approached, his head still bowed, snuffling fruitlessly in the dead soil. We stood over him, and dropped a banana just in front of his snout. He recoiled in fear as it bounced on the hard ground. *What the hell is that?* He looked around, side to side, suspiciously. He turned around. *Where on earth did this come from?* He seemed utterly nonplussed. The strangest thing was, he didn't think to look upwards, in the direction the banana had come from.

US: We are right here, Skinny Pig. We are RIGHT HERE. You see those two enormous bipedal mammals standing over you? That's us. We're doing this. Look up!

Nope, thought Skinny Pig. *I've had a look, left and right – nothing. Nothing around. Weird.*

His next emotion appeared to be fear, perhaps a rising panic that he was going to be attacked by the other pigs. He hung back, his tiny corkscrew of a tail windmilling in the breeze, ready to scarper. But there was silence. There were no other pigs around.

Shit, thought Skinny Pig, *this might actually be for me* . . .

I am not lying when I say that that pig TIPTOED towards that banana like something out of an old Warner Bros. cartoon. He made it to within grabbing distance, then, scarcely believing his luck, he bit into it, timidly at first – then desperately scoffed the lot.

We let him settle for a moment. Then we drop another banana.

There's the same routine: confusion, terror, cartoon scuttle, scoff.

We drop another.

> SKINNY PIG: Jesus, where's that come from? It's happened again! Bloody hell! OK, don't panic. Just breathe. Nothing to my left, nothing to my right – nothing behind me . . . Ahead is all clear . . .

And this time, having finally exhausted all other options, he gazes up and spots us. But the look he gives us isn't the look of a pig who knows we are feeding it, who connects the actions of the human to the dropping of the food. It's the look of a pig that has met The Rapture. A pig so STONE-COLD STUPID, it thinks we have nothing to do with the banana downpour and are merely bystanders.

> SKINNY PIG: Hey, you! Are you getting this? Can you see this? Incredible, isn't it? There are bananas falling from the sky!

You could literally make out the shocked, gleeful expression on its face.

> SKINNY PIG: Come on, guys – is that all you got? Can't you be just a little more excited? It's raining bananas! It's raining fucking bananas! Get 'em. Come on, get 'em!

We drop another, and it is then that Skinny Pig goes properly loco. Gone is the reticence, and in its place, something new. Mania.

We drop another and notice he is no longer questioning where the food is coming from, or even worrying about another pig getting hold of it – he is just ramming the food into his mouth, gorging and dribbling as he does so.

Five bananas down. Ten, fifteen. He is getting cocky now, catching them on the bounce and swallowing them whole. His belly is no longer sunken, but beginning to swell and glint in the sunshine.

Twenty. Twenty-five. Twenty-six. Twenty-seven. Sweet God, this pig is the Cool Hand Luke of Ratanakiri province.

After the twenty-seventh, Skinny Pig stops dead in his tracks. For a second I wonder whether he's about to keel over. Then, he sniffs the air and lets loose the most impressive belch I've ever heard. The air hangs heavy with banana funk.

Twenty minutes later, Skinny Pig (thankfully Skinny no longer, so I renamed him Simon) waddled back to the group, his balls swinging in the air like dried figs. There was a certain swagger in his step. I headed back to the car, laughing, imagining his peers' reaction on seeing him:

PIGS: Simon? SIMON? WTF? Simon, is that you? What the fuck's happened? You're twice the size!

SIMON: Long story, guys. You wouldn't believe me if I told you. Some crazy shit went down at the edge of the village.

PIGS: No way.

SIMON: Believe.

PIGS: Don't leave us hanging, dude . . . Like what?

SIMON: Bear with me, OK, cos this is going to sound weird.

(*Long dramatic pause, the other pigs lean in expectantly.*)

SIMON: It just rained bananas.

ALL: Bullshit.

SIMON: For real.

PIG 1: Stop mugging us off, Simon.

SIMON: I shit you not. It rained bananas.

PIG 1: What? From the sky?

PIG 2: Where else it gonna rain from, you pig-shit thicko?

PIG 1: All right! Keep your scratchings on! Proof, Simon, or it didn't happen.

SIMON: I got witnesses. A couple of humans saw it and everything.

PIGS: Really?

SIMON: Yep, they watched the whole thing.

PIGS: Wow, that's incredible.

(*Simon's nemesis, an Alpha Pig named Trevor, walks in.*)

TREVOR: What's all the noise in here? Simon? Is that you? What the fuck you doing here? Get out . . .

SIMON: I ain't going nowhere, Trevor.

TREVOR: What you say?

SIMON: Things are gonna change around here.

TREVOR: Like hell they are. What's happened to you? Where your ribs gone?

SIMON: I gone got me some bananas, Trevor. From heaven.

TREVOR: You takin' the piss out of me, Simon? Cos I am one second away from biting your ham ass.

SIMON: Be my guest, yesterday-pig.

(*A brief fight ensues. There is a loud squeal. Trevor has been bitten. He runs away, terrified. Simon stands there, as the other pigs corral around him. They have a new leader now. All is happy ever after.*)

I am woken from my reverie by a tap on the window. It's Claire. I am aware I have a stupid grin on my face.

CLAIRE: You OK?
ME: Sure.

I don't tell her I've been playing out an imaginary piggy power struggle in my head. I just nod.

CLAIRE: C'mon. It's time.

Matt picked up the camera, Olly gave the thumbs-up, and Claire gestured into the distance, where a semicircle of village women were sitting, chatting.

'Speed,' said Matt.

I started walking towards the group, when I realized we were missing something.

ME: Where are the translators?

We were in such a remote area, we needed two translators; one to translate English into Khmer, then another who could relay Khmer into the minority Kreung dialect. I was set to be outnumbered by interpreters.

CLAIRE: I can't see them, but don't worry, they're here somewhere.

Well, wherever they were, they didn't come anywhere near us. Ever. I was walking into a tribal clearing with nothing more than an arsenal of facial expressions, some rudimentary mime and a couple of generic sound effects to make myself understood.

As I approached the women, there was a burst of chatter and high-pitched laughter. They gestured for me to sit down in front of them. I did as I was told, stiffly parking myself cross-legged at their feet.

The moment I hit the ground, I was met with the most violent stink.

'God, what's that smell?' I asked, waving my hand in front of my nose in the internationally recognized mime of 'God, that honks.'

They laughed.

Keep going, I thought. *Keep going. I'm going to find out what that smell is if it kills me.*

'What is that?' I said again, this time exaggerating my hand gestures and grimacing for comic effect.

They laughed again. The sort of laughter that isn't travelling with you, but towards you.

I could feel a sudden damp sensation in my trousers. That's never a positive. After a little buttock manoeuvring, it transpired I'd sat directly on a fat pig-pat, sun-baked on the outside, but still deeply gooey within. Texturally, think dung fondant.

This monumental Babe-dump had crumbled under the considerable weight of my backside and was now leaking into my combats. The Kreung were now roaring – rocking back and forth in hysterics.

As first meetings go, sure, it had none of the historic grandeur of Edison meeting Ford, or Stalin meeting Roosevelt – but, let me tell you, if you ever find yourself in a clearing with a remote hill tribe, do park up on a turd. It turns out it's a real ice-breaker.

After the laughter came the lull. What to do? Television abhors a vacuum (as indeed does my auntie Margaret, but that's another story), and awkward silences were simply not going to cut it. I smiled. They smiled back. I gave a thumbs-up. They did the same. There was a pause as I considered my next move. I decided to do what I do anywhere in the world when stuck for a communication inroad. I started loudly counting to ten. I raised my index finger.

ME: One!
KREUNG: One!
ME: Two!
KREUNG: Two!

Thank goodness they were going to play ball.

And on we went.

I took the glorious chorus of 'TEN!' as my cue to get up and, as I did, plunged my flip-flop deep into yet another voluminous turd just to my left. Once again, great peals of laughter rang out through the forest clearing. This seemed to set the template for the rest of the day. I would sit in something, knock over something, or eat something I shouldn't, and they would roar through it all at my grotesque ineptitude.

One of the great pleasures in meeting people from different worlds is the chance you get to observe their routines, the tiny, ritualized moments that add together to make a life. The only problem comes when they invite you to *participate* in those routines. And so I followed the women as they went about their day – revealing, at every turn, how thoroughly ill equipped I was to be a Kreung.

– Lighting a fire? Shit at it.
– Dyeing thread? Shit at it.
– Picking vegetables? Shit at it.
– Weaving? Yep, you got it. Shit at it.

The unofficial spokesperson and *de facto* leader of the group was Seebagh, a fine-boned, beautiful woman of indeterminate age. She could have been anything between thirty and sixty-five. No matter. Within seconds of meeting her I was utterly in love with her. She was special.

There are people in your life, not many, whom you meet for the briefest instant, but who stay with you for ever. Seebagh was one of those people.

I don't think I've ever met anyone so light and yet so deep, as content with herself as with the situation and circumstance she found herself in. Her voice was like a song, the words I didn't know but the tune was familiar and reassuring; it gladdened my heart to hear it.

In contrast, I don't think she'd ever met anyone so panoramically inept – this hulking, lumpy foreigner with zero skills and zero strength. I'm not sure whether she felt entertained by me or sorry for me, but I suspect it was a combination of the two.

For the next twelve hours we gabbled and giggled like old friends. As the sun dipped a little, she marshalled her merry band of women and led me into the forest. As she did so, she reached out and took my hand. It never ceases to make me catch my breath – that simple gesture: a stranger placing their open palm against mine and leaving it there, without agenda, awkwardness or shame.

As we walked through the boulevards of cashew trees, one of the women brought out an enormous clay pipe and sucked deep on it, wreathing the pathways with smoke.

I felt this incredible sense of sorority. Peace. My heart rate slowed, my arms relaxed and began swinging in time with my stride. My hand melted into hers – soft white and hard brown all as one. Seebagh looked at me and smiled, then picked a flower from a passing bush and put it behind my ear. We walked on.

'I feel like I've known you all my life,' I said, grinning like a loon.

She looked at me, muttered something in return, and we carried on into the forest.

It was not until many weeks later, once the footage had been assembled in the edit, that the translator came in to provide the subtitles. It was only then I got to understand her reply.

ME: I feel like I've known you all my life.

And then she speaks. The translation appears underneath.

SEEBAGH: I feel like I've known you all my life.

Synchronicity: the energy that comes from sharing a moment, a feeling, with a fellow human.

As I watched it on the screen, I realized I hadn't needed the translation. I had always known, in my heart, that she had shared that moment with me.

A couple of hundred metres into the forest, Mrs Pipe came to an abrupt halt and began frantically pointing at her bosoms. I wondered if her basket strap was chafing, but kept my distance in case my instincts were incorrect. The last thing I wanted was an international incident.

Is she OK? Is she all right?

The others soon followed suit, pointing to their bosoms. What? What were they trying to tell me? Was there something wrong with *my* bosoms? I looked down. Both jugs present and correct. Still in a bra, still under wraps. Definitely not out and about in the open. Tick. I had signed my BBC Safeguarding Trust Modules, you see, and was very aware that exposing yourself to hill tribes in rural South East Asia was not the sort of behaviour likely to be looked on favourably by the Corporation's documentary department.

These Safeguarding Trust Modules came into force around 2008, and took the form of an online multiple-choice question-and-answer quiz. They were developed to ensure that producers showed footage in the same order as it was shot – putting an end to the occasional, but misleading, time-shifts seen in the now infamous footage of Her Majesty the Queen.

Even though these questions were for members of the production team, for some reason presenters were, for a short time, required to complete them too. In fact, if you didn't complete them and get your mandatory passcode, you were not allowed to proceed with the shoot. These modules featured questions such as:

> Q: You are producing a Reality Medieval Re-Enactment and Jousting Show. During filming, one of the contributors is gored by a jousting pole (non-serious). This footage, however, was crucially *not* captured on film. Do you:
>
> (a) Ask the injured party if they would mind recreating the accident, only this time with the cameras rolling?
>
> (b) Show the aftermath of the accident and explain what happened in voiceover?
>
> (c) Recast your contributor and re-shoot the jousting scene?

Silly, isn't it? However, I did learn a few things – such as getting an injured person to be re-stabbed by an outsized knitting needle is *not* the right answer. That's why I'm not a producer. I'm just here for the jazz-hands, folks.

I'm digressing – but, hey, you're familiar with that by now.

So. I'm in a cashew forest, surrounded by the women of

the Kreung, all pointing frantically towards their breasts and shouting at me. This carries on for some time before it dawns on me what's going on.

ME: Oh, I see! You want another English lesson!

An image flashes into my mind. I am with the director general. He is crying. I am crying. Bulldozers begin demolishing New Broadcasting House as we weep in each other's arms.

I'd better check I'm right before I continue.

ME: These?

I pop an index finger on each nipple, just for emphasis. They murmur.

ME: You want to know the English for these?

The entire gang nod vigorously in agreement.

ME: THEY'RE BOOBS!

I realize this may have come across as too gleeful a response. I try again, this time at a more appropriate pitch.

ME: They're boobs.

'Poooooobs,' reply the Kreung, in an awed unison. 'Pooooooobs.' They sound not dissimilar to the aliens at the Pizza Planet Restaurant in *Toy Story*.

KREUNG: Poooooobs! Poooooobs!

ME: Yes, that's right. Excellent.

If I'd thought that the anatomy lesson was over then, boy, was I in for a surprise. On learning the correct word for boobs, Mrs Pipe proceeded to bring her hands down below her waist, and start manically pointing at her crotch.

ME: Oh, God.

There was a crunch of dry leaves as Matt moved towards me, giving me a salutary reminder that the next few minutes of my life were being committed to film.

At this point, in this situation, most normal people would have said 'Vagina', and that would be that. Job done. Not me. I am never knowingly under-thought. Why answer spontaneously when you can spend hours, even days, painstakingly analysing and angsting over the minutiae?

Here's what my brain made of that simple request:

SUBCONSCIOUS: Well, the first word that comes to mind is vagina.

CONSCIOUS: That's rather clinical, isn't it? This isn't a clinical environment. These women are women of the world, they're savvy. They need something more colloquial.

SUBCONSCIOUS: But it's the obvious word . . .

CONSCIOUS: You're not thinking of your audience.

SUBCONSCIOUS: What?

CONSCIOUS: Think! Vagina is SO BBC4 and we're going out on BBC2 at 9 p.m.

SUBCONSCIOUS: God, I hadn't thought of that.

CONSCIOUS: Plus, you've got to factor in that certain units of sound, or phonemes . . .

SUBCONSCIOUS: I know what a phoneme is. Don't patronize me.

CONSCIOUS: Certain sounds don't travel well. For instance, in Cambodia, the V phoneme is often made into a W.

SUBCONSCIOUS: Oh, OK. That's a good point. So 'vagina' will sound like . . .

BOTH: Wagina.

CONSCIOUS: Mmm. That's no good.

SUBCONSCIOUS: Wagina. Perfect if Wayne Sleep and Angelina Jolie ever get together, though. Hang on, I know what word you can use . . .

CONSCIOUS: What?

SUBCONSCIOUS: C—

CONSCIOUS: No!

SUBCONSCIOUS: Why not? Hard Cs work well in Khmer.

CONSCIOUS: Don't go there.

SUBCONSCIOUS: You're post watershed!

CONSCIOUS: I could probably say it. Once – and if there was a continuity announcement warning before the programme. But who wants that? It's a divisive word.

SUBCONSCIOUS: Fanny?

CONSCIOUS: It's *so* BBC2.

SUBCONSCIOUS: Twat?

CONSCIOUS: Harsh. Feels too pejorative. Reminds me of teen comedies of the late nineties or mockney cop shows of the early 2000s.

SUBCONSCIOUS: Minge.

CONSCIOUS: Too youth. Bit BBC3.

SUBCONSCIOUS: Foof? Minnie?

CONSCIOUS: What? Is this CBeebies?

SUBCONSCIOUS: Tuppence?

CONSCIOUS: I'm not listening to you now.

And so it went on. Welcome to my Vagina Mind Palace, where all words for the female anatomy are stored; technical, medical, and just plain colloquial. If you're interested in my list, it ran as follows:

BBC1
(broad brushstrokes, mass appeal)

– Crotch
– Privates

BBC2
(strong content, still approachable)

– Duff
– Bonnet
– Front bottom
– Noo-noo

BBC3
(more urban, youthful, and direct)

– Gash
– Clunge
– Minge
– Nipper
– Parking lot
– Growler
– Kid shitter

BBC4
(serious-minded, detailed, historical)

– Nature's Tufted Treasure
– Daisy Den
– Mrs Fubb's Parlour
– The Ivory Gate
– Cupid's Warehouse
– Chuck Hole

– Chapel of Ease
– Bluebeard's Closet

While I wrangled with this meaty minefield, the Kreung women waited patiently. Mrs Pipe kept rhythmically pointing to her genitals by way of an aide-memoire, as if somehow I might have forgotten the word they needed translating.

I'd just settled on either 'love-box' or 'fun hatch' (inclusive, warm, with a hint of anatomical rigour) when I realized I'd made the classic presenter mistake. I had failed to be Nations and Regions inclusive. Here's me with my metropolitan media elite mind-set having not even considered 'quim' (possibly derived from the Welsh *cwm*, meaning 'hollow' or 'valley') or 'gee' (from the ancient Irish Síle na Gig) or –

'FUD,' I blurted out. I don't know why. I was thinking of Scotland. I am always thinking of Scotland.

'FUD,' said the ladies, mesmerized. 'FUD. FUD. Fud, fud, fud, fud, fud.'

And so it was set in stone. There endeth the lesson. You've learned numbers one through to ten, boobs and fud. You can now negotiate most social situations in the United Kingdom. Job done.

The ladies resumed their walk, intoning, every other step, 'FUD'. It became like a mantra. Two steps, 'FUD', another two steps, 'FUD'.

At the end of the long boulevard of cashews was an open, undulating space, loosely bounded by makeshift wooden fencing. It took a while to realize it was their vegetable garden. There was no Western cultivation here, no orderly lines of brassicas, legumes and alliums. This was the haphazard bounty of Mother Nature.

'What's this? Ooh, what's this? Oh, is that . . . ?' I

blethered, like a six-year-old, while the adults wandered silently through the patch, plucking shoots from the dry soil and throwing them into their panniers. I followed behind, occasionally prodding at a rogue stem.

ME: What's this?

A translator had now miraculously appeared, called, no doubt, by Claire – who had started to despair at the direction the film was taking. We'd learned a word for vagina, and it was still only 10 in the morning. Who knows what vocabulary we'd get to by midday.

I stumbled over a plant.

ME: What's this?
TRANSLATOR: That? It's garlic.

What a muppet – I couldn't even recognize garlic here. I fired it backwards into my pannier. A shout went up behind me.

ME: And this?
TRANSLATOR: It's lemongrass.

I plucked it and tossed it over my shoulder. A second shout went up.

ME: What's this?
TRANSLATOR: Galangal.

I threw again. Yet another shout.

It took me ten minutes to connect the act of throwing the veg into the basket and the cry coming from behind me – but when I did, I turned round to see Mrs Pipe covered with mud and dust from where I had mis-aimed my harvest.

She laughed. And all of them followed. All of them. They just laughed.

I retired to the edge of the vegetable garden and watched Seebagh and her mates clawing at the dirt, gathering their food for the night. It was clear that things were very different for women here. It starts in childhood, of course. Kreung girls are empowered to love their bodies and to enjoy sex as part of romantic love. Their fathers even build them 'love huts' once they hit puberty, and they can choose whether or not to let boys come in to visit them. They are in charge of who is allowed to touch them. Men are taught from birth to respect the agency and choices of women. Sexual violence is rare, rape is unheard of, and couples don't divorce. Of all the places I visited in South East Asia, this felt the most open and tolerant. I didn't feel afraid. Gangs of men didn't follow me around, staring at me. Judging me. For the first time in a long time, I could relax and be myself.

It was time for my end-piece to camera. Time to sum up this beautiful, fragile place and its wonderful people.

'Speed,' said Matt.

As I opened my mouth, a gentle breeze hit my face, bringing with it two distinct sounds. First Seebagh, singing as she gathered up the long stalks of lemongrass, and then, more faint at first, but growing in intensity, the crunch of metal teeth chewing through forest. Men were coming. Men with chainsaws. I wanted to explode with the pain of it all.

When I'm doing a sum-up, I try to be in the moment, to simply say what I feel – but sometimes, at the end of a film, you need a little structure in your head, a peg on which to hang the odd thought or feeling. During my reading on the region, I'd come across a quote from a former American ambassador, Joseph Mussomeli. When I came to speak, that was what came out of my mouth because, borrowed as it was, it felt like the truest thing to say.

'Cambodia is the most dangerous place on earth. You will fall in love with it and it will break your heart.'

I loved it. I couldn't wait to leave. I hated it. I can't wait to go back.

It took nearly eight hours to get to the airport, but even inside the cool neutrality of the terminal I could feel Cambodia hanging over me, like a curse. I sat on a plastic moulded chair waiting for our flight to be called, and rang a friend.

'Some places stick,' she said. 'They just hang off you. And over time, the heaviness weighs you down. You need to shake it off. You need to come home, to the things you love.'

And I did come home. I came home to find my darling dog Pickle was dying.

Laos

15. The Lost Souls

The piece to camera at the start of a new film is always hard to get right. Essentially, you're listing the stereotypical expectations of a place you've not been to yet, in the hope that, once you arrive, your preconceptions might get shaken and redefined. Thankfully for my viewers, the Mekong greets Laos at the top of a large mountain, where it roars down the side in a furious, beautiful waterfall. This meant that most of my on-screen banalities were, thankfully, swallowed up by the sound of the torrent.

Laotians are famously mellow folk. Some say the Lao PDR (People's Democratic Republic) actually stands for Please Don't Rush. Their favourite phrase '*bor pen nyang*', even translates as 'no worries' or 'no problem'.

If 'no worries' is the mantra of Laos, then, on reflection, our crew motto would be: *Don't order the milkshake.*

South East Asia is home to many culinary gems – green papaya salad, *pad Ga pao*, *laap*, *pho* – but despite their French colonial past, they're not big on cow-juice. Because we Westerners love a bit of dairy, local restaurant owners try their very best to replicate creamy classics for the tourist population. Sometimes however, their very best gives you *e.coli*.

Next tip, and this one is key: if you go ahead, regardless of my warnings, and order the strawberry milkshake and it happens to taste of strawberries and *fish*, stop drinking right there. Just at the point where the taste-buds are going 'Mmm, that's *wonderfully* creamy – but is that a back-note of mackerel I'm detecting?' that's the time to put the glass down and walk away. Always remember: hope is not enough of a reason to continue drinking something that tastes of something other than it should.

I speak from bitter experience, because the first thing Matt, Olly and I like to do on arriving at a new place is to get food poisoning. *En masse.* You know, get it all over and done with.

That night, we chose to have a drink in a spit-and-sawdust bar on the riverbank, decked with a neon sign that intermittently fizzed on and off. From far away, it looked magical. But, then, so does the Death Star – and you wouldn't necessarily want to order from its cafeteria.

At the entrance way, a sumo-sized lady was standing at a large wooden block, steel cleavers in each hand, alternating left and right as she pounded up and down on a pile of raw chicken flesh. She was making the famed national dish, *laap.* As she hurled the blades downwards, I noticed several beetles and the odd mosquito getting minced alongside the meat. Still, it's all protein, I suppose – and I'd long since given up being fussy.

We sat down and browsed the laminated menus, greasy with a thousand fingerprints. I noticed a cluster of black flies now milling around the work surface. In retrospect, they were obviously returning to what was a habitual breeding ground. We plumped for the strawberry milkshakes, but it was only after placing the order that I noticed the fridge door was hanging off its hinges, the warm air wafting within.

The first gulp was as refreshingly rich and filling as you could want. It was only then, after that initial mouthful, that I registered the somewhat piscatorial twang. Matt noticed it, Olly too, both smacking their lips up and down in the vain hope their initial perceptions had been wrong. And yet, despite the oceanic after-burn, we carried on drinking. After all, what was the worst that could happen?

Bor pen nyang.

Bor pen nyang.

The sun started to melt into the river, casting an eerie yellow light across the water. We retired for the night. Home was, that evening, a row of wooden shacks on jetties connected, like fairy lights, one to another. From every window, all you could see was the river. How romantic. In reality, it was like being individually spoon-fed to the mosquitoes. I was in the Malaria Suite. Olly and Matt were either side in the Chikungunya and Dengue Rooms respectively. Because each pod was connected, every step you took, every move you made, the entire structure rocked from side to side, like a creaky boat. If Olly got up for a wee, my bed vibrated. If Matt leant over to switch his light off I felt a faint tremor in the walls.

My stomach had begun to feel decidedly sour, but I decided not to dwell on it. Instead I got into bed, turned the lights out and tried to sleep it off.

I was woken at around 3 a.m. by a rhythmic juddering coming from my left. Matt's room. What could it be? Minutes later, it was accompanied by a lurching sensation coming from the right. Olly. The boys had started vomiting, and I was party to each and every heave. The floor shook violently with each motion.

This was shortly followed by a more subtle shimmering sensation. I figured it was the aftershock from a chunder further down the row, possibly emanating from Lucy's room.*

* Lucy was our fabulous director on this third shoot. She is so wonderfully mellow she should be prescribed on the NHS for people suffering with anxiety.

Then it was my turn. Without warning, I was violently sick. The lampshade fell to the floor. I was sick again. My mobile phone slipped off the bed. Now we were all at it, every heave creating ripples along the row, until it felt like we were all on some kind of giant puker's Power Plate.

Three hours later, I returned to bed with the taste of river fish still heavy on my palate. Ten minutes after that and the light fitting started vibrating as poor Fred, two doors down, stepped up to the bowl.

Fred was our assistant producer and is the nicest man on earth: mild-mannered, polite – the quintessential English gentleman. Weighing in at around ten stone, he was also the lightest in the group, very much in the helium-weight category. Fred got *really* sick. In fact, he was green for a week. He woke up green. He went to bed green. He spent his days meeting and greeting hill tribes green. For some of these remote communities, this was the first time they'd ever met a Westerner, so they assumed, after seeing Fred's nauseous chops, that we were all that colour. They seemed genuinely surprised when some pink folk followed on behind.

What made it worse was that most of this episode was filmed on the water – day after day spent on boats, rocking in the intense heat, with only one basic toilet between us. Poor Fred. Poor bloody Fred.

It turns out that television doesn't care whether you've been up all night rocked by the vigour of your neighbour's regurgitations. Television has a schedule to follow. And so, at seven o'clock the next morning, we began our journey to Si Phan Don and the Four Thousand Islands, a river archipelago where the Mekong is at its widest. The water winds its way round thousands of little islands (hence the name), some disappearing and reappearing with the rainy and dry seasons, others inhabitable all year round. This place, this little paradise, is the Asia that people hold in their imagination, that they dream of when they buy their tickets east, with its promise of soft skies, white sands, and an easy pace of life.

It's true, everything happens slowly here. Your muscles relax, your senses dull, all sense of urgency leaves the building. Everything in the world achieves a sudden and perfect perspective.

We felt stoned on arrival, like we'd walked into a cliché. Everywhere we looked there were the easy signifiers of chill – yin and yang, tie-dye, fresh tattoos with the skin still proud from the puncture. Backpackers lolloped past, decked with coral necklaces, their burnished faces freckled with sand. Everyone held a beer. There were tight huddles of tourists dozing in the heat, the sudden localized burst of transistors and laughter, and the sneak of couples trying to find an uninhabited dune to shag in.

I knew only one thing about our first day filming here: I was to meet a certain Mr Bounsom, a local fisherman. I won't lie, I was expecting someone in a similar vein to the other fishermen I'd met along my travels: shy, silent types, their rheumy eyes trained wistfully on the waterline as I bombarded them with questions. I could not have been more mistaken. You see, Mr Bounsom was not just a fisherman, Mr Bounsom, as he would be at pains to point out, was an *entrepreneur*.

Mr Bounsom was as charismatic as he was handsome. He was also a little drunk. It was nine o'clock in the morning. I mention that not to be unduly judgemental but because if I'd known he was going to be four sheets to the wind throughout my time with him I wouldn't have turned down the opportunity to have a little tot of whisky with my breakfast noodles.

It became immediately clear I'd encountered a fellow klutz. Bounsom was as utterly inept as I was – all zest and no skills – a chaotic, imploding mass around which orbited a collection of dutiful and capable women. He would chide his wife and sisters, barracking them for the benefit of the camera, but his alpha-male posturings failed to obscure the reality that they were the ones doing everything, quietly going about the business of choreographing and producing his day.

After an awful lot of hugging and shouting, Bounsom gestured in the direction of a wooden boat, long, lean and curved at the ends – like an ironic smile. He seemed awfully keen to get me onboard and demonstrate his fishing skills. Our embarkation was slightly hampered by the fact that neither of us could stand upright on the vessel, me due to a critical lack of core strength, him due to a surfeit of Laos beer.

Once underway (the womenfolk had to push us from the shoreline), Bounsom took the opportunity to ask for my hand in marriage. We had known each other for approximately seven minutes. I tried to explain some of the many things standing in the way of our union, not least:

(a) he was married already (I'd just said hello to his wife)
(b) I'm not genetically engineered for commitment, especially in the form of matrimony
(c) THE OBVIOUS, and
(d) he was carrying a loaded harpoon gun, which made him deeply intimidating.

'You, beautiful,' he said – as the arrow-tip glinted in the sunshine mere inches from my face.

Bounsom was an extremely excitable sausage, and the slightest thing would send him giddy with delight. Now he was armed the last thing I wanted to do was agitate him further. 'Gosh. Thank you,' I said – more in fear than acquiescence.

As we chugged into the sunlight, I could see the effort scored on Bounsom's face. He looked worn out. This isn't paradise at all, is it, mate? This is graft. I noticed the myriad lines around his eyes – the price he paid for those endless shit-eating grins – plastered on for the sake of us tourists. We're on holiday, though, yeah? We're taking a break. We're taking a year off. We're on a gap year.

A year off from what? I thought. God only knows there are no gap years here. No downtime. For these people, it never stops. Jesus, we don't know how lucky we are.

'Weeeeeeeeeeeeeeeee!'

I started from my reverie.

'Weeeeeeeeeeeeeeeee!' screamed Bounsom, as our boat smashed into some rocks. I flinched as the harpoon muzzle grazed my left ear.

'Weeeeeeeeeeeeeeeee!' he screeched again, jumping off the vessel and running up through the sandy hillocks to the cliff above. I followed slowly, feet stumbling on the uneven ground until I finally reached the top. From there, we had a perfect view of the river. It felt more ferocious, misdirected and thwarted by a million rocks as it fired its way downstream. I noticed a few wooden traps nestled into the stone, capturing the tiny shad and croakers as they hurled down the rapids.

'Time to fish!' said Bounsom, brandishing his spear aloft. I'd not seen one fish pulled live from the Mekong in my entire trip – and the largest I'd seen in the nets was only around six inches long. A harpoon gun felt like overkill; like taking a howitzer to a grouse shoot or a trebuchet to a fox hunt.

A woman in a lampshade hat sat on one of the rocks at the water's edge. The river tumbled around her, the spray hitting her hems and lashing at her fingers. In her hand she held a net, just two bamboo poles lashed together in a V-shape, with a scoop of mesh in between. The sort of net you'd get the kids to fish for crab with at Brixham Harbour. Except she wasn't fishing for fun, she was fishing for her life.

'Whhaaaaaaayyy!' bellowed Bounsom, at maximum decibels, waving his spare hand in the air. 'Time to fish!'

And with that, he reached across and grabbed the woman's net from her. Inside, two silver tiddlers were flick-flacking as they tried frantically to breathe. And that was Mr Bounsom's fishing done.

These were the first fish I had seen taken live from the river, caught by a woman whose face I never saw, a woman who had given up her catch without so much as a word or gesture.

'Fish!' cried Bounsom, waving the net triumphantly in the air, as if the act of possession alone made it his catch, his achievement. 'Now we barbecue!'

The fish were still thrashing about. I wondered if this was when Bounsom would use the harpoon – to silence them for good. Perhaps he'd brought along a grenade or surface-to-surface missile for that job. Who knew? Instead, he simply passed the net back to the woman, who duly rapped the fish on the head and returned them, dead.

A fire was lit – a Bounsom sort of a fire. No dried moss and flint, no careful eking of a spark, just a casual squirt of petrol and a cigarette lighter. Boom. The fish were suspended in a grill cage over the flame, where they began their rapid transformation into carbon.

Bounsom cracked open a beer, then another. He started talking. I tried to interject, interview him, get a conversation going, but he wasn't interested in a formal back and forth. The alcohol had made him both bold and unfocused. He wanted to broadcast. He wanted to preach. His speech was an angry, tangential mess, each sentence empowering a new train of thought. We sat back, as the acrid smoke from the fire enveloped us, and let him rant. He talked about political corruption, his outlandish conspiracy theories on the Thai government, and what life was really like on the islands. On and on in the dizzying heat.

After a while, I noticed Olly had removed his headphones. Olly listens to everything, so if the phones are off, he is no longer recording. I turned and saw that Matt had lowered his lens. I stopped even trying to prompt or ask questions. To record Mr Bounsom from here on in was to get him into trouble, even if he was too drunk to know it. So we just sat there, listening to his wild ideas, his rantings, his unshaped, raw pain – all of it dutifully translated back to us. This meant, of course, it took double the amount of time.

Imagine listening to David Icke. TWICE.

We listened until the sun grew too hot, even for him. I could feel the end of my nose going crispy.

The fish were now cremated, lumps of black crumble where the flesh had been. I stared at the woman, now silhouetted in the afternoon sun, and mouthed an apology. I don't have a God, but I prayed that hers would, at the very least, send her a replacement catch she could make a meal out of.

'Wheeeeeeeeey! Paaaarty time!' shrieked Bounsom,

seemingly now bored by his own monologue. He grabbed his harpoon and ran headlong down the bank back to the boat.

Back at the beach café, a now battered Bounsom was keen to show me his karaoke skills. He cracked open yet another beer and stood there watching as the womenfolk unfurled metres of black cabling, set up the microphone and rigged the speaker system. Then he clicked his fingers, and they retreated, silently, back into the walls, whereupon he took centre stage and began belting out some stone-cold Laotian classics.

This was classic Bounsom, all sound and fury. He would trumpet his brilliance to anyone in range, yet in the whole time I was with him he never caught a fish or cooked a meal or served a guest or lifted a finger – unless it was to raise a Lao beer to his lips. If he was an entrepreneur, then he was the goddamn laziest entrepreneur in all of Laos.

My dog Pickle died shortly before I flew out for this leg of the journey. While I was away in Cambodia a hard, cancerous lump had formed in her throat, and by the time I came back cachexia had set in. Her muscles were melting into her bones, and the skin hung like an old curtain from the pole of her spine. She died in my arms, on our bed. Ten days later I got on a plane again. Her death was still so raw, so new, that I would routinely howl on the cool marble floor of the hotel toilet once the long filming days were over and I was on my own again.

That afternoon, as Bounsom began what turned out to be a two-hour session at the mic, a little pup bounced over to me, big-pawed and cocky, the colour of sand with a white bib that began under her jaw and ended mid-belly. Just like Pickle. She came and sought me out, fat tail swinging, needle teeth biting in play. She wound in and around my legs as if to say, I love you, but I knew that wasn't true. She was merely using me, and the coarseness of my denim trousers, to provide temporary relief from the fleas.

Then, when the heat of the sun became too much, she crawled into my arms and passed out, her long legs dangling in the breeze. Bounsom had now changed tack, and was using his public platform to regale the audience with his plans for a hotel complex and retail park. (God, his wife was going to be busy.)

But I am no longer listening to him. I am no longer listening to anything. I am merely cradling this dog, and trying to calculate the practical, logistical and financial implications of taking her home with me on the plane.

It is another hour before she wakes again, by which point I am up and dancing with her still in my grasp, as Bounsom belts out another South East Asian floor-filler.

So, a question. What naturally follows three hours of tub-thumping karaoke? That's right, you got it: an intense spiritual communion. It was now time to roll headlong into something known as a Baci ceremony.

A Baci is a Buddhist ritual in which a holy man recalls the thirty-two spirits that supposedly inhabit each human body (in this instance, mine). Laotians believe these spirits are responsible for our thirty-two organs, so when they drift away from us, it can have a profound effect on our mental and physical wellbeing. The rite effectively calls the spirits home to where they belong so that one's life might function fully again.

In order to attract these wayward souls, a large, handmade pyramid of marigolds was erected. I sat cross-legged underneath it, while the monk, a man well into his eighties, began to chant and intone. Dozens of villagers appeared, taking their place alongside me, bowing their heads and muttering along. Bounsom would occasionally interject – his booming bulldozer of a voice ensuring that any building sense of the spiritual was quickly kicked into touch.

Candles were lit, and offerings made: a little cash, a little whisky. Spirits love spirits. More villagers arrived, encircling me, protecting me, casting out the bad, and welcoming in the good.

Fifteen minutes in, and I was nudged gently in the ribs. A villager proffered his arm so I took the cue and did the same. I held out my left arm, and one by one the villagers tied thin cotton bracelets around my wrist in pink, red, orange and white. The strings ensure that the recalled spirits stay with you. I thanked each celebrant as they completed their knot, and they responded by pressing lightly on my pulse point and saying a blessing. After a couple of minutes, my arm was full, almost to the elbow. The right was next, and that too was quickly covered. By the time they had finished I looked like I was wearing a pair of ethnic, hand-woven gauntlets.

The holy men say that if you want your wishes to come true, you have to wait for at least three days before you remove the strings. When it comes time to remove them, they should be untied, rather than cut, as cutting the strings means the good wishes might be severed. The best option, though, is to leave them and let them fall off naturally. The guys all cut theirs off that night. In fact, I'm not sure Olly even waited until the end of the ceremony before he took his Leatherman out and started hacking at the strings. Stuff and nonsense, he said.

Yes, of course, you're right. It is stuff and nonsense. Yet I kept mine on nonetheless – all of them. I couldn't tell you why. An element of politeness? For sure. Superstition? Maybe. Because no attempt to try to rationalize the universe is too 'out there' for me? Why, yes indeed.

But it was more potent than that. There was something about that day – that concentration of feeling, that purity of intent – that really stayed with me. I liked them, plain and simple. I liked those gentle villagers, who gave up a piece of their day for me, to commune with me, to make me whole again.

So the strings stayed on. And on. Occasionally one would break off, or unravel, until the last one remained.

The final braid fell off this January, 2018, seconds after I'd released a seismic fart into the bathtub. Ah, the majesty of the cosmos. After looking through my diaries, I noticed it was exactly four years on from that Baci ceremony. It had taken 1,461 days for my unruly spirits to reunite.

And as it fell, down the side of the bath onto the mat beneath, Tig was there, out of nowhere, to lick my naked wrist. Tig, the brindled Staffie, who steals food and sneaks about, who is wilful and needy and believes, despite the trauma of her early years, that the world spins just for her. Exactly like Pickle – the reincarnation of naughty Pickle.

It's OK, I thought – staring at the newly exposed pale circle of skin – your souls are home.

We're all home.

16. Lies, Dam Lies and Statistics

One of the fundamental rules of documentary film-making seems to be that a presenter must never be allowed to get comfortable – either physically or mentally. And while that can prove troublesome and disruptive, I guess it means I have to constantly challenge my ideas and feelings about a place.

We left the peace and tranquillity of Si Phan Don – and, just in case I was getting too used to the finer things in life, like fresh air and vegetables, Steve decided to change it up a little. He wasn't on this shoot in person, but was still busy operating the levers from back home. As I've said before, I like to think of him as a shadowy figure, Charlie from *Charlie's Angels* – back to camera, surrounded by gorgeous women – giving us some God-awful assignment by Western Electric speakerphone before hopping on a surfboard and catching some good ol' Gower waves.

STEVE: So, how is Sue?
PRODUCER: Great. She's having a wonderful time in the Four Thousand Islands, hanging with some stray puppies and singing karaoke.
STEVE: I see. Then it's time to send her down a sewer, or a mine – or maybe to a building site. Yes, a really messy, noisy building site. Do it.

Steve didn't just send me to any old building site: he sent me to one of the largest, and most controversial, in Asia – the Xayaburi Dam. This was the first dam to cross the main stem of the Lower Mekong, and would end up completely blocking the flow of the river – a river that fifty million people depend on for their livelihoods. In order to learn a little more, I had an appointment to meet the spectacularly monikered Mr Virapong Viravong, the vice minister for energy and mines.

It may surprise you to know that I don't get to speak to many ministers on account of the fact that:

(a) I am deeply suspicious of anyone in government and their motives.
(b) I have a compulsion to tell them that I am deeply suspicious of them and their motives.

I am not the person you send in to speak to a minister. I am the sort of person you get to stand outside the minister's office with a megaphone and luxuriantly punned protest sign until the police turn up and move them on.

My interfaces with those in positions of power have been brief but eventful: a red-faced outburst at Tory MP John Whittingdale, a rant in a lift to Tory MP Ed Vaizey and a misdial when working as a temp, which saw me get inadvertently connected to the finance minister of the Estonian National Government.

This is a sensitive subject, and complex, too. Dams are deeply controversial in Laos. The Mekong is a river shared: it flows through six nations, rich and poor, Communist and capitalist, through cities and paddy fields. The action taken at one single point can have a catastrophic effect on the millions who rely on it for their livelihood.*

* As I write this, news is breaking about the collapse of an auxiliary dam at the Xe Pian Xe Namnoy plant. We may never know how many innocent people have lost their lives as a result.

We headed to the site, the tarmac pathway widening to a vast concrete boulevard. I was treated like a five-star general: the roads were cleared; I had my own security detail, and men in uniform saluted as I drove past. I saluted back at them – it was a reflex, I'll be honest – I'm not trained. As I reached the head office at Xayaburi, there was a halo of flash-bulbs, as a load of silent men in skinny jeans trained their camcorders and iPhones on me. It soon became clear that we were not only making a documentary about the dam officials, but the dam officials were making a documentary about us.

Incredible, isn't it, that you can travel to the poorest regions on earth, and you'll still find 'information officers' and 'media managers' there to make sure I stay on message and the party line is toed.

Mr Virapong was waiting to greet me, stiff-backed and gracious. I bowed in greeting, then shook his hand. If he was surprised at my scruffiness (I was in double-denim and a neck buff – what was I thinking?) then he gave nothing away. Although, as I walked through the door and he caught a glimpse of my ill-advised harem pants, I thought I could detect a faint twitch in the corner of his eye.

There was precious little time for formalities: this was business. No sooner had I said my hellos than I was propelled headlong into a rather formal and intense presentation on the technical specifications of the hydroelectric plant.

It will not surprise you to learn that I am not good in formal settings – specifically, anywhere there's a PowerPoint presentation, a plethora of biros or a whiteboard. In fact, I'm pretty dreadful in any organized situation where the main driver is 'work'. There is something about the expectation of application that makes me panic. Certain business-oriented trigger words, when spoken in a conference room or meeting space, will make me so anxious I've been known to make my excuses and run. Here's a brief run-down:

- **Agenda** – literally translated from the Latin as 'the things that must be done'. Things. Plural. There is more than one thing I need to do. I might be here for days. I feel claustrophobic. Get out. Now
- **Brand Strategy** – I don't care. I just want to make jokes. Now look what you've made me do – I am drawing a cock and balls on a napkin.
- **Let's schedule a catch-up** – So you want to repeat what we've just discussed in one week's time? My life is slowly ebbing away. I was young once.
- **Feedback** – You said 'feedback'. You mean 'criticism'. Let's never speak again.
- **Get-together** – A 'get-together'? You bastard. This is a meeting in disguise. You think I don't know that? You are cloaking a meeting in a social setting. This is like a Matryoshka doll of work. Well, I've rumbled you, pal.
- **Inventory** – See List.
- **Itinerary** – See Agenda.
- **List** – Right, first up, show it to me. I need to see it. I need to see how long it is. If I don't know how long it is then how will I know it is nearly at its end? I am sweating. I am actually sweating. SHOW IT TO ME. SHOW ME THE LIST.
- **Mission statement** – Tone it down, will you? This isn't Cape Canaveral. Mission statement – honestly. Anyway, why do we need a plan? Plans are death. Where's the room for improvisation or manoeuvre?

Live a little. OK. You still want to run with 'mission statement'? Fine, mine is to be in front of a bag of crisps within the next fifteen minutes.

- **Recap** – See Catch-up. I have already moved on and I can no longer remember your name.

The meeting room was long and thin. You could smell the torpor in the air. The whole place looked like it had been built as an internment camp for middle managers – prefab white walls, endless projector-screens and wires. You could hear the electricity pulsing through the walls. The whole set-up was like an ennui installation as realized by a Turner Prize-winning artist.

The space was dominated by a vast and heavily lacquered table surrounded by a jumble of black office chairs. More than a dozen cameramen stood around me, filming, as I took my seat opposite Mr Virapong. As soon as his gentlemanly buttocks hit the cushion, he launched, full throttle, into the presentation – accompanied by a dizzying selection of slides.

I tried to calm myself. I focused on my breathing. Just be in the moment, I thought. Be mindful, be mindful.

It turned out that the office chairs were not only comfy but swivelled – and I realized that if I could angle mine towards the projector screen, rest my chin on my hands with my fingers covering my left eye, then no one would notice if I drifted off a little.

I descended into a comfortable trance state. Technical drawings flashed in front of my eyes: radial gates, spillways, navigation locks, sand flushing. I seem to remember an awful lot about sand flushing.

Halfway into the presentation, I was pulled from the

depths of an alpha wave by a single, ridiculous sentence: 'Blah, blah, blah, blah FISH LIFT,' said Mr Virapong.

I was suddenly awake, my curiosity piqued.

ME: Sorry, Mr Virapong. Did you say 'fish lift'?

MR V: Yes!

He waved his arms in the air emphatically.

MR V: The doors open, the fish come in, the lift takes them up and then releases them!

ME: But who will operate the buttons?

I thought, but didn't say. I was obviously still half asleep.

This is insane. I am in Laos, in the middle of nowhere, in a massive conference suite with a senior member of the Lao People's Revolutionary Party, telling me they are spending billions building a lift. For fish. I felt like I was in an aquatic episode of *Are You Being Served?* 'Ground floor, pangasius, striped barb and *pa pao luang*, perch and *anabantidae*, catfish and *khop*. Going up!'

The meeting ended as abruptly as it had begun. The film crew and government personnel got up and headed outside, and I duly followed. A line of freshly waxed cars stood idling by the front doors, waiting to take us to our next location. After a few minutes' drive, we arrived at the entrance to the site. I donned a hard hat, ear defenders and a pair of acrylic goggles, and approached.

Nothing had prepared me for the scale of the thing. It was as if Nature had all but given up. Below me, I could see the river, stemmed by a gargantuan concrete platform, its banks stripped of their customary green to reveal mountains of exposed scree. Nine thousand people worked on this site round the clock, day in, day out. The air was thick with dust as drills akin to those from *Journey to the Centre of the Earth* bored endless holes into the ground. I was simultaneously amazed at the industry, the technology and drive, and dismayed by the utter destruction of the environment around me.

MR V: Incredible, isn't it?

He was shouting to be heard over the incessant grinding and whirring.

I don't think I said anything in reply. I was still struggling to take in the enormity of the scene.

MR V: Go, go wherever you want. You can go on your own!
ME: On my own? Really?

If I sounded somewhat suspicious, it was only because we had become used to the legion of government officials following us around.

MR V: Yes! Of course! Wherever you want! Just go!

It turns out that when Mr Virapong said,

MR V: You can go on your own!

What he *really* meant was:

MR V: You can go on your own, as long as you are OK with being followed by a fleet of ten white jeeps brimful of Communist Party lackeys tracking your every move.

We arrived at one of the resettlement villages, Ban Talong, and parked up. The ten jeeps parked behind us in single file and, as we got out, I saw ten doors open in perfect synchronicity in my rear-view mirror. If this was being left alone, then I sure as hell didn't want to experience what it was like to be accompanied.

As I walked into the village, a crowd was already forming. I approached what I assumed was one of the villagers and said hello. After some to-ing and fro-ing, it transpired he wasn't a villager at all but a property developer. I moved on and greeted the man next to him – who also turned out to be a property developer. I introduced myself to a third man – who didn't say much, but who, thankfully, appeared to be entirely unconnected with the construction of the new settlement. Finally, a genuine resident of Ban Talong. We sat down for a chat, just me, the contributor and a dozen observers.

After exchanging a few pleasantries, it turned out he wasn't a villager either, but a member of the government – in fact, out of the eight people seated in front of me, all but one was an official of one kind or another. Three henchmen were writing in notebooks; the others were whispering advice and key buzz-phrases down the line. The extraordinary thing was how brazen it all was – they simply didn't care that we could see how obvious the coercion was.

ME: Is there anyone from the village actually here? Anyone who lives in Ban Talong? Is there a representative of this community at this table? Or anywhere?

There was a lot of huffing and puffing and some frantic scribbling in the notebook.

Finally, one of the men opposite me lifted his hand.

ME: You're a villager here?

The man nodded. The other men nodded. It was hard not to feel a little intimidated, but I carried on. The building company had requested that *they* provide the translator, rather than us using our own. This would, of course, save any embarrassment should the villager say something that wasn't appropriate for translation – or should the response need to be finessed into something that was more 'on message'. To this day, I have no idea whether what the guy said and what the translator *said he had said* were one and the same thing.

I asked him about his new life, and what it felt like for his community to be resettled away from the water's edge where they had lived for centuries. As soon as he heard each question in his mother tongue, his eyes flickered around the table. Sometimes he didn't bother to reply at all. Instead the answer was simply provided for him by one of the developers or government officials crowding around me. Once again, everything was being videoed, and a rather old-school Party member with a Fu Manchu beard was making notes on a clipboard. I felt bad. I knew this was an uncomfortable experience for the villager, and I didn't want to stress him out, but at the same time, there were questions that needed to be asked. Matt did a great job of getting shots of the collusion around me – and, to be honest, those images say more about the duress we were under than any amount of my fruitless probing could.

Down by the water, you could still see the traditional shacks, raised on timber stilts with steep thatched roofs and rickety verandas. But there was no sign of life, no thin plumes of smoke emerging from the kitchen stoves, no screams of children as they dived in and out of the river, no snort and snuffle of pigs or cluck of chickens. The ancient village of Ban Talong, as was, lay empty. Abandoned.

Up on the bank, however, and winding up into the hills, you could see a Brave New World. Freshly built concrete houses, in perfect rows, with shiny gravel pathways, and, most exciting of all . . .

Electricity.

This was what it was all for, this degradation of the landscape, this mass construction, this exodus from the old ways of water and land towards tarmacked roads, plastic bags and retail opportunities, all for this.

Power. It was finally this community's turn to have power – and all at the touch of a button.

I was taken to one of the new houses, surrounded by the gabble of minders and the flash of cameras. There was no denying it was a cut above any village hut I'd seen before. The ceramic floor was cool and clean, the wooden beams straight and strong. We stood, not on loose boards suspended above the earth but on concrete foundations, sturdy and enduring, set well away from rising water and flood risk.

I felt joy and sadness in equal measure. Joy for the villagers, because their lives were about to get easier. After all, who wouldn't want to flick a switch and have light? Or be able to flush a toilet or have your clothes washed for you by an automated steel drum?

But I felt sad for us, for our 'developed' world that keeps on developing and developing and doesn't know when to stop, that cannot help but expand without end. A world defined by acquisition and insatiable need, where our houses are filled with baubles, and where we pay for out-of-town storage outlets to contain the overspill of our excess possessions. But where, in our endless plans for expansion, do we consider or pursue the intangible? Happiness? Community? Mutual respect? Can we ever reclaim a time when we weren't fearful and insular?

We're all in this together. Those of us fortunate enough to live in a place where we want for little have a responsibility to support those in need. But we also have another responsibility, one that we have never embraced. We need to finesse the end goal of it all. We need to work out what we're chasing, and what really matters. We need to know when enough is enough.

We need to know when to stop.

The main switch was flicked. There was a fizz as the long fluorescents hanging from the beams sparked to life. There was the sudden hum of fridge and television as the room filled with white noise.

The government officials applauded. So did the developers. So did the villager. Then they looked at me, and I applauded too.

17. It's Oh So Quiet

The dam might have come as a shock, but there was no question that something in Laos needed to change. Laos is the poorest of all the Mekong nations and education is simply out of reach for large sections of the population. Approximately one in every four Lao kids is illiterate, putting them at a distinct disadvantage to their rapidly developing neighbours.

Where the state is struggling, independent non-government organizations intervene to take up the slack. Community Learning International is a small NGO set up by an American called Bob but run by locals, with a mission to provide educational outreach to the more remote and rural areas of the country. One of its projects is a book boat, which visits more than a hundred riverside villages. Think floating library and you're almost there.

This library, however, turned out to bear none of the traditional beige, municipal trimmings of its Western cousins. This library was a belting baby blue, with vast cartoon murals on each side in gaudy yellows and reds. Inside, racks of shiny, colourful paperbacks lined the walls, all with slightly forbidding titles, such as:

– *New, Improved Buffalo!*
– *The Dead Tiger Who Killed A Princess*
– *The Frog Who Unbuttons His Shirt*

And my own personal favourite, the uplifting kids' classic:

– *Life in Hell*

This waterborne learning centre also shunned conventional rules on sound pollution. There were none of your twin-set, horn-rimmed librarians scuttling about, frantically ssshing. In fact, it turned out to be the noisiest library ever. From the moment I got on, it was basically a non-stop party with the odd paperback thrown in.

One of the volunteers had been a famous cabaret singer in Thailand in her youth, so we were treated to some solid-gold Bangkok folk classics, all delivered in a shrill soprano that could have shattered glass and put the local dog population on high alert. After a two-hour uninterrupted set of her greatest hits (I had started to wonder just how many more she had in the tank), we came to a rather abrupt halt.

ME: Oh. Are we here already?

I made as if to get up, but stalled on seeing the concerned look on my fellow travellers' faces. It was clear that something had gone very wrong.

ME: Is this where we get off?
SINGER: No.
ME: So we're not here?
SINGER: No.

The driver turned towards us with a look of desperation on his face. He yelled something to the volunteers. They mumbled something in return. I waited for some kind of explanation, but none was forthcoming. In truth, the atmosphere had become a little awkward. I broke the silence.

ME: Is everything OK?

The volunteers stared at me, wordlessly. I tried again.

ME: Is there a problem?

Still nothing.

ME: Guys, why have we stopped?

What on earth was going on? Why were the crew so reluctant to speak?

ME: Is this normal?

Eventually, one of them shook their head.

ME: OK. So, what's going on?

It turned out we had crashed into some large rocks on the bank and the boatman was having difficulty extricating us from the shoreline.

ME: What can we do? How can we help?

That awkward silence descended again. More staring.

ME: Hello? Anyone? What can we do to help?

It took me a good few minutes to figure out that the problem was me – or, specifically, my heft. The volunteers had been either too polite or too embarrassed to tell me. With old Lumbertubs here as passenger, the boat was lower in the water than usual, so it had snagged on the boulders at the water's edge.

ME: Ah. I think I see what's going on. Shall I move?

The entire crew nodded in emphatic unison.

Bless them all for trying to spare my blushes. I vowed to treat them to an a cappella version of 'Kumbaya' on the way home, by way of a cultural exchange and thank you.

It's true, I was packing a little more timber than I should.

Years of relentless power-eating on *Bake Off*, where I'd spend every summer feasting on Ukrainian funeral breads, Chechnyan meringues and obscure English puddings, had, it's fair to say, laid waste to my waist.

I manoeuvred my way, clumsily, to the rear of the boat, shuffling my buttocks along until I was past the centre line. Suddenly a victory cry went up. The front of the boat reared upwards, no longer weighed down by my Anglo-Saxon podge, we freed ourselves from the rocks and were able to push back into the river.

We puttered for a couple more hours, along the river's least-travelled backwaters. It was here, in one of its most remote windings, that the hill people of the Hmong lived, one of forty-nine ethnic-minority tribes in Laos.

'We're here,' said the singer. It was the first time she had stopped singing in nearly four hours.

As we approached, I could see hundreds of little kids running down the hillside to the sandy banks below, their faces smudged, clothes hanging off them like rags. They were all waving and cheering, not for the cameras, not for the pale Westerner, not for any of that circus. They were cheering, quite simply, because the books had arrived. My eyes pricked with tears. We take it for granted, our access to learning, to betterment. What a way to be shocked out of my complacency, to see these kids, tumbling down rocks barefoot, rushing towards us, desperate to lay their hands on a book.

My tears didn't have a chance to make it down my cheeks, as the sight of the children had set the singer off again, this time with a shrill welcome song that appeared to have no fixed key and, more worryingly, no seeming end.

This charity doesn't just deliver books, it runs an impromptu school on the riverbank, where the Hmong children can learn

Lao. This means that the younger generation will have a chance in life: to travel, to be understood, to be connected with the rest of their countrymen. No sooner had we moored than we were conducting lessons on the beach – a call-and-response class, which introduced them to the benefits of learning. The beach exploded into a riot of song and movement. Out came a tambourine, a drum, and an awful lot of props. I was in heaven.

ME: What are we doing?

I was shouting to be heard over the sound of the class, whose excitement had reached fever pitch.

WOMAN: We are finishing our welcome song, and then we will perform a play.
ME: YES! Can I join in? Can I?

The volunteer looked slightly piteous in the face of my epic enthusiasm.

ME: Can I? I'll do anything! Can I?

I don't like to beg, but this came pretty close. Finally, after some fairly intense lobbying, she caved in.

WOMAN: OK. You can play the part of the tree.
ME: Yes! YES! Now, what *kind* of tree? Do you want something generic, or would you like me to be more region specific? I could be a Dalat pine? Or a Chinese plum? You're the director, so it's your vision . . .

She ignored me. Well, your call, I thought, but don't blame me if my performance is a little less nuanced than it should be.

I do like to get into character. For me it's important. I have had no formal training, but I tend towards being a little method in my approach.

I remember, fondly, a casting for a tea commercial where I was auditioning for the role of Maggie the Pigeon. It was one of the two most embarrassing casting calls of my life.* It transpired I hadn't needed to rent the outfit – but you learn, don't you? I wasn't sure what kind of an accent pigeons might have, but a little research (and it really was a little) yielded the surprising fact that, although feral pigeon populations tend to be very concentrated in cities, their numbers are actually greater in rural areas. Anyway, to cut a long story short, I gave her a West Country burr – like she was the distant cousin of the Cadbury's Caramel bunny, or at least lived in the same postcode. I also made her gluten-intolerant, which I thought was a counter-intuitive and unexpected little twist.

I arrived at the audition to see the usual bunch of downcast actors, fidgeting and muttering to themselves while reading the script. I said a quick hello, and then settled myself down to begin my deep-breathing exercises. What I wasn't expecting was for an assistant to emerge and hand me a character breakdown, a full A4 sheet, listing Maggie's likes and dislikes. This was a last-minute blow. I had, of course, created my *own* back story for the character (abandoned at birth, fostered by doves, a chequered series of relationships with older pigeons that hinted at a father-complex) so it was somewhat annoying to have to rethink the role at such short notice.

I shall always remember the first line on that sheet:

* I have only ever had two casting calls in my life.

Maggie is an organized and well-kept pigeon who goes to the gym regularly – at least twice a week.

This stumped me. In all my calculations, I had not factored in that Maggie might be a *gym-goer*. What an oversight. I stared down at my midriff. It was too late to get in shape for the role. Mind you, what pigeon has a six-pack?

Finally, I was called in. It became clear early on that the West Country accent was surplus to requirement. One of the casting directors even said 'The Geordie wasn't working,' which I thought was a little unkind.

ME: I can do other voices.
DIRECTOR: Your own is fine.
PRODUCER: Can you make her more clipped? Brusque?
ME: Sure.
PRODUCER: She needs to be abrasive and uncomfortable in her own skin.
DIRECTOR: That's why we asked you in.

After about fifteen minutes of ad-libbing around Maggie's busy schedule (popping the washing in the drum, sorting the shopping, organizing work diaries), they decided to ask another actor in to audition with me. This is called a Chemistry Test, I think, which ascertains whether or not you have the requisite sparky, *je ne sais quoi* with another performer.

In walked a lovely Irish guy I'd met in Reception, called Dave.

DIRECTOR: Dave's going to be playing the part of Tom, the obese owl.

I looked over at Dave, who wasn't obese in the slightest. Dave looked down at his belly and then up again.

'Hi, Tom – you massive owl,' I said, trying to help him into character.

'Hi, Maggie, you big fat pigeon,' said Dave, returning the compliment.

We shook hands. I welded my fingers together to form a claw as I did so – just to get us into the part.

DIRECTOR: OK, you two. Tom and Maggie have the hots for one another. It's an unspoken thing. Unconsummated. Think Dempsey and Makepeace, or that couple off *Moonlighting*.

DAVE: (*awkwardly*) Cool.

ME: Right . . .

I was suddenly feeling a little hot under the collar.

DIRECTOR: They're obsessed. They have that ache, that yearning inside them. So, why don't you have a role-play around that, really feel the sexual tension, and let's see what happens.

It was just your average casting session: a gay man playing an overweight raptor and a gay woman playing an uptight pigeon, both locked in a love that could never be. Standard stuff.

We sat on the sofa and tremulously began. The lines, which were mainly about the rich brew being an excellent source of flavonoids, didn't really lend themselves to a sexual subtext, but we did our best. In the end, Dave just gave up and simply laid his head in my lap – leaving me to carry on with a speech about how comforting a cup of tea is after a stressful house move.

We both got the job.

My only other casting call was somewhat different. This was for the BBC's flagship blood-and-guts drama series,

Casualty. Instead of a generic audition invite going out to all and sundry, my agent received a call requesting me, specifically, and asking if I could act. Call me old-fashioned, but I always think the safest thing is to find out whether that person can act *before* putting in the call. In any event, it's a silly thing to ask an agent because they are invested, to the tune of 15 per cent of your gross earnings, in saying you are good at absolutely everything. Their job is to say yes. Your job is to turn up, disappoint and be vilified in the national press.

Rather than go through a formal audition, I simply went and had a nice chat with the director. I let him know how committed I was to the defence and maintenance of a public health service free at the point of entry. I thought that was important to mention, in the context. In fact, I talked about it so much that we didn't get round to discussing acting at all. The first sign that I'd got the role, and that everything was, indeed, happening, was when the script landed on my doormat.

Now, knowing me, as you do, what kind of part do you imagine the good folk at *Casualty* had dreamt up for me? Well, here's what I had expected:

1. A drunken oaf dressed as a nun suffering from concussion following an accident during a student pantomime.
2. A mute.
3. Someone who had been driving behind an industrial truck carrying acid, failed to brake and was covered with corrosive liquid, who therefore spent the episode wailing under a payload of latex FX make-up.
4. A myopic cretin who had been too vain to wear their glasses to a party, got off their tits on ketamine

and copped-off with a fork. (The fork would be sticking out of my face, giving the props department a challenge I'm sure they'd embrace with relish).

Sadly none of those roles were offered. Instead, I was horrified to learn that I'd be playing a police doctor in a very gritty scene involving a sexual assault. Two things occurred to me on first glance:

1. I patently don't have the gravitas to carry off playing a person with proper qualifications.
2. The grim sexual-assault scenario was not going to play to my limited range of skills – namely punning and gurning.

Still, I thought, they must have seen something in me. Some potential. I shall give it my all. I prepared for weeks and turned up on set, on time, with my lines learnt, ready to go.

I stood in the costume department staring at my outfit, which was a rather drab affair. 'Where's the full scrubs?' I asked, a tad disappointed.

'Oh, you're a police doctor – they wouldn't wear those,' said the wardrobe lady.

Once again, I had to start from scratch. I had envisaged the character in a full hazmat suit with a cheeky kitten heel poking out of the bottom – serious, but with a frivolous side. I would have to speedily rethink the way I played her.

I turned up at location, ready to go. The actress playing the assault victim was sitting on the bed.

ME: Hello, everyone.
ALL: Hello!

They really were a bloody friendly bunch.

DIRECTOR: OK, are we ready? Let's go for a take. Sue, you're going to be swabbing round the mouth, remember? And . . . action!

I steadied myself, then let fly my opening line.

ME: That's it. Just open a little wider, please . . .

There was a pause. I waited. Why wasn't the actress saying her lines? Why was she shaking? Was she choking? Had I pushed the cotton bud too far down her throat? It was then I realized she was heaving with laughter – as was everybody else in the room.

DIRECTOR: Cut!

Five takes later and there was total hysteria in the house. I have no idea why. I just maintained my professionalism and carried on. They'll settle down, I thought.

Well, they didn't. In the end we had to make a compromise. I delivered my line to the wall, not looking at the actress, and she bit down on the swab so the microphone couldn't pick up the sound of her guffaws.

That was the last time I graced the set of a serious drama.

Anyway, let us depart the heady glamour of Elstree Studios and head back to the sweltering banks of the Mekong, back to my latest starring role – a tree. I hadn't been given anything in the way of direction, so I had to find my own way with the character. I was just in the middle of assigning a voice (gruff, strong, possibly Northern Irish), when the volunteer stepped forward and unceremoniously popped a large sheet, hung from a bamboo pole, in front of my face.

ME: Oh. Really? A sheet? I'm a tree, not a mattress . . .

They carried on, ignoring me.

There had obviously been some crossed wires in the translation. When they said 'tree' what they really meant was 'canvas'. It became clear that my job was to simply hold up the sheet while the rest of the group performed a puppet show. On me.

Theatre can be such a cruel mistress.

After I'd stood behind this histrionic windbreak for an hour, the show wound to a close. There was a big farewell, with lots of waving and shouting, then we all enjoyed an impromptu hula-hoop session. As you do.

Once the formalities were over, the children scattered like marbles to the hills above, clutching their library books of choice. From what I could see, the most popular titles appeared to be *Pirates Attacked Dr Dolittle As He Was Sailing Home*, *The Wasp With A Stick In Its Eye* and *Eat Teeth!* – a treatise on dental decay and how to avoid it.

A silence descended over the landscape, the crags of rock dotted with colour as the children settled into the outcrops and began to turn the pages. You could feel the concentration in the air, the silent fascination of a hundred children whose imaginations were being stirred.

My eyes filled again as I saw the unmistakable cover of Eric Carle's *The Hungry Caterpillar.* My favourite book, sent through time and space to this remote beach. I picked it up, my fingers poking through the cut-out holes in the watermelon and strawberries and as I did so, I felt it again – like a distant rumble – that excitement when I first sat on my mum's lap, held a book in my hands, and started.

Once Upon A Time.

18. The School of Hard Knocks

I didn't know it, but I wasn't done with schooling just yet. We left the banks of the Hmong village and headed further up the river, to the ancient city of Luang Prabang.

I'd heard about the extraordinary energy of this place, the strange hypnotic effect it has on its visitors, but had been sceptical. I was so brimful of the crusty witterings of backpackers that I no longer took anything at face value.

Prabang? Oh, man, it's *soooooooo* mellow.

Whatever.

And yet, less than an hour into wandering its streets, I was captivated. Everything you've heard about this place is true. Linear time doesn't seem to exist here. It is the in-between place. It is the every-place. You are caught between worlds, ancient and modern – the time-honoured rhythms of Asia and the modern interventions of its erstwhile French overlords, both happily coexisting, yet apart. Here you can meditate, grab a croissant and sit in the lotus position for a fortnight listening to an Edith Piaf tribute act without feeling incongruous.

This gentle, almost somnambulant city is the place where you begin to understand the feeling, if not the philosophy, of Buddhism. It starts to make sense here, not only because of the concentration of temples, but because you are surrounded by water. The city is built at the confluence of the Mekong and its tributary the Nam Kam, and everywhere you turn you can see the snaking silver of the river.

'Lao-ness' is defined by Buddhism, Theravada Buddhism to be more specific, which advocates a calming of emotions. The basic premise appears to be that it's not a good idea to get worked up by strong feelings, or worry about the future. The water seems to be the perfect metaphor for this view of life. Trying to contain or hold on to it is a fool's errand – best to relish the moment it touches your fingers, and, with love, let it go.

I suffer from crippling anxiety – there aren't many days when I don't succumb to the adrenalized spike of a panic attack. The headaches, the dry mouth, the pounding chest, they are the physical signs, but it begins way down beneath the surface. There will be a misguided thought, a negative connection forged in the subconscious that slowly and perniciously works its way upwards, causing chaos at the surface – at the point where you meet the outside world. After years of trying to be better, here, in this venerable city, I was able to release my mind from its familiar traps, be in the moment, and experience something approaching true relief.

We approached the central monastery, its towering roof sweeping up and down from the ridge, like the crest of a wave. From a distance it looked like the trees outside were weighed down with strange orange fruit. As we drew nearer you could see they were decked with monks' robes, hung and slung onto every available bough. It was obviously washing day for the spiritual community – either that or someone had accidentally put one monastic robe in on a white wash, in which case someone was in deep, deep trouble.

I wandered in. A young man, bent like a river-willow, was too busy sweeping the courtyard to take any notice of us, so a rather beautiful white mutt took it upon himself to be the welcoming committee. He lolloped over, rolled in one of the dust-piles the novice had so meticulously created and exposed his belly to me for a tickle. You've lucked out here, mate, I thought. Good for you. Animals tend to congregate around temples. There's food, of course – but, more than that, they get to be calm and safe for a little while, away from the beatings and constant, unpredictable menace of cars, bikes and tuk-tuks. I sat with the dog while the others set up, picking the fleas from the base of his tail and crushing them in my fingers. A pointless task, perhaps – the poor thing was riddled – but, in the monastery context, a completely understandable and valid one. After all, the end is not the reward: the *process* is reward in itself. It is the journey, rather than the destination, that must take our attention. However fruitless it may appear, there is a point to everything if you are sufficiently invested in the moment.

The monastery has another attraction, of course: education. The sons sent here won't have to break their backs on their parents' farms. Instead they will sit in orderly rows meditating and learning English. And from there – after a respectable period of veneration – the world is their oyster.

As soon as we headed for the classrooms, a low-slung concrete block that provided some much-needed shade, I knew they were going to make me teach a lesson. This time, however, I would stand in front of a group of older boys, who would hopefully make sure the tables were moved before we played Head, Shoulders, Knees and Toes.

'It's fine,' said Lucy. 'I think the lesson is all worked out.'

ME: That's a relief – I am not sure I have any more songs in me.

LUCY: Honestly, it's just a vocab class. All you have to do is look at what's on the board and teach them the words.

ME: That sounds easy enough. Leave it with me. Are we good to go?
MATT: Speed.

I screwed my courage to the sticking place, took a deep breath and strode into the room.

ME: *Sabai dee!*

'*Sabai dee!*' replied the class, somewhat taken aback at the sight of this bumptious Westerner marching through the door.

I approached the teacher.

ME: *Sabai dee!*
TEACHER: *Sabai dee!*

He bowed in greeting, and stepped away from the front of the class, joining the rows of pupils waiting expectantly.

OK. Deep breath. Here we go. It's fine, I thought. *It's really fine. Just look at the whiteboard, say the words out loud, give a simple context for those words, then move on. You can do it. Sure you've had no training, but you can do it. How hard can it be?*

It *was* fine. Right up to the point I glanced at the lesson set out on the whiteboard. At that moment it became clear that this was not going to be like any lesson I'd ever taught before. If I were to sum up first impressions, I would go with 'hostile'. It resembled a serial killer's mood board. Scribbled across it, in red marker, was the sort of alarmist vocabulary I'd expect someone like my mum to use when describing traffic at Hyde Park Corner.

I could make out 'wound', 'accident', 'ambulance', 'car crash', 'collision', 'scar' . . .

What kind of lesson had I wandered in on? Whatever happened to good old Peter and Jane?

I tried to joke a little, to break the mood, which was, I have to say, pretty intense.

ME: Now obviously you've already done the what-happens-if-I-get-attacked-by-bears session – and you're about to attend the I-have-to-perform-open-heart-surgery-in-the-frozen-tundra workshop – but this class, this one here, is all about car accidents!

These monks were obviously going to be tough novices to crack. Undeterred, I tried again.

ME: Right. Well, this is one extreme syllabus. First things first, has everyone done their Psychopath Module One homework?

Still nothing. One man with a wisp of a beard nodded, which I took as both a positive and worrying sign.

There was nothing for it but to get on with the class. I began by working my way down the words, trying to find a suitable sentence in which each one would sit. But every time I located the words within a context, it seemed to make things worse.

ME: When a wound doesn't heal, you get a . . . scar.

'Scaaar,' murmured the class, their monotonous repetition only adding to the feeling that I'd wandered into a death cult.

ME: That's right. And when you've ripped your LEG off in an ACCIDENT, you need an AMBULANCE.
CLASS: AMBUUULANCE.

I proceeded to deliver thirty minutes of hearty improvisation, based around the words on the whiteboard. It was like a really violent episode of *Just a Minute*, where I would speak, without hesitation, deviation or repetition on the subject of multiple car pile-ups to a load of Laotian trainee monks.

At the end of the lesson, one man was rocking slowly, back and forward, muttering 'Wound', repeatedly.

Mercifully, the bell rang just as I got to the last word on the vocab list.

ME: SUTURE.

CLASS: SHOOCHURE.

ME: Before you go, as a parting shot, I just need you to know that the UK is very safe.

MONK: Wound . . .

ME: It's highly unlikely that you'll ever need a lot of this vocabulary.

MONK: Wound . . .

ME: It's a pretty welcoming place, with well-established traffic rules so you should be fine. OK. Enjoy the rest of your day.

And with that, I turned to leave and smashed headlong into the boom pole.

CLASS: WOOOOUND.

ME: (*trying to suppress a roar of pain*) That's right. Well done. Well done! Class dismissed!

I was sad to leave Luang Prabang: it had afforded us a little peace in what was an arduous journey. We usually moved hotel or house every day, getting up at first light to pack the endless batteries, drives and lenses we needed, so to have the chance to be in the same place for a few days was bliss.

We boarded a boat and set off on a two-day journey north. After recording a couple of reflective pieces to camera, and a few in expectation of what was to come, there was nothing to be done but laze in the sunshine or drift off on one of the mattresses onboard. You'd catch the odd dot of saffron on the landscape, as a monk headed to the banks to wash his robes, but in the main the landscape was free from all human activity. Buffalo munched their way along the ridges of the banks. Birds circled and dived around us. It was a truly special few days.

As I woke the next morning, I sensed something had changed. The air was thick and humid. There was no sound of birds or insects. I went above deck and, sure enough, the landscape was altered. The land had been stripped, the lush vegetation replaced by dust and sand.

I can feel the pull of Laos's superpower northern neighbour. I can feel the breath of China on my face.

19. All That Glitters

We maundered upstream for a day to Pakbeng, overnighted there, and the next morning set off northwards for Bokeo province and the Golden Triangle. We were literally on a slow boat to China. The Golden Triangle is where the borders of Laos, Thailand and Myanmar meet, although the name is more commonly used in reference to the region's major export: heroin.

On nearing our destination, I transferred from our wooden vessel to a gleaming white powerboat with a plastic roof. I felt like a ready-meal – hermetically sealed and sweating in a synthetic tray waiting for the full microwave experience. Through the vinyl flaps I could see the heat radiating from the pavements beyond, the earth scalped of any living things that could mitigate the rising temperature. The skyline, usually so dominated by trees, was now owned by a vast gold dome atop a concrete monstrosity. I had arrived at the Casino.

If building dams and selling green energy to the Thai government was one way of earning money, this was another. This was the Golden Triangle Special Economic Zone. There are at least ten SEZs in Laos, with many more planned over the next decade. These are parcels of rural land developed with foreign investment, with unique low tariffs and flexible free-market-oriented economic policies. That's just a fancy way of saying that the rules don't apply here. It's a free-for-all. Essentially, this place is an annexe, a *de facto* Chinese state in the heart of Laos.

The Casino attracts hundreds of visitors each week from mainland China, where gambling is banned outside Macau. Most travel by road from Yunnan, or fly to northern Thailand, then cross the Mekong on speedboats laid on by the gambling firm. Despite its location in the tropical hills of Laos, the casino clock is set to Beijing time, one hour ahead of Laos. Mandarin is the *lingua franca* here, and the local shops only accept Thai *baht* or Chinese *yuan*, rather than the Laotian *kip*.

I pulled up at the dock. Young Chinese women in pink dresses and kitten heels wandered the concrete walkways alongside the river, shielding their alabaster skin from the scorching sun with branded parasols. I was met by an army of business representatives who ushered me towards a glistening black stretch limo.

'What, this? You want me to get into this?' I gestured to the car, but the men were no longer listening, turning their backs and returning to the boat. I stood, somewhat confused, next to this elongated obscenity of a vehicle. It took me nearly five minutes to work out where the door was. Thank God I never got that *Top Gear* job, eh? It would have been an hour on BBC2 of me saying things like 'Where's reverse?'. 'I can't find the ignition' and 'What do you mean it's an automatic? I've just rammed it into second gear.'

I half expected to see Sean Coombs turn up and oust me from my ride, but after a few minutes of dazed silence, and a lack of any other passengers materializing, I managed to find the handle and jumped in.

For months I had lived with, and around, subsistence farmers and fishermen. I had seen their world; matchbox houses, tarpaulin shanties, kids with ribs overhanging their bellies like bone roofs. And now I found myself here, in a stretch limo, my face blasted by Arctic air-con, a champagne-chiller to my right and a state-of-the-art sound system to my left. If anything summed up more what is wrong in this world then I have yet to find it.

I was met outside the casino by the general manager, Mr Abbas, a courteous gentleman, although, if I may say, a tad liberal with the hair pomade. We passed through the vast revolving doors and I entered another world.

The air was suddenly cold and processed and carried the relentless beat of tills, tellers and Muzak. There were polished marble floors in a riot of beige as far as the eye could see. Above me, giant frescos depicted the hand of God reaching for, but not quite meeting, the hand of humanity. What a perfect metaphor for this soulless venture. Everywhere you looked there was Italian Renaissance statuary, topped by a vast mock-marble rendering of Zeus at the top of the stairs. He appeared to have shrugged off his role as defender of mankind and charitable protector of the poor and was now, thunderbolt in hand, waiting to punish anyone marking cards or manhandling the croupiers.

'We wanted it to feel like the West,' said Mr Abbas, with no hint of irony.

The casino was made up of twelve thousand feet of gambling space, VIP rooms and private spaces where the high-rollers could get their 'special needs' met. I asked Mr Abbas what 'special needs' these might be, but he quickly changed the subject. I was ushered in to a side room where a vertiginous blonde Russian with a face like set concrete proceeded to deal me some cards.

WOMAN: Baccarat. Yes?

ME: Actually, I won't play, if that's OK.

WOMAN: This casino. You play.

ME: Really, I . . .

WOMAN: You don't know rules? I show you. Listen . . .

ME: No, I know the rules, I just don't want . . .

WOMAN: You no fun. No fun.

As consumer experiences go, this one was up there with the bleakest.

WOMAN: Bad customer. So goodbye.

Outside the casino, the developers had also been busy. There were long, formal gardens, planted in haste, with shrubs at right angles, their roots exposed, drying in the heat. Gaudy cement pagodas popped up here and there, cracked and faltering. There was even a miniature Forbidden City, which managed the extraordinary feat of being less well preserved than the original, despite the fact it had technically been standing for only a matter of months. All around me was a concrete simulacrum, a shoddy grey replica, where the natural world, where beauty, should have been.

I wandered around. I felt displaced and uncomfortable. Something about this barren theme park felt menacing. I didn't know then what I know now: that the SEZ is a haven for child-trafficking, illegal wildlife trading and sex tourism. I just knew that I hated it.

Somebody mentioned that an airport and shopping mall were on their way. A zoo was planned too. My heart sank. I imagined a snow leopard pacing up and down on the boiling aggregate, a polar bear rocking from side to side, while gawping tourists took snapshots for family and friends back home.

That night we headed off to find somewhere to eat, but couldn't find anywhere half decent. Later I learned that some of the restaurants sell bear paws and pangolin. The boutiques openly stock ivory. I had even heard that live tigers were traded for skins, meat and tiger-bone wine. What a basin of hell this place was – a habitat so lawless and godforsaken that even the designers of *Westworld* would have found it *de trop*.

We wandered to the edge of the strip, to what felt like a shanty town, a place where the thousands of casino workers lived and ate. It was edgy – TVs blaring, motorbikes revving. Sex workers patrolled the humid streets. There was no *laap* here, no fresh papaya or fish, just a vending machine, monitored by some kids in flip-flops with buckets of attitude. When it came to paying, we didn't even have the right currency. '*Yuan* only,' said the server. '*Yuan* or *baht*.'

We stayed in the hotel complex, a brutalist block designed around a waterfall with no water in it. The rooms were painted black, and the walls hummed with electrical cabling. I could hear the couple next door having a fight. Then having sex. Then having a fight again. Maybe it was all sex, I don't know. I can't tell any more.

I couldn't sleep. The air was too thick and I felt too anxious. I walked around the courtyard – the stars that had accompanied me throughout my travels seemingly gone, the eastern upside-down moon obscured by cloud.

I rang London. I knew it was the middle of the night. I knew I would just get Anna's voicemail. It didn't matter. I got to hear her voice. I got to say how I felt.

It's me. Sorry, I know it's late.

Baby, I want to come home. Please. I want to come home. I just want to come home.

China

20. Yunnan

We flew from Kunming to Jinghong, the capital of Xishuangbanna Dai Autonomous Prefecture. It was my first trip to China and the only thing I knew about it so far was that Xishuangbanna Dai Autonomous Prefecture is a *total shit* to pronounce on camera first thing in the morning after approximately three hours' sleep.

We arrived to a skyline broken by the vertical scars of cranes and tower blocks. I heard that a new skyscraper goes up every five days in China. Whether that's factually correct, I don't know – but the nomenclature is off, that's for sure. These things don't scrape the sky, they punch right through it. They burst through the clouds and get their concrete faces into God's grill, good and proper.

The story of Jinghong is a familiar one, repeated time and time again across this country. Just over fifteen years ago it had been a fishing village, nestled in the jungle – alive to the sound of temple bells. Now, it resembled a tropical Gotham. Plants struggled to mature in the cancerous gloom, tourists strolled through the streets in face-masks, the birds hung their nests in JCBs, not trees.

From the second we woke, we were serenaded by angle-grinders and the endless beep, beep, beep of reversing haulage trucks. Everything you touched was covered with a thin film of concrete dust. Your throat tickled as you talked, and in the dead of night you'd wake, choking on the particles lining your sinuses.

Our hotel was a vast compound unlike anything I have seen before. When I say vast, I mean vast – it was larger than a village and verging on the size of your average suburban town. The Citadel of a Thousand Trouser Presses. To give you a sense of scale, it took just over ten minutes to walk to my room from Reception. You had to put walking shoes on to get to the gym. By the time you got there, some fifteen minutes later, in the thick, oppressive heat, you felt your workout was already done, so you could simply turn around and head back again.

The hike to breakfast had to be planned with military precision, making note of the right and left turns in the endless and identical breezeblock boulevards. Golf carts stood idly in the roads that connected each residential unit, so if you got too knackered you could make like Bob Hope, hop in one and career over to the restaurant.

Everywhere I went in this grey metropolis I felt dwarfed – like a Borrower on a building site. I would walk to the end of a corridor, only to return the next day and find builders hard at work extending it still further. Perhaps this is how it ends, this endgame of capitalism – with a hotel that expands ever outwards, covering every hamlet, village, city and country in the world with its asphalt fingers, until we are all interconnected by vast grey tunnels punctuated with conference rooms, 'meeting spaces' and restrooms.

How can I help you, madam?

All this walking, from lobby to room and back again, makes a girl hungry. Thankfully, there were multiple restaurants to choose from, although only one technically completed. I am not exaggerating when I say it was the size of an aircraft hangar with a buffet laid out as far as the eye could see: endless metres of immaculately sliced dragon fruit, melon, pineapple and papaya. A depressed woman stood making pancakes at a crepe station. A depressed woman stood making bespoke omelettes at an egg station. A depressed woman stood dunking grey pork balls into dish-water at the noodle station. There were huge lengths of sliced meat curling in the heat; pitchers of concentrated orange juice stagnating, topped with an inch-thick neon meniscus. And who was there to eat all this food – this never-ending sumptuous spectacle?

Twenty people.

Twenty of us, sitting at six or seven different tables spread out in the cavernous space: our crew, a party of six from Beijing, a single-child family from Hong Kong and a silent couple. All with a concrete acre of space between each of us. I could have played a tennis match in there and been unconcerned that the ball would hit a fellow diner.

It was as despairing a sight as I've ever seen, a paean to waste and excess and basic bourgeous crapitude. As we left, the flies started to descend. Normally, I'd be appalled. Here, I was just glad that something, at least, got to polish off the buffet.

Our first day involved getting the boat from Jinghong to one of Xishuangbanna's major tourist destinations. The boat was a pleasure cruiser, a floating party rammed with Han Chinese out for a good time. Han Chinese are the majority Chinese, making up around 92 per cent of China's population. This day trip was to allow them to see a different side of their great nation. On each table there was more wasted food and a pile of plastic trinkets that celebrated 'ethnic culture'. The PA whined into life and a couple, resembling a tribal Donny and Marie Osmond, embarked on a gruelling half-hour set of traditional folksong. There is something searing about the Chinese scale, that shrill pentatonic, which, when combined with a microphone and a loose cable connection, can provide a brain-damaging audio onslaught. This trip ended up feeling like one stress-position short of an aquatic Guantánamo.

We were headed to a visitor experience called the Dai Minority Park. Take a wild guess at the main attraction . . .

I'll give you a clue – 'minority'.

Yes, this is a theme park celebrating the ancient traditions and ways of the Dai ethnic tribe. But the Dai weren't played by actors, recreating the past – oh, no. The Dai were playing themselves. This tribe have lived by the water for millennia, until one day someone popped a fence around them and started charging tourists an entry fee. Essentially, their community was now living a simulated version of their traditional existence under the watchful gaze of coach parties and day-trippers.

There is no other way of putting this: it's a human zoo, with visiting times and feeding times. You're not gawping at jaguars or a greater one-horned rhino. You're gawping at people, real people, going about the same daily routines that their ancestors have enjoyed for thousands of years.

It's hard to find a point of comparison in the Western world for this. We no longer have members of the hunter-gathering Caucasoid Europeans on our shores. There are no existent Celts or Germanic tribes living off the land. Our indigenous communities no longer exist, if indeed the term 'indigenous' can be accurately applied to our nation in the first place.

Of course, the reason there is no parallel is because the rapidity of change in China itself is unparalleled. It's outrunning its own yesterdays at a pace the rest of us can only marvel at – evolving so fast, in fact, that it feels like an entirely different country from the one of even a decade ago. In that context, of course you'd want to make a feature, an exhibit, out of what has been so suddenly abandoned or outdated.

The state of Britain, say, fifteen years ago is a recognizable spectacle. We can easily join the dots between then and now, and find the through-line. We certainly wouldn't look back on 2003 and think anything back then had enough historic or cultural rarity to merit creating a visitor attraction around it. Can you imagine a VERITAS theme park, devoted to Robert Kilroy-Silk's anti-immigration party? Or a Littlewoods ride, commemorating the loss of the 119 stores sold to Associated British Foods? Or would you and the family like to pop to BOOZE WORLD, celebrating the law change meaning pubs in England and Wales were finally allowed to open twenty-four hours a day?

Not exactly scintillating, is it? You wouldn't hop on a boat and go and check out any of those, would you?*

We paid for our tickets at the visitor centre and entered the park. A sleek black coupé sped past, nearly knocking us over.

VICKY: Dai.
ME: What? Really? In a sports car?
VICKY: Really.

And she was right. It turned out that the income from till receipts had raised the living standards of the Dai so rapidly they now drove flashy cars – with an income way beyond the imaginings of even their parents. I watched them wandering through their town. Surely it's now impossible for them to live their life like they used to. Surely they have now become actors playing themselves in a performance of life as they

* I am actually interested in Booze World. I'd definitely visit there.

used to know it – the reality and its simulacrum almost indistinguishable from one another.

We wandered around the wooden houses and the golden temples. I wondered how much of the building material was real and historic, and how much was painted plastic tubing made to look like bamboo. It's hard to know what is genuine and what has been fabricated for the tourist *yuan*.

My guides for this part of the trip were the utterly fabulous Wendy and Echo, China's most magnificent female double-act. Echo was whippet-thin, fluent in English, with a sense of humour drier than silica. Wendy, by contrast, looked exactly like Velma from *Scooby Doo*, spoke no English whatsoever and had an appetite quite unlike anyone I'd ever met. Whatever Wendy encountered, she put into her mouth – be it animal, vegetable or mineral. If we walked past a shrub, she'd pull off the leaves and munch them, she would lick walls, put her hand in pans and tubs and vats. Once I saw her make a drive-by swipe of a spatchcocked frog at a market and swallow it whole. That's my kinda girl.

Of course, I'm not averse to adventurous eating myself: I'm known not only for screaming 'BAKE' in a marquee but also for my ability to eat the inedible, particularly during my stint on *Supersizers*, the chaotic gastronomic gag-fest I presented with Giles Coren. People often come up to me on the street and ask, 'Sue, what's the worst thing you've put in your mouth?' Well, that's a very long answer. But here, by way of a brief diversion, is my top five:

Ancient Rome (eighth century BC to fifth century AD)

Nothing said 'I'm a rich Roman' at a banquet more than a platter of pigs' sex organs, which were not only ostentatious, but a real conversation starter. Let me tell you from personal experience, you're never lost for things to say when there's a prostate tempura in your eye-line. In this case, we were sitting down to a classic BC feast of porcine fallopian tubes. Gosh, I thought, they're really spoiling us with this. After three flagons of wine, I plucked up the courage to sample one. Grim. Think inner tube with slightly faecal back-note. It was then, and only then, that I remembered to ask the key question:

ME: Where on earth did you get these?

There was a nervous pause. The producer looked at the researcher. The researcher looked back. It was a conspiracy.

ME: Seriously, how on earth did you get hold of fallopian tubes. In Rome. In *winter*?

I said the last bit to try and look clever, as if to say, 'They never harvest fallopian tubes in winter. It's more of a spring thing . . .'

The researcher broke the silence.

RESEARCHER: Errrr . . . Well . . . We didn't get them in Rome. We got them in London, from the bottom of a freezer in Chinatown. The restaurant owner said he thought it was uterus. We think it's uterus.

ME: You *think* it's uterus?

RESEARCHER: Yes. We think so.

Of course, the issue of provenance was redundant, since I'd

already eaten it. I decided not to dwell, finished a plate of sow's udder pâté, then headed off to my vestal virgin dance class.

Coffin Pie (Restoration Period 1660–89)

Well, if ever a name sold a dish, it was surely this one. What's not to love about the sound of Coffin Pie? This mortuary mash-up featured a tombola of grey dead stuff, including whole chicken heads, cockscombs and braised pig teats. Oh, and the thick pastry crust was reusable. Imagine that – the hot-water crust that keeps on giving.

Bread and Butter Pudding (Restoration Period 1660–89)

Sounds delicious, doesn't it? That evergreen British pudding, rich with butter and raisins. Now imagine it without the sweetness of raisins and substitute bone marrow for the butter – so that once cooked down it looks like a hot and leaky beef duvet. It was a favourite of the Puritans, and certainly accounts for the rather pursed look on their chops.

Eel (Lamprey) Pie (Restoration Period 1660–89)

What could be more wonderful than an eel, fresh from the Thames? I have a list. Come round my house and I will read it to you.

The first thing that alerted me to this dish was not the smell, but the sound – to be more specific, the sound of chef Allegra

McEvedy screaming downstairs. I rushed to the kitchen to find her convulsed at the sight of chunks of eel, freshly killed, bouncing around the pie crust. They didn't stop moving for another twenty minutes. If Stephen King did pastry . . .

Battalia Pie (Elizabethan Era, 1558–1603)

This was described, by historical recipe books, as a pie filled with 'small, blessed objects'. The mind runs riot, conjuring all the small, blessed things it can think of – a Cadbury's Mini Egg, the Ashes trophy, Janette Krankie. Nope. Not even close.

Translation: testicles, mainly testicles, an avalanche of testicles spilling all their gonad-y goodness as they tumbled forth from the pastry.

I followed that up with Carp with a Pudding in Its Belly, before vomiting in a bucket and heading off to a lute lesson.

And finally, as an addition:

Butterscotch Angel Delight (1967–)

I know. How could I? It's outrageous. How could I demean the food of our youth, the very nectar of childhood! Well, let me pose a question. When was the last time you tasted it? Twenty years ago? Thirty even? Prepare for the sweetest of napalms to lay waste to your taste-buds as this cocktail of e-numbers hits you in the mush.

Back to the Human Zoo.

It turned out that Wendy was *not* one of the 0.0285714285714 per cent of the global population who'd tuned in to watch the *Supersizers* series. She didn't know I'd eaten weird stuff in a corset for money. She just had this sixth sense that I was a fellow gastronomic adventurer. Either that or she'd witnessed me eating that odd fried thing at the theme park, and after that saw me as a worthy wing-man and eating partner. If true, this worried me – because it meant that the odd fried thing must have been something truly, impressively awful.

Wendy would sense that I was coming to the end of an interview and would wander off to a stall or market. Out of the corner of my eye, as I wrapped things up, I could see her buying deep-fried rats from a roadside trader and proffering them in my direction. I'd do a piece to camera, and her hand would venture into shot holding a tangle of noodles bathed in what looked like engine oil. I'd be silently communing with a bunch of animists in the forest and she'd hove into view with a fistful of ants for me to try (citrus flavour, surprisingly tasty). She'd half crunch something left on a table as we took our seats in a restaurant and pop the rest, unbidden, into my mouth. We had nothing in common other than our piratical palates, and the fact that the very sight of one another caused us to spontaneously roar with laughter. We didn't need translators – everything we needed to say got more than adequately expressed in a giggle, a grimace or a mouthful.

Wendy and Echo led me to the main concourse where the tribal celebrations were to begin. In Dai culture, there is a large water festival each New Year, to bless the community and thank the river gods. Of course, tourists can't be expected to wait twelve months for such an experience, so now, in the theme park, this meaningful ceremony takes place at 2 p.m. and 4 p.m. every day, including weekends. Instead of praying, meditating and making offerings over a three-day period, here you dress up in an acid-pink frock, stand in a swimming pool and pour buckets of chlorinated water over each other for ten minutes, while a man shouts frenetically on a microphone and an abused elephant walks past carrying a bunch of VIPs.

The festival, which is over seven hundred years old, originates from a legend that once upon a time, a demon, who wished to do great harm to the world, forced seven princesses to marry him. The youngest got her revenge by chopping off his head with his hair, and the others held the demon's head in their hands until it had entirely rotted away. Happier, simpler times.*

Which is not to say that the whole thing wasn't fun. What's not to like about being issued with a plastic bucket, standing in a fountain and trying to soak your neighbour? Especially if your neighbour is the four-year-old kid you saw trying to kick the poor, wretched elephant earlier that day.

Wendy's greatest moment came after the Dai water celebrations. We dried ourselves off and headed to one of the wooden huts on stilts, where several of the womenfolk had prepared a traditional feast of things that (a) I didn't recognize, (b) couldn't name, and (c) was frightened of. Wendy bent over the assembled plates, wiped the steam from her bottle-bottom glasses, and dived in, sucking chickens' feet, slurping at soups and occasionally roaring as the chilli burn came upon her.

* Potential visitors should note that this decapitation ritual is *not* performed 2 p.m. and 4 p.m. every day including weekends.

I was a little more cautious. I now approached all hospitality with a light unease. The schedule was so tight I couldn't afford to get sick again, so I would routinely rub every chopstick and utensil in hand-sanitizing gel before I tucked in. This meant that everything tasted faintly of ethanol and an old lady's knicker-drawer. After this massive banquet, I settled down, cross-legged, to get serious with the community, talking to them about their ancient traditions and whether or not they felt they were being eroded or compromised by the Park.

Things started out well enough, but around about five minutes in, I became aware of a deep rumbling noise to my right. I carried on, gamely, until I started to notice that both Olly and Matt were shaking with laughter, the boom and camera with them. I persisted, desperately trying to rein the conversation back to the traditional customs of ancient Yunnan. The rumbling was loud now, rhythmic and deep. The Dai women started laughing too. I looked over in the direction of the noise, and there was Wendy, flat on her back, magnificent stomach in the air, dead to the world and snoring her head off. Not just any snore. This snoring was the stuff of legend. The sort of snore you'd imagine Brian Blessed or Tom Baker would produce, after eating a cheese fondue in the middle of a sinus infection. The sort of snore that no one, not even the most skilful of editors, could remove from the proceedings.

Wendy finally awoke, with a fulsome belch, jackknifed upwards and dipped her finger into a boiling pot. We watched her, transfixed. After a few minutes of sucking and slurping she looked up as if to say, 'What are you looking at? Seriously, have you guys got nothing else to do?'

Then she laughed, coughed something up from deep within her lungs, chewed on it, spat the rest out on to her hand – and without thinking passed it over for me to try.

21. You Don't Know What You've Got Until . . .

Next morning, Wendy and Echo took me to see their mate Li-jin, a proud curator of Aini custom who lived in a traditional shack perched on a newly tarmacked A-road. I was used to the co-existence of old and new but, boy, this was a tight-knit collaboration. Her bamboo cottage rocked every thirty seconds as another vast haulage truck sped past on the freshly laid asphalt outside.

Li-jin's passion for all things Aini stemmed from an awkward dinner party many years earlier, when a fellow guest had started asking her questions about her culture. She found she was unable to give an answer. She was so ashamed that she decided to devote her entire life to the commemoration and preservation of the traditional Aini way. I remember a similar thing happened to me when a fellow diner asked me why the westernmost corner of the second level of the NCP car park in Croydon was being used as a latrine. I am ashamed to say I did not go on to devote the rest of my life to finding out the reason why.

The deal was simple here. I'd ask some questions. Echo would then translate those questions from English to Mandarin. Wendy would handle the translation from Mandarin into the local tribal language, whereupon Li-jin would answer. Then the process would get reversed. It was *literally* a game of Chinese whispers.

That's how it was *supposed* to work.

Once we'd arrived and said hello, and I'd been hugged, prodded and laughed at (a ritual that accompanied me for the entirety of my trip), we sat down for a meal. The Aini are famed for their hospitality. It turns out Li-jin was making fourteen different dishes, all while giving me the low-down on the local menfolk (to cut a long story short, she claimed they were only good at two things – hunting and bullshitting. And hunting, it transpires, is illegal). I pounded red chillies with a pestle, and tried to ask relevant questions, but found myself distracted by the horrific sight of Li-jin casually ripping the heads off live shellfish.

I was prodded again. Li-jin said something and Echo and Wendy laughed. I knew, from her tone of voice, that it wasn't a compliment, but I had to sit there with an idiotic grin on my face until the official English version of the insult landed.

'Soft body!' came the interpretation.

SOFT BODY. Man, that's harsh.

We tottered down the wooden stairs, bearing plates of freshly decapitated shellfish, and headed to the courtyard below. The table was laid. Two metres away, an articulated lorry roared past, sending a cascade of loose chippings into the seafood gravy.

Once again, the first part of the translation process went well – Echo seamlessly doing her bit. But when it got to Wendy's turn, she'd be too distracted, either sucking crabs' brains out of their shell or gnawing at what looked suspiciously like an obese squirrel. Added to which, my interviewee, Li-jin, had produced a two-litre bottle of moonshine from under her voluminous skirt, and was more intent on forcing it down our throats than discussing the complexities of cultural erosion in the face of profit-driven homogeneity. And, frankly, who could blame her?

Each time a drink was poured, we'd say the Aini equivalent of 'Cheers' – a rather extended ritual, which involved Li-jin saying '*Gibaduo*', then '*Swae*', five times. We would join in on the sixth. Then the grog would get tipped down our throats and off we'd go again.

Around about the third shot, even Echo started to break down. By the fifth she informed me she'd gone blind in her right eye. I tried, desperately, to be a professional and carry on with the interview, but I was losing the battle of sobriety. Here is a potted version of how the conversation progressed from thereon in:

ME: So, Li-jin, what was it that kick-started your interest in preserving Aini culture?

(*Echo translates to Wendy. We look at Wendy to do her bit. Wendy is nibbling at a leg of something, oblivious. Li-jin refills our glasses.*)

LI-JIN: (*raising her glass and toasting*) *Swae swae swae swae swae.*

ALL: *SWAE!*

(*We down it. It tastes of fire. Li-jin mutters something to Wendy. Echo waits expectantly for the translation. Nothing is forthcoming. Wendy does a little burp. She looks at me and laughs. I can't help but laugh back. My head is starting to swim. A silence descends that may have lasted a few seconds or a full hour. I can't tell. Time is becoming increasingly meaningless. Still no answer, so I decide to venture another question.*)

ME: Do you worry that the next generation will lose their identity? That they will be assimilated into mainstream Han society?

(*Li-jin is already pouring another glass. Her left eye is completely shut. Wendy starts talking to her. Echo kicks her. Wendy laughs again. I laugh. Echo looks at me, glassily, and asks me to repeat the question. I can't remember the question.*)

LI-JIN: *Swae, swae, swae, swae, swae . . .*

ALL: *SWAE!*

(*Down it goes and I get to my feet, quickly, like a reflex – in case I need to vomit or sprint to the local hospital.*)

LI-JIN: *Swae, swae, swae, swae, swae . . .*

ALL: *SWAE!*

(*By now, I realize there will be no answers to any of my questions, but I carry on, regardless. Weirdly, the drunker I'm getting, the more interminable and pretentious my questions are becoming.*)

ME: Do you think that all cultural artefacts are worthy of preserving, or do we tend, as societies, to only want to keep those that appear the most totemic?

(*Echo looks at me, as if to say, 'How am I supposed to translate that, you utter prick?' Wendy laughs and upends the booze bottle into her face. Li-jin grabs me round the waist and we start dancing to a hypnotic guttural tune she is singing. It may be a famous Aini folk song, or it may be gibberish she is making up as she goes along. Equally it may just be a vocal symptom of gastric distress.*)

LI-JIN: *Swae, swae, swae, swae, swae . . .*

ALL: *SWAE!*

I am, indeed, *swae*-ing, at this point – barely able to keep my feet. One side of my face has become numb, and I keep slapping it in an increasingly desperate manner. I cannot feel a thing. Is it palsy? Is it reversible? Will my girlfriend leave me? I am never going to leave this goddamn continent alive. They are all trying to kill me.

Wendy is hunched over a bowl of noodle soup, ramming it into her mouth at breakneck speed. She looks at me and guffaws, spitting a long carb-worm back into the bowl as she does so. I laugh right back at her as Li-jin hands me another drink.

LI-JIN: *Swae, swae, swae, swae, swae . . .*

ALL: *SWAE!*

It's at this point that Li-jin suddenly gets *incredibly* animated. She tells me that there is no written tradition in Aini culture – that their history is woven, literally, into the detailed embroidery of their clothing.

I can no longer speak, but listen with interest. Just before I lose consciousness, I think, *No wonder they have to embroider everything. With refreshments this strong they'd never be able to remember a bloody thing otherwise.*

And black.

I believe the next day involved a drive to Tacheng, where we caught sight of the mighty Yangtze river. I say I believe, because I personally don't remember any of it. I'm so sorry. Simon Reeve or Ben Fogle would never have behaved like that. They are professional broadcasters. They don't drink a litre of bootlegged home brew and collapse unconscious on a load of highly embroidered wristbands.

What I do remember is that Vicky decided I should do a reflective chat to camera at six o'clock the next morning, in a nightmare piece of documentary-making that we now all jokingly refer to as the 'Culture in the Car Park Piece to Camera'. The Culture in the Car Park PTC is a classic example of how *not* to make television.

VICKY: (*behind camera*) OK, Sue. What are your thoughts on your time with the Aini?

I tried to open my mouth, but realized my lips were glued shut by some sort of resinous gum. I ran my tongue over them, delivering some much-needed moisture, and began.

I noticed, after a couple of minutes' opining, that everyone was just staring at me. What on earth was their problem?

This is what I *thought* I was saying:

ME: We cherry-picked the cultural artefacts that define 'Britishness' years ago. How strange to be in a country that is in the process of doing exactly that in the twenty-first century – of negotiating what is saved in the public cultural consciousness, and what is lost.

But this is what I was *actually* saying:

ME: Because because you know I don't need to say because you know and you know you know it's culture isn't it and that can change will it I don't know she made me a really nice embroidered gauntlet because not all is written down will it be lost yes or then again no I think yes I think that sorry I've got a burp coming.

Forty-eight hours later, and whatever hellfire my body had ingested had now been fully expunged. We said goodbye to Echo and Wendy, and I had a pain in my heart as I hugged them. It's a strange truth but, sometimes, the less verbal your communication is with someone, the more you bond on a deeper, more intuitive level. Wendy and I never exchanged more than the odd grunt or giggle, yet every time I pop some new-found nugget into my mouth, I remember her face, and see her, hands on belly, laughing, laughing, like her face is going to split.

22. Ho Goes There?

We pointed the car towards the heavens, and drove for six hundred miles until we were enveloped by cloud. As we wound round the mountains, I noticed the river below. She had changed. Gone was the calm and steady companion that had flowed alongside me at Luang Prabang. Now I had a more agitated and restless escort. Her name was even different here. She was no longer the Mekong, or Mother Water. Here she is known as the Lancang Jiang, or Turbulent River.

We climbed into the chilly reaches of the Himalayas, where the air let slip its oxygen. I began to feel the squeeze in my chest. Everything felt fierce and raw here – the landscape as clean and white as bones.

We arrived in Baisha, at the foot of the rather splendidly named Jade Dragon Snow Mountain. I wanted to stretch my legs, so took off for a stroll around town. I was drawn to a gap in a row of low-slung buildings, through which I could hear the faintest pull of music. I ventured down the alleyway towards the sound and, as I reached its source, came out into an open-air venue to find what could only be described as a pensioners' line dance in progress. The women of the Naxi tribe were in full swing at their weekly exercise class.

It was a beautiful, spontaneous moment: dozens of elderly women in traditional dress – blue caps, dark jerkins, with white scarves criss-crossing their torsos, whirling in perfect synchronicity. I joined them for a while, but soon became too wheezy to continue. I stood back and watched them in awe, septuagenarians, octogenarians together – all still at one with their bodies. What a thing, not to be at war with your physical self.

This area of Yunnan has been famous for herbalists and botanists ever since the Victorian plant hunters first beat a path to it in search of the exotic. I imagined how they would have found this exposed landscape, the thinness of the air – the utter otherness of its people. Everything is available to us now, of course, the world's topography shrunken by the internet – but how magnificently, beautifully curious this place must have seemed back then. Nowadays, these plants, the clematis, rhododendrons and peonies, are familiar residents of our back gardens. Back in the nineteenth and early twentieth century, they were alien species to the European travellers, prized and fantastical. So prized, in fact, that the appropriately named George Forrest escaped with a couple of arrows through his hat while trying to get his hands on a local speciality. The rest of his party were killed. I'm no botanist, but that seems a somewhat high price to pay for a flowering *Camellia saluenensis*, lovely though it is.

Perhaps that's what's missing from *Gardeners' Question Time* – that element of jeopardy. Maybe that's the way to wrest the show from its ageing audience and give it a more contemporary edge. Younger viewers might tune in if Bob Flowerdew risked a spear to the ribs every time he ventured towards a contributor's *Jasminum polyanthum*. Or if Bunny Guinness had to dodge crossbow bolts fired from the Cambridgeshire branch of the WI as she went in search of a rare fenland fern.

I was due to meet Dr Ho, a famed herbalist in the region – over ninety years old and still busy practising Chinese herbal medicine from his roadside dispensary. If the Cambodian

Hermit resembled Grasshopper, then Dr Ho was a dead ringer for Fu Manchu as played by Peter Sellers in *The Fiendish Plot of Fu Manchu*. He was barely four foot tall, mere skin and bone, with a wispy white beard that travelled from his lower lip down as far as his midriff.

But make no mistake: this was no frail old man.

I am always conscious that having a camera shoved in your face can be a disconcerting and intimidating experience, so I always try to be as gentle in my approaches with interviewees as possible. In this particular case, I needn't have bothered. From the moment we arrived, Dr Ho was camera-ready. In fact, I suspect Dr Ho had been camera-ready for several decades before this little show-off was even born.

'*Ni hao!*' I placed my palms together in greeting and bowed towards him.

Dr Ho looked towards us blankly. Perhaps he hadn't heard me.

'*Ni hao!*'

Silence. Dr Ho didn't seem remotely interested in me, but he was interested in the camera lens, which he beetled towards at breakneck speed. What on earth is fuelling the pensioners here? They're all super-charged. There must be something in the water.

I tried again. '*Ni hao! Dr Ho!*' Still nothing. '*Ni hao!*' In truth, my hellos were now starting to sound more like a cry for help than a greeting.

Dr Ho carried on towards the camera until his nose was mere millimetres from the lens. As his face filled the frame, his mouth widened to a grin that only just stopped short of the full Tony Blair. He then launched, unprompted, into a lengthy monologue about the variety of TV programmes he had featured in. The list was seemingly endless. Jesus, I thought, his IMDb profile must go on for pages. It appeared there was no presenter in either hemisphere who hadn't beaten a path to his front door in search of an interview. In fact, I appeared to be the very last documentarian to learn of his existence.

He gestured upwards, to the wall – which turned out to be covered in newspaper articles, all of them about Dr Ho. There was Dr Ho posing in a white coat, Dr Ho stroking his beard in quiet contemplation, Dr Ho smelling a plant looking intrigued. He had been a *National Geographic* centrefold, and there was not one, but *two* signed photos addressed to him personally from Michael Palin no less.

I laughed out loud. There really is no such thing as a new idea in television – no place on earth spared its glittering reach.

After a solid five minutes of showbiz chit-chat he paused for breath – and, just at the point where I thought I could get a word in . . .

He got out his cuttings.

The first book contained page after yellowing page of newspaper articles, photos and profile pieces. Dr Ho was about to open the second book when he was overtaken by a hearty cough. I took this break in his monologue as an opportunity to ask him a question about the collapse of herbal plant stocks. Michael Palin beamed down on me. God, the pressure. Had he, the Godfather of the Modern Travel Documentary, asked this question before me? Was it even worthy of his unrelenting gaze?

Dr Ho responded to the question by simply laying a hand on my shoulder. What had started out as me trying to be solicitous of his feelings ended up with him being solicitous of mine. His touch was basically saying, 'I'm sorry, you're the four hundredth person to have interviewed me, Sue – but I shall go easy on you, as you're patently a novice at all of this.'

Dr Ho ushered me outside, pausing only to introduce me to his silent wife, who was also in her mid-nineties. I am not sure whether she was silent by choice, or whether experience had taught her she was unlikely to get a word in edgeways regardless. He then proceeded, unprompted, to give me a full medical. He grabbed my tongue with his thumb and forefinger, dragged it out of my mouth and inspected it. He put his hand on my pulse. There was some earnest nodding. Then, out of nowhere, he rammed his thumb deep into a pressure point on my philtrum – that hollowed strip between your nose and top lip – and I jumped out of my chair, howling.

'Headache,' he said, satisfied with his diagnosis.

And he was right. I did now have a headache.

Dr Ho seemed to be some sort of reverse-doctor. You came in completely fine, but left with a dazzling array of symptoms.

It was then the turn of the equally wonderful Dr Ho the Younger (who was probably sixty, but had the boundless energy of a pre-teen). This was a man for whom the phrase 'Personal Boundaries' had little or no meaning. He crushed me in an intense embrace, then whirled me to and fro – desperate to introduce me to his rare plant and shrub collections. There was an urgency about him that was both compelling and intimidating: he delivered everything in a breathless monologue, as if, any minute now, someone was going to shut him up for ever. His English was excellent, although he put the emphasis on strange words, which tended to give each sentence a somewhat shocking jolt.

HO JNR: This – very good FOR the colon. COLON! You see and this flower is for THE breast, disease of the BREAST, disease OF the breast.

He brought me to his garden, a compact and serene space containing some ten thousand species of medicinal plants and herbs. Round the edges were wicker baskets, full to the brim with multi-coloured seeds, flowers and roots, all drying in the sunshine. Just being there made you feel well.

HO JNR: What DO you need from PLANTS?

ME: Do you have anything for a wrenched tongue and a banging migraine?

Dr Ho reached into one of the baskets and lunged at me with something that resembled orange peel. I think he was aiming for my mouth, but instead I took a glancing blow to my eye socket.

ME: Oh, and something for corneal damage too, if you have it.

He pirouetted off in the direction of a lobelia. I sat in the garden and drank in its peace. And then I left, before Simon Reeve arrived for his shoot at 6 p.m.

23. The Miracle at Cizhong

As we became more remote, as we drifted further from the major towns and cities, I'd expected the roads to peter out, the wide boulevards to give way to dust and loose chippings. Not here. Here the roads were brand new, the slick stink of freshly laid tarmac still hanging in the air. We drove from Tacheng to Cizhong on one of these brutal highways that cut deep into the range. It started to rain, and the vast mounds of aggregate leached their endless grey into the surrounding earth. To the right, we noticed scree and, above it, exposed flanks of mountain flayed by landslides. I recognized these scars. They were familiar.

We were entering dam country.

Here you can see, first-hand, the violent ingress made by man on the landscape – the terraced farms, fashioned over centuries, scored with fallen rubble. Over one hundred thousand ethnic people displaced. For this.

For progress.

We were not alone. The Chinese government had demanded that a guide be assigned to our crew. From now on, as we moved into politically sensitive territory, we were to be monitored. Of course, it wasn't only the dam that was politically sensitive: we were approaching the border between China and the Tibetan Autonomous Region. Enter our official watchman, Mr Li.

Mr Li was a nervous, waxy-faced man, who could well have come straight from the pens of Trey Parker and Matt

Stone. Mr Li redefined fastidiousness, and his desire to cross every *t* and dot every *i* sadly didn't end with his job. Pathological pernicketiness, it transpires, doesn't begin at 9 a.m. and finish at 5 p.m. sharp. At dinner every night he would regurgitate statistics and facts in an unrelenting monologue, desperately designed to assure us how open and tolerant Chinese society was. He never seemed to realize the irony of the situation – that his very presence told the magnitude of that lie. In the end, I felt rather sorry for him – after all, his life was spent watching others rather than participating himself, always the spectator, never the player.

As we spiralled upwards, you'd find the odd, comforting counterpoint to the filth and the noise. There would be the occasional white pagoda on the hills above, decked with brightly coloured prayer flags flapping in the gusting wind. This would indicate we were entering a Tibetan village, that a certain serenity could be found there, amid the modern maelstrom that circled the mountains.

We were starting to ascend to proper altitude now, over three and a half thousand metres above sea level and counting. When I walked, I could hear a little wheeze in my throat – like a wasp trapped in my larynx, struggling to get out. I arrived in Cizhong, exhausted – having taken some surreptitious shots of the construction site and the scope of the building works in the rare moment our car managed to break away from Mr Li's convoy.

Cizhong is home to a population of ethnic Lisu, Yi and Tibetan people – 80 per cent of whom are Catholic. The remaining 20 per cent of Tibetan Buddhists join the Catholics during their celebration of Christmas and vice versa during the Tibetan New Year. It's a happy, peaceful mix.

That evening, I attended mass in a beautiful, ornate little church that had been built by the French missionaries in the nineteenth century. It was a rather improvised affair, from what I could gather. There were no bells, no smells and no priest either, just a layman orchestrating responses from the pulpit. Women sat on the left, men on the right, all singing Catholic songs in Tibetan, like the missionaries had taught their ancestors over a hundred years ago. I say all, I just moved my mouth up and down like a ventriloquist's dummy.

The guy I was scheduled to interview the next day, Mr Yi, was among the congregation, but I avoided saying hello. I like to meet people for the first time on camera, so you get all the rough edges and genuine connection.

Next to me on the pew was the cutest baby I'd ever seen, a riot of chubby ruddy cheeks topped with a bobble hat. Her mum was on the phone for the entire service, the screen casting an eerie blue light towards the altar, like a Tibetan remake of *Poltergeist*. It's that odd contrast of new and old and painful and funny that makes this place so extraordinary. I love it. I had grown addicted to it.

The next day we trudged along muddy pathways down to a small clearing by the river. Mr Yi was there, beret plonked with the requisite degree of jaunt on his head, chatting to his chickens, who pecked around him in the dust. He has been a practising Catholic all his life. He had also been a schoolteacher. When the Cultural Revolution swept across China, he was arrested, and duly sentenced to hard labour in a 're-education camp'. For thirty years.

I tried to imagine what it would be like to believe in anything strongly enough that I'd be prepared to relinquish my freedom for it. I failed.

In the middle of our chat, Mr Yi shuffled off into his house and emerged, minutes later, with a pile of documents. One was an official letter, folded and bound in faded red velvet. The script inside was printed on brightly coloured floral paper. In all honesty, I thought it was an invite to the local fete.

'What's that?' I asked, somewhat confused.

'It's my certificate,' he said, proudly.

A certificate? Excellent, I thought, with relish. This is where we're now about to career spectacularly off piste. This is going to be fun.

ME: Mr Yi, what's it a certificate for?

YI: It's from the government . . .

ME: Really? What for?

YI: It's a thank-you. It's thanking me for my service to my country.

There was suddenly a cold feeling in the pit of my stomach. It dawned on me that this certificate was, in fact, the official rebranding of his prison sentence. His penal servitude had simply been reclassified as state service. And instead of the righteous indignation and fury that you or I might feel after being robbed of decades of our life, Mr Yi sat there, grinning, as pleased and proud as Punch.

I tend to go into interviews with just one simple question that I want answered, maybe a theme that needs unpicking. Once again, nothing prepared me for the casual horror of Mr Yi's story and the lack of self-pity with which he disclosed it. You wait, thinking there'll be a coda of 'Poor me' or 'I'm so angry' – but what sets these people apart from any I'd met before is the total absence of hatred or the desire for retribution. Horrors had come and gone, and could well come again – but there existed no trace of bitterness. Pain is part of life: you deal with it, even embrace it. You can't insulate yourself from it. The Tibetans neither fetishize it nor expend energy trying to hide from it, like we do.

Then, almost as if he could sense my confusion, and in a testament to how little he held on to the horrors of the past, he whisked me up off my chair and started dancing. It was a strange dance, and a stranger tune, a little like 'The Birdy Song', delivered in a high-pitched wheeze that sounded like a Franco-Mandarin hybrid.

So there we were, two people from two entirely different worlds, bound to each other by the international superglue of music and movement. Same as it ever was.

After a couple of minutes we sat down again, both wheezing – him through age, me through altitude sickness. He got out his prayer book. I haven't been to church in thirty-four years, yet he and I sang through that plainsong in Latin, long after Olly and Matt had stopped committing it to tape.

I sing through the Kyrie and the Gloria. I am eight years old. I am rocking my sore buttocks from side to side on the hard wooden bench, the rich tickle of incense in my nose. I sing the Credo, the Sanctus. I see my dad at the end of the pew check his watch and roll his eyes. I know he is bored and wants to go play golf. I sing the Agnus Dei. Dad sees me looking at him and winks. We stifle a laugh. I finish singing. Hallelujah. Hallelujah. Amen.

There's something in my eye. Bloody chickens. I must be allergic to bloody chickens.

The church was surrounded by vineyards, planted by the French missionaries some hundred and fifty years ago, and each household owns a plot. Some villagers sell the grapes in the nearby village of Badi, and others still make red wine following the techniques taught to their ancestors by the priests.

That afternoon, I pottered down to talk to the workers tending the vines. As I approached one of the houses, a tiny Tibetan mastiff puppy, a blur of black fur with sandy points, danced towards me on his back legs at the end of a long chain.

'Can't you let him off?' I asked the couple standing next to him. 'To play?'

They laughed, hard. As if the request was crazy. As if anyone, or anything, would want to do something as pointless as play.

I sat with the pup for a while, tickling his back legs, feigning hurt as his milk teeth pressed either side of my fingers.

ME: When will you let him off? Surely he has to get used to the other dogs.

They laughed again. That little dog would grow into a big dog. And that big dog would one day be a dead dog, and only then would they take it off the leash.

Before I could head down that melancholy side-road, my attention was drawn to a young girl, poking her head between the gateposts and laughing at me. I laughed back and blew a raspberry, for good measure. She stuck out her tongue. I lifted up the end of my nose, exposing my gums and nostrils and gurned. She did the same. We clicked, immediately, profoundly – to the point that Vicky was impatient to separate us so I could actually get on with some work.

My interview was with a quiet, soulful guy who whispered his name. The wind took it before it reached my ears. I say he was quiet. I mean silent. I was not upset. I was starting to learn the foolishness of asking big questions to those who lived a life of subsistence. There was no sound in the valley, save the snip of his rusty shears on the vines, and an occasional burst of my inane babble. Around us, the little girl – who I assumed was his daughter – danced, her arms outstretched in the faint breeze. I caught her eye, and before long, we were dancing together, and playing tag through the tumble of vines. I did not know her name. I do not remember being told it. She held my hand, and I felt a tug that went beyond the temporal. It was the tug I feel every time a little one grabs my palm – the faint twinge of loss, the faint echo of what might have been.

It was an odd day. Baggy. Usually I'm up and at it – but today the crew needed to take sweeping shots of the mountains, of the ancient road scarred by the hydroelectric dam being built. I found myself with very little to do, and with very little energy to do it with.

I asked to be driven to the top of the village, to the temple overlooking the valley. I wanted to be alone. I wanted to think. I walked out onto the thick flat rock that extended from the mountain's edge. Beyond, a carpet of endless green punctuated by the occasional whitewashed *stupa*. I cleared my mind. I tried to meditate. To my surprise I began to cry.

Then, out of nowhere, the wind got up – sharp and sudden. The flaccid boughs of prayer flags around me tautened and the air was filled with furious noise – like the beating of a million wings.

I started from my meditation. I looked over to my right, sensing something new on the landscape.

And there she was, the little girl from the vineyard.

What the hell? How on earth had she got up here so quickly? I was driven and it took at least five or six minutes. She must have sprinted, yet her chest wasn't heaving. She wasn't even out of breath.

She extended her right arm and beckoned me over with a twitch of her hand. I got up and wandered towards her, suddenly light-headed. I clasped her little fingers in mine, and together we walked back down the mountainside in silence. After fifteen minutes or so, we came to an abrupt halt by a tiny concrete dwelling. Outside were two old women, sitting either side of the door, like gatekeepers. Both were dressed in emerald green and knitting furiously.

I was starting to feel that this reel of my life was being directed by David Lynch.

The pensioners looked at me with trepidation as I approached. The little girl said something to them in a low voice. They relaxed and nodded. I was ushered through the open doorway to the single room beyond. The little girl gestured towards a wooden chair, draped in a yak-hair blanket. I sat.

'STAY,' she seemed to be saying. Yet her mouth didn't open.

She dragged a chair across the room, stood on it and, with great difficulty, stretched up to a little cupboard mounted high on the wall. From inside she brought down a candy bar and a plastic juice carton.

She removed the straw from its wrapper, punched it through the silver disc at the top of the container and handed it to me. Same with the biscuit: she ripped the foil, exposed a bright pink cake beneath and pressed it into my palm. Then she returned the chair to its place and sat next to me, her hand resting on my knee. I looked at her and was shocked to find she was viewing me with a mixture of curiosity and . . . and sympathy.

It's like I'm a patient, I thought.

It's like I'm her patient.

The long silence was broken by a woman entering the room. I assumed she must be the girl's mother. I bowed.

'*Tashi delek*,' I muttered.

'*Tashi delek*,' she replied.

Yet the child didn't behave like a daughter. And the woman seemed deferential, timid. Even a little afraid.

The girl spoke once more, in a low whisper. The woman left.

She reached for a remote and turned the television on. The room exploded with noise and colour. She slipped her hand back into mine and we stared at the screen, wordlessly, occasionally slurping our juice.

I began to feel distinctly woozy. It must be the heat. The lack of oxygen. Or poison. Has she poisoned me? Has she?

We sat there, holding hands, for what seemed like hours – the endless, high-octane adverts washing over us.

Finally, she moved. She turned to face me, handed me the remote control and said: 'Sue. You can change channels any time you want, you know.'

In English. In plain, uninflected English.

My heart was racing. *I've gone mad. I've lost it. I've come all this way and I have lost my mind.*

ME: Did you speak? Did you speak just then? I heard you! How come you know English? How come you can say that? How? What are you? What are you?

The little girl just smiled, and lightly touched my cheek with her palm. Then, she got up, gestured for me to follow and led me out into the afternoon air. I stood there, gasping in the light, whereupon she ran down the hill until I lost sight of her.

I still struggle with that day. I struggle to make sense of it. Did I imagine that voice, even though I saw it come out of her mouth? Even though I could hear it as clear as day? Was I hallucinating? Had I temporarily taken leave of my senses in that strange, otherworldly high place?

The unknowable is frightening. That's why we're hard-wired to rationalize, to find answers. But with that little girl, I chose to believe something else – something fantastical, that which is unprovable, random and crazy. I chose to believe that she was an angel. My angel. And, yes, she may have been born from the fires of madness, sadness, or plain and simple oxygen starvation. She may have been a projection of a brain now badly malfunctioning with prolactin overload. But she remains an angel, nonetheless.

And when I came home, I did, indeed, change channel.

24. It's Not What You Do – It's the Way That You Do It

We ascend again, still further into the Himalayas, four thousand metres and counting. We climb as far as Shangri-La, the most exotic place name on the planet, a citadel in the yellow plains, where wild dogs roam and people spin round and round on a vast prayer wheel to the point of collapse. Whatever you believe, we are near the heavens, for sure.

My voice had gone from wheezy to full-blown Dalek. The lack of oxygen meant that everything I said now had the sinister overtone of a tin-can Kaled, hell-bent on destroying all known planets in the galaxy.

'WHERE IS THE NEA-REST TOI-LET?' I'd ask, and people would jump. I'd become used to the fact my new Davros voice prompted fear.

After a few days acclimatizing, the headache finally went. I felt clean and clear. We journeyed onwards as far as the border between Yunnan and Zogang but could not process any further. A thick barricade of prayer flags greeted me at the pass. In front of me lay the majestic Khawa Karpo, the mountain sacred to all Tibetans – but, sadly, it was wreathed in thick cloud, so I didn't get so much as a peek at it.

There are direct flights from Shangri-La to Lhasa twice a day. It takes, on average, a mere two hours to get there. Easy, yes?

Easy, that is, if you're given permission by the Chinese

government. We weren't given that permission. Instead we had to take four flights, skirting round the edges of the Tibetan Autonomous Region.

- From Diqing to Kumming (that's 1 hour)
- From Kumming to Chongqing (that's another 1 hour 15 minutes)
- From Chongqing to Xining (add an extra 1 hour 40)
- From Xining to Yushu Batang (and finish it off with a final 1 hour and 15)

President Xi Jinping – sir – with the greatest respect, I want you to know that I hold you personally responsible for my deep-vein thrombosis, lumpy legs and spider veins.

Landing in Yushu was like landing on another planet. The runway was a simple strip mown into an endless pasture of soft yellow grass – so yellow you felt you were descending into custard.

The terminal was empty save a couple of kids, with pinched, flushed cheeks, and their grandfather, all sitting in silence waiting for their relatives to descend from the sky. Chinese guards in thick gabardine uniforms were holding their automatic weapons at the ready, in an airport the size of your average restaurant.

I was picked up by a wonderful guide named Tashi. We drove past a vast herd of yak, heads down, munching as far as the eye could see.

ME: You know there are around twelve million yaks in this area?

TASHI: Yes.

ME: And only six million Tibetans.

TASHI: OK.

ME: You know what that means. If the yaks get their shit together . . .

TASHI: It's over for us . . .

It was a four-hour drive to our overnight stop in Sharda. On the way we saw small groups of men and women walking at the edge of the road, mumbling mantras to themselves, hands raised to the heavens. They would take three small steps, drop to their knees, lie face down on the earth, then stand again. Then they would take another three small steps and repeat the process. Walk, kneel, lie, walk, kneel, lie. Most wore red and orange robes; some were in animal skins. Others had wooden paddles attached to their hands. This was to protect their palms from the sharp gravel, but also, so that when they raised their hands to the heavens they could clap.

ME: Where are they going?

TASHI: Lhasa. To the holy temple of Jokang.

ME: And they do this the whole way?

TASHI: Yes. Of course. They will be there in about five months.

Through rain, snow and dizzying heat they walk, breaking the momentum with devotional prostration. A reminder to be mindful of each step and be present in the now rather than the later.

I thought about me in the car in Kentish Town, screaming if I didn't make the lights.

Finally, we hit the edge of town and the familiar dusty streets. The hotel felt familiar too; young kids smoking on Reception, the customary whine of an old TV. I'd never been there, but I'd seen it all before – the polished marble floors in the entranceway, the lacquered, ornate hardwood chairs . . . a wilful distraction from the horror of the actual rooms upstairs.

I was given the honour of the Presidential Suite. Sure, there was still the mandatory overflowing toilet that I'd had in every other Chinese hostel. The difference was this was a *large* overflowing toilet – and that's what puts the P in Presidential, folks. I spent the night in a vast carved bed strapped to a tank of oxygen, watching the puffs of dust emerge through the broken windows as the lorries rumbled through the streets in an endless line.

The most wonderful thing for me about this part of the journey was that no one could agree on its exact end point. For hundreds of years, locals have recognized 94°18'14E, 33°34'15N as the source of the Mekong, or Dza Chu, as it's known there. In 2001, a Japanese research team published the source as some forty kilometres away from the Tibetan recognized points. Then, in 2002, a Chinese expedition claimed the location as six kilometres away from the Japanese location, and on an entirely different mountain altogether.

Either the Mekong is having a laugh and moving every now and then, or weather and climatic conditions make pinpointing it virtually impossible.

Two things were clear; first, the start of the Mekong is found somewhere in the centre of Dzado County, in one of the most rugged and remote spots on the planet, and second, this was as near as I was going to get to it. *

* There had been the outside possibility of a two-week trek on horseback and foot – but I can't find my car keys most days, so the idea I was going to beat the expeditionary teams of some of the greatest scientific powers in the world was . . . well, somewhat unlikely.

We set off the next morning to the most north-eastern part of the plateau, arriving at a tiny outpost some four kilometres from the town of Nyalga to meet the first family of the Mekong. They were yak herders. In the winter they stay here, and in the warmer months they are nomadic, following their animals across the vast plateau.

I knew they had never seen a Westerner before. I had thought long and hard about the impression I wanted to make on them – but I never got the chance. As soon as I opened the car door, I was grabbed by the entire family – two at each arm and several at my back – and manoeuvred into the house. It was my very first Tibetan love-bomb, and I crave it still.

The house was a single-storey concrete dwelling with two rooms, one a bedroom with low-slung wooden cots, the other a living space with a roaring open fire at its heart. A thin, sweet fog filled the air, as the mother, Ama, got busy with the kettle.

'She's making your drink,' said Tashi. 'It's the local speciality.'

Ama opened a pot, delved inside and pulled out a fistful of yellow fat. It squelched between her brown fingers. She put a clod of this butter in the pot, along with some barley powder and what looked like milk curd, then poured on some tea. Yak butter tea, the Tibetan staple. The result was an earthy, nutty brew full of fat and salt. I could get quite used to it.

A man called Dave Asprey tried yak butter tea in the Autonomous Region in 2004. He liked it so much, he added grass-fed butter to his morning brew and the Bulletproof Coffee was born – the beverage that launched a million wellness blogs. I thought of life up here – the simplicity of limited ingredients, the integrity of their farming practices and life in general, and then I thought of the pitiful ways we have tried to deconstruct it at home with our barley 'mylk' and bone broths.

We left at midday and climbed the mountainous plain next to the house. The sun snarled at my cheeks and turned them red. It's strange up there – you're simultaneously hot and cold. I had now acclimatized, so finally had the chance to relax and be transported by the beauty of it all.

The land was dotted with black, as the yak spread like marbles across the plains. The husband, Aba, looked on at his herd in pride. Occasionally, if one of the brutes got out of line, he would send a stone skimming, at lightning speed, to its hocks, and it would rumble off, duly disciplined.

I noticed that several of the yaks had brightly coloured ribbons in their ears. I asked him what that meant.

> ABA: It means they are safe. They are untouched. They are our gift to the gods and we will look after them until they die a natural death here in the mountains.

We wandered to the river, a river I had spent the last four months looking at. I had seen it filthy and clogged in Ho Chi Minh, raging in Laos, dammed in China – and here . . . Here it was like the purest of streams, bounded by white rocks and soaring mountains.

I have never been anywhere on this earth that I loved more, save perhaps the furthest reaches of Cornwall and the Scottish Highlands.

I stood back as Aba knelt by the water. He washed his face three times, took three bowlfuls and threw each of them back, one by one.

Me: Do you fish?

I was optimistic. Surely here I'd be able to see fish taken from the Mekong.

ABA: No. We take nothing from the water. We want to preserve it for the others downstream. We want to keep it pure.

I wanted to tell him what I'd seen. The endless outboard motors leaching fuel, the plastic bags like indestructible lilies floating by. *They're killing it. While you preserve it, they are killing it. Your love, your dutiful respect of this ancient river, counts for nothing.*

I remained silent.

We never included the pieces to camera we shot by the bank, as I couldn't stop my eyes leaking. I was so overwhelmed by the sadness of it all.

As dusk fell, we tethered the yaks so they would be kept safe from the clutches of wolves and bears. It's impossible to overestimate the worth of these gentle beasts. They provide food, clothing and fuel; their butter is offered to the gods and their wool woven into prayer flags. Tashi and the Tibetan crew had bought a range of fresh vegetables from town – none of which could be grown here – and made a delicious stew on the stove in the centre of the house. It was fed with dried manure that gave off a gentle sweet smell. Ama handed round a giant yak leg for us to gnaw on, like a carnivorous game of Pass the Parcel.

Darkness was descending. From outside came the occasional grunt of the tethered yaks – deep and guttural. As the sky grew inky, the candles were lit and prayers began. I have rarely felt more content, my head bowed, listening to Ama's nasal intonation as she sent her mantra out into the wilderness beyond. It was pitch black now, yet barely 7.30 p.m. The young lads came in from the other room, stripped down to their long johns, and got into their bunks. I lay on my yak-hair mattress, cushioned by the wooden crib around me.

I awoke an hour later to the sound of five men snoring. There was something hot and furry on my chest.

ME: (*hissing*) VICKY!!!

Poor Vicky, she was forever being woken by me. Her head-torch switched on.

VICKY: What is it?
ME: What the fuck is on me?
VICKY: Hang on . . . Let me see . . . OK . . . It's either a rat or a cat. It's big though. Don't worry – it likes you.

We didn't sleep a wink. The high altitude meant your bladder was on overdrive, so you constantly needed to wee. It wasn't safe to go outside on your own – wild Tibetan mastiffs hunt in packs – so you needed a wing-man on your nocturnal sorties, just in case. Every hour or so, Vicky or I would wake the other so we could have company while we pissed against the wall in the howling gale.

The next day it was snowing, thick, soft flakes that burrowed into your clothes. Kids walked past carrying piles of hay taller than they were, and old men in bobble hats spun their prayer wheels as they began the first incantations of the day.

We were in the fields by 4.30 a.m., milking and collecting dung. Ama put on a makeshift mask, grabbed a rake and flung each dry bolus of shit backwards into the pannier on her back. Then she took the dung and smeared it by hand onto the grass so it could dry in the wind.

She then wiped her hands on her skirts and headed in. Whereupon she reached into the jar of yak butter and started to make tea for us all.

It was then that I realized – that this was the exact point in her daily routine that I had walked in on yesterday. I looked at her brown fingernails. I looked at her. And I handed her my cup.

India

25. Kolkata: Arrivals

I meet up with Steve in a coffee bar in Soho. He looks shifty, like he is selling something. God, I love him. I love the fact he is so uncomfortable in a job he has actively chosen and pursued. I recognize the feeling.

His cappuccino arrives. He views it with suspicion throughout the entirety of our meeting.

STEVE: Sue, we're thinking India next.

This is fabulous news. I've never been to India before, but I've heard so much about it. This is a composite of what I've heard:

PEOPLE: Oh, my God, India! The colours, Sue! The colours! The colours are *incredible*. And the smells! The colour and the smells! And the food! Oh, my God! The colour and the smells and the food! The people, Sue! And the colours! The colours are *incredible*! *The colours are incredible!*

So, to sum up India: colour, food and people. Well, I bring news. *Everywhere* has colour, food and people. So, what else?

I wondered where I'd be sent. The tranquil waterways of Kerala? The sandy beaches of Goa? The ancient temples of Rajasthan? Nope. This was Steve and, as we know by now, it is Steve's avowed mission in life to make me suffer. And so I was sent to a city deemed the very signifier of what it means to be poor and disenfranchised – Kolkata.

With time an issue (I had only twelve days to make the film) Steve thought the best thing to do would be to take me straight from the airport into the busiest part of town and simply start shooting.

STEVE: It'll be great. We'll get your initial reactions to all the hustle and bustle and go from there.

ME: Cool. That sounds pleasingly chaotic. What's it like?

STEVE: It's mental. I mean, it's great. Honestly, you'll love it.

I got off the plane after an eleven-hour flight, hurled myself headlong into a taxi, and forty minutes later I was slap-bang in the middle of a city of fourteen million people – most of whom seemed to be in the very street I was filming my opening piece to camera in.

It was the biggest culture shock of my life. There was barely room to breathe, let alone walk, in that thoroughfare. Tuk-tuks in the bright red, yellow and green of the nation's flag beeped and swerved like luminous beetles. Traders, laden with bolts of fabric and panniers of garlic, elbowed me as they jostled past. Delivery boys ran at me with pushcarts full of papers and plastic, desperate to find a space in which to manoeuvre. And, in the midst of it all, cows – merrily sauntering in front of lorries, tiptoeing over tram lines, and nonchalantly chewing bin bags in the path of oncoming traffic. The cows don't care: they know they are safe. They're the only ones guaranteed to make it out of this goddamn street alive.

Within seconds, my entire body started flaring with allergies, my sinuses set like concrete and red pimples burst through my skin in violent protest at the heat.

Kolkata had been a sleepy village right up to the point us Brits showed up and decided it was the perfect place to start an empire. In its Victorian heyday, it was a thriving port, where fortunes could be made, and immigrants flocked from all over the world in search of work and a better life. To avoid any cultural 'unpleasantness', the British devised a system whereby they divided the city according to colour. There was the 'White Town', made up of European (mainly British) settlers, which looked a little like Kensington, with its stucco buildings and wide boulevards. There was the 'Black Town', where the Indians lived. And then there was the 'Grey Area' where everyone else got put. It's now called Bowbazar, and remains a wonderful, jumbled mish-mash of nationalities and ethnicities.

Bowbazar is both chaotic and harmonious, fractious and tolerant. This tight-knit mix, where everyone eats, shops and works together, may well account for the fact that when Prime Minister Indira Gandhi was shot by her bodyguards thirty years ago Kolkata was the only place in India that didn't see reprisals against the Sikh community.

To walk around the district of Bowbazar is to tour the world: there are churches and synagogues, minarets and stupas. One moment you're in a classic Indian street, commuters savouring their clay cups of sweet chai, then you're in Parsee territory, walking past the Zoroastrian temple, where a sacred flame has burnt since 1912. There's a wedding cake of an Armenian church, a baby-pink Jain temple and a red and cream coloured synagogue, built in Kolkata's Raj heyday, when the city had a population of some ten thousand Jews. Today there are fewer than thirty, barely enough for a service. There is no rabbi to light the Shabbat lamps, so this sacred duty is carried out by a Muslim family.

We wander further. The imam calls the faithful to prayer. Ten thousand men fill the streets, get down on their knees and stop the traffic. Moments later, they get up, and the bustle begins again.

We enter the Nakhoda Masjid Mosque and the temperature drops. I welcome the sudden cool. I remove my boots and sit them next to the hundred or so dusty sandals that crown the entranceway. My hot feet spread on the chilled tiles. There are dozens of men lounging by the Ablution Pool, and others lie fast asleep on their backs, snoring, in the shade of the main courtyard.

A girl approaches, drawn to the spectacle of a television crew. She says in perfect English that she wants to be a journalist. I don't want to tell her this, but with two fluent languages and a can-do attitude, she is already over-qualified.

ME: Well, this, I am ashamed to say, is my very first mosque experience. You'd do me a great honour if you showed me around.

She takes me round the ground floor, pointing out the finer architectural details of the building. Around her the men snarl and chomp in their sleep. We walk up the wide stone steps to the first floor, where my eye is caught by a narrow door in the far corner.

ME: What's that?

GIRL: It's the staircase up to the minaret. I've never been up there. I don't know if we are allowed.

ME: Well, I think we are allowed. We can allow one another. Shall we?

She giggles, then puts her hand over her mouth, as if to stifle a full-blown laugh. I open the door, fine dust falling from the lintel onto our heads, and we make our way up the narrow stone spiral.

We come out onto a rooftop by the minaret. Below, the entire world is going about its business, unaware of this silent act of rebellion.

ME: Shall we?

I point up to the minaret once more. And we laugh all the way to the top.

Abhra started out as our fixer, then became an on-screen contributor and then a friend. We ended up working with him on every film we made in India – and I can't think of a better, sweeter guy to hang out with.

We hit the clogged arteries of Bowbazar once more, with him as our guide. We turned a typical Indian street corner, and suddenly entered Chinatown. Hawkers were selling prawn crackers, noodles and fish-ball soup. The signs were in Mandarin, and red flags hung over the doorways. We could have been in Shanghai.

The Chinese community has been in Kolkata for over two hundred years. Their population originally numbered around twenty thousand; nowadays it's about a tenth of that. But, despite the fall in numbers, this temple is still going strong.

Abhra ushered me inside. It was cool and serene. Red candles burned next to stagnant cups of jasmine and *pu'er* tea. On the opposing wall, there were gold drapes, vast floral arrangements in silk and an engraved altar, decked with gilded vases and candlesticks, at the centre of which sat an ebony-faced figure in the lotus pose.

I was met by a very friendly dude, whose name, rather unfortunately, appeared to be Attack.

ME: Sorry. Attack?
ATTACK: Attack.
ME: *A-ttack?*
ATTACK: YES. ATTACK.

I have no idea whether this was indeed the case, but that's what it sounded like, so for the rest of the afternoon that's what I called him. It was a shame, as he really was a delightful gent – though not a patch on his older brother, Onslaught.

I had barely got through the door before Attack offered to tell my fortune. *Why not?* I thought. After all, I am at the beginning of another journey – there's no harm in seeing what's in store for me and my fellow adventurers.

An elderly lady with advanced politeness issues materialized from behind a curtain and handed me a large tub with some bamboo sticks poking out of it.

'Oh, hello,' I said, taking the tub. 'What do I do with this?'

The question provoked a heated debate between Attack and the lady. As with all the holy places I have visited around the world, there seemed to be a fair amount of disagreement as to the procedural elements involved in the ceremony.

ATTACK: You have to pray three times and then ask once.

'No!' said the woman, who was so furious that everything she said sounded like it should have an exclamation mark at the end of it.

WOMAN: NO! You have to say your name! Say your name!

Attack was suitably admonished.

ATTACK: Yes, she is right. Say your name!
ME: OK. OK!

Now I was shouting.

I was incredibly confused, but desperate, nonetheless, to get it right. I attempted to get myself into a respectful headspace for what was to come, but couldn't tune out the intense Mandarin mutterings between the two – which, to be honest, were turning out to be a bit of a spiritual-buzz kill. The lady turned to me again.

WOMAN: You! Now! Say your age!

I wonder if she had requested this information more out of spite than tradition.

ME: I have to say my age?
WOMAN: Yes!
ME: Really? (*Suddenly panicking*) What? Out *loud*?

This is not a number that should be uttered in public.

WOMAN: Yes! Say!

Attack stepped in to spare my modesty.

ATTACK: No. Not to us. To the gods.

That's perfect, I thought, because only the gods know my real age.

Abhra was now getting involved – trying to interpret – but even he was struggling to make sense of the conflicting information I was receiving.

ABHRA: Say your name and shake it once.
WOMAN: No! Three times!
ATTACK: OK, shake it – think about your age and whatever, however you want.

'Whatever, however you want' sounded somewhat vague, even to a non-believer like me. The barracking continued:

WOMAN: Face the shrine! Say your name!

I took a deep breath and approached the deity.

ATTACK: Shake it.
WOMAN: Shake it!
ATTACK: Shake it three times . . .
WOMAN: SHAKE IT! More! More!

Another argument broke out behind me. I carried on regardless, shaking, then saying my name and my age.

ATTACK: Keep shaking.
WOMAN: More! More shaking! SHAKE!

This was certainly the most high-pressured spiritual event I'd ever attended. At one point I thought I might be having a panic attack. Finally, one of the sticks broke away from the others and hit the floor.

ME: Yes! YES!

I was just relieved the whole thing was over. The atmosphere cleared a little, everyone calmer now the process was finished. There was a moment of congratulatory silence, and then Attack spoke up.

ATTACK: What did you ask for?
ME: Oh.
ABHRA: What?
ME: Oh, no . . .
WOMAN: WHAT!?

ME: I didn't ask for anything.

And with that, the whole thing kicked off again.

WOMAN: NO!
ABHRA: You were supposed to ask the gods . . .
ME: But you didn't tell me I had to ask for anything . . .
WOMAN: She is an idiot!
ME: How am I supposed to know? I've never had my fortune read in a Chinese temple in Kolkata before!
WOMAN: She is an idiot!
ME: OK, OK . . .
ATTACK: Let's do it again.
ABHRA: Remember, your name, your age and . . .
WOMAN: Go now!
ABHRA: . . . and what you are looking for in your fortune.
WOMAN: Shake! Go! Now!

I panicked, violently rattling the pot, and spilling the contents onto the floor. I was now surrounded by sticks.

WOMAN: NO! God! No!
ATTACK: Which stick came out?
WOMAN: All of them. You see? Idiot!

Attack came forward and picked up the first stick he came across. He no longer seemed to care about due process. Why worry about authenticity, eh? Just pick up any old stick and crack on. He examined the end of it.

ATTACK: Number sixty-two.

I was ushered to a stand on which were stacked various numbered sheets of paper. So this is how the goddess manifests her fortune-telling – through the power of the photocopier. I found the corresponding sheet for number sixty-two and read the prophecy aloud: 'This will be a fruitful year for farming and marriage.'

I gulped. As an urbanite and commitment-phobe this was a double blow.

Underneath that, there followed the rather ominous divination: 'Your family will be liquid.'

As predictions go, it was a hard one to forget. To this day, I have no idea whether or not it was a typo or a genuine warning – but on hot days I keep an eye on them, just in case.

26. Bow Barracks

Even now, some seventy years after the Indian Independence Act, there's some corner of Kolkata that is for ever England.

The air in the tiny streets of Bow Barracks is thick with the stink of boiled milk and sugar, the terracotta buildings a somewhat faded spectacle from the russet pomp of their heyday. There are thick bars on all the windows – a salutary reminder of the building's heritage. The Barracks were originally built as military housing for the British Army during the First World War. When the soldiers left, they handed over the apartment blocks to the Anglo-Indians, those with mixed British and Indian parentage.

During the East India Company's rule in India, it was fairly common for British officers and soldiers to take Indian wives and have Eurasian children. Over generations, this Anglo-Indian community developed a culture of its own: it established a school system focused on the English language, and formed social clubs and associations to run functions on special occasions like Christmas and Easter.

Kolkata's Anglo-Indian community grew to nearly three hundred thousand strong, enjoying, thanks to their fluent English, some of the best positions in the colonial government. Following Independence, however, they found themselves increasingly displaced, mistrusted by nationalists and unwanted by the motherland.

Today, more than a hundred families continue to live in

the Barracks, 80 per cent of whom are Anglo-Indian. I was here to meet one of them.

I entered the building, turned sharp left and walked into one of the flats. The family were there, waiting, ready to greet me. I was somewhat taken aback by the sight of one of the sons, who was wearing full England football strip. I'm not sure it was official merchandise, as the three lions seemed to have been replaced by a pair of obese crocodiles.

The moment I set foot inside, I was set upon by a pair of distinctly wheezy Pugs, one of which went for my ankles.

FATHER: Don't worry about her. She is curious, but she will soon lose interest.

I'd heard that before.

ME: What's she called?

I flinched as her snotty muzzle brushed across my flip-flops.

FATHER: Ah – that's Brooke Shields.
ME: *Brooke Shields?*
FATHER: Yes. Brooke Shields.

It was an act of will not to laugh. I thankfully maintained my composure. Standards.

FATHER: And this . . .

He pointed towards the second dog, which was busy licking my big toe like a lolly.

FATHER: This is . . .

He muttered a name. I couldn't quite make it out over the din of the street, but it sounded an awful lot like Moira Stewart.

Brooke Shields was now desperately trying to gnaw my fibula, but her face was so flat her teeth couldn't gain purchase. Instead, she decided to gum the hem of my trousers until they became soggy. It was like being savaged by an asthmatic draught excluder. Moira Stewart had seemingly given up on trying to dissolve my foot with her acrid saliva, so retired to the corner of the room and set free a heady, high-pitched fart.

I sat down. Marion, the matriarch of the family, approached.

MARION: Would you like some Christmas cake?

It was early October and 35 degrees in the shade.

'Of course,' I said – as if that were the most normal request in the world. 'That would be wonderful.' I was keen to not offend my generous hosts. I wondered if they served Simnel cake in January and birthday cake at funerals. It didn't matter: cake is always wonderful, however anachronous.

FATHER: We love Christmas.
MARION: Yes. It is our favourite time.
SON: (*proudly*) We can sing 'Jingle Bells'.

Great, I thought. *Please don't.*

Around me were stationed myriad pictures of the Queen, and other, less luminescent, royals, fashioned on commemorative china plates and cups. They were everywhere, mounted on walls, adorning shelves and bookcases.

FATHER: We love the Queen.
ME: So I see.
MARION: We love her.
SON: Yes. We love her.

There was an expectant pause. Everyone stared at me.

ME: Oh, yes. Sorry. Yes. I love her too. Of course. She's wonderful.
FATHER: Have you met her?

The family leant forward in eager anticipation.

ME: No. No, I haven't.

A volley of dry crumbs erupted from my mouth as I spoke.

FATHER: Oh.
MARION: Oh.

The sense of disappointment in the room was palpable. Even Brooke Shields paused from her damp mouthings to reflect on my lack of prestige. I started wondering whether someone in production had lied to the family in order to secure the interview – implying, perhaps, that I had royal connections. Maybe they'd been led to believe that I'd played real tennis with the Earl of Wessex, or at the very least been on an all-night Jägermeister bender at Chinawhite's with Princess Eugenie.

No one moved to cover the silence. I filled the awkward pause by mainlining what remained of the fruitcake into my mush.

Then out came the photos. First a black-and-white snapshot of a quintessential Englishman in Royal Navy dress uniform, arms folded and smoking a pipe. It transpired this was the father's grandfather. His son had been the only survivor of a torpedo attack off the Sri Lankan coast in the Second World War. Then came a photocopied sheet, seemingly tracing the family name back to Elvidge – a rare Anglo-Saxon Old English and pre-seventh-century moniker.

FATHER: We may even be royalty.

Even he didn't sound convinced.

ME: Really?

FATHER: Yes. Henry VIII had many more wives than we know about.

I'm not sure he did, I thought – but it wasn't for me to piss on their parade.

Another of the sons drifted in, also in full England football strip. I was now at the stage where, if a Beefeater had walked through the door singing 'Greensleeves' and morris dancing, I wouldn't have batted an eyelid.

I started again, desperate to keep the interview on track.

ME: So, have you ever been to England?

FATHER: No.

ME: Do you think about it?

ALL: Yes.

ME: And what do you think about it? What do you think it's like?

FATHER: Good.

SON: Green.

SON 2: Home.

Everyone in the room nodded sagely.

FATHER: Yes. Home.

I tried to speak, but no words came. I am rarely lost for words, but that response just felled me.

Home.

We abandoned these people. They are the sons and daughters of Mother India and Empire, who return, time and time again, to a crystalline version of our traditions, faithfully observing what we, in the UK, are beginning to neglect.

I returned to the cake, full of more questions than my little brain could answer. Then, once the last piece of marzipan had been swallowed, I put on my dog-dampened flip-flops and, like all the other white Brits before me, I turned on my heels and left.

27. Faith, Hope and Love

Kolkata has long been synonymous with desperate, grinding poverty, and although things have improved since the dark days of Mother Teresa's mission, there is, even to the casual visitor's eye, still much to do. The bulk of this work falls to charities, and we were about to embark on a night shoot with one of them: the Hope Foundation. We set off at 10 p.m. with social worker Geeta and her team, driving their ambulance around, checking on children and vulnerable families living in the most desperate conditions.

We headed for the Hastings Underpass, a ten-kilometre stretch of road and wasteland that provides shelter for approximately ten thousand people. Many of the homeless sleeping here are domestic workers, tending other people's houses by day, with no roof over their own heads at night.

Blankets, saris and tarpaulin sag from wonky bamboo poles. Makeshift washing lines are decked with clothing burnished black by the pollution and ambient filth. Kids sleep on urine-soaked blankets, atop raw sewage, while drug addicts and alcoholics brawl around them. Welcome to a hell more vivid and terrifying than Bruegel or Bosch. A hell wrought by something more prosaic than Satan: inequality.

We walk from the ambulance towards a large gathering. Small fires punctuate the gloom. I can see women, silhouetted in the flames, rocking. There are kids hobbling in the dust with legs bent like plumbers' pipes.

I ask Geeta if I can talk to some of the young mothers.

One approaches. She looks no more than a child herself, her skin glued so tightly to her skull that, from a distance, she looks like nothing more than a bronzed skeleton.

She does not give me her name – names are superfluous here since all experience is identical. She tells me she was born in this place, in the shadow of the underpass, and that she will live out her days without a second's respite from its horror and sadness. As she begins to speak, more women start to join us, then more, until there are so many that Geeta struggles to interpret all the different voices that surround us.

I can smell the fear on them. I can smell it on myself. Even as we talk I become aware of the men in the shadows, the unpredictable, lurching men high on glue – kicking dogs, swearing – coming for us. The women respond by chattering ever louder, some grabbing at me for attention, pulling at my hands and shoulders.

One woman rushes towards us, holding a photo. The others part to let her through. They all begin jabbing their fingers at the image she is holding.

'Yes' I say. 'I can see.'

It is a picture of a child, a beautiful child, maybe two years old at most, wearing an ornate dress. She is sleeping.

The babble is becoming hysterical, the gesticulating more and more frantic.

'Yes,' I say. 'It's all right. It's OK. I can see.'

I am holding their hands. I am holding as many hands as I can.

And then Geeta speaks. It is easy for her to translate the message, because the women are all saying exactly the same thing.

GEETA: This child is not sleeping, Sue. This child is dead. She was abducted and raped to death.

Raped. To death.

Dead.

It's raining, I think. *Thank God, it's raining. Let it come in a roar, in a deluge, let it wash all of this away and me along with it.*

And then comes the slow understanding that emerges from beneath the shock and horror: that there is no rain, that the steady drips that hit the sand beneath me are coming from my eyes. I have gone into shock, but my eyes are still working – still pumping tears. I want to scream until my lungs burn out, but I stand there and I listen. I feel dizzy. But I will not faint. I will stand here and bear witness.

After that abduction, these women now tie themselves to their children by the wrist at night. Imagine that for a second – the place you call home is so unsafe you tether your family like animals so that if someone tries to steal them in the night, the jerk of your limbs will sound the alarm.

We hug. We listen. Finally, we have to move on, the ambulance chugging through the sepia gloom of the streetlights.

Through the murk I can see hundreds more silhouettes. These are the shadow people, those who live in the city under the city. They fall with the sun to the ground. When the last deal is done, when the last trader has hawked his wares, they sink like ash into the earth, where they lie with the dogs in the shit and the plastic. And at first light they rise again – back to clean your house, to fix your car, to serve your breakfast.

Welcome to the boulevards of the dispossessed – the left-behinds, the unwanted.

Welcome to capitalism's forgotten children.

Geeta is the calmest, kindest soul you could ever wish to meet. When the ambulance wheezes to a halt and she gets out, a crowd immediately forms around her – mainly children, who hold her hand and laugh. She begins her rounds, visiting the street families and asking how they are, enquiring about this child's health, this mother's mental state, this father's drug abuse and so on. She explains to me that her role is to listen, to allow people to unburden themselves, share their problems. She is an ear on wheels.

I want to have a role, and it doesn't take long before one presents itself.

Of course, I am a curiosity here. I'm the plump white girl who doesn't look much like a girl at all. I have squeaky new shoes. I have glasses made for me that I can actually see out of. The kids emerge from the margins of the street, desperate to poke at my pale flesh, dozens of them – they grab my hands and twirl around me, giggling, and it's not long before we all start to play.

For hours I run up and down the pavement, catching one, tickling another, throwing another upside down. I chase them through the human huddles, past the smoking fires and cooking pots, past the weaving men on solvent highs. We laugh so much we nearly throw up, pausing for breath, before the hide and seek begins again.

Their mothers are hunched together on the pavement, chopping vegetables, trying to get the youngest kids to bed – exactly the same sorts of tasks as we'd be performing at this time of night, except these women are making their evening meal on a pavement, by the side of one of the most congested roads in the world. Kids with matted hair weave in and out of the traffic, oblivious to danger. This is their home. This toxic highway is their manor. There are white rabbits, crammed into cages, piled five high – dinner, no doubt. I can't look at them. I can't even summon any extra pity for them, because nothing lives or dies well here.

Each family has a chunk of concrete pavement to call their own, divided into kitchen, sleeping area and so on. Of course, there are no walls, but you can tell, where the pots give way to blankets, that you are entering a bedroom. Toothbrushes hang from an electrical pole – that'll be the bathroom. There are even shrines set up in the gutter.

After midnight, the traffic thins. The children take to their beds in groups. The lucky ones have roll-up mattresses, a centimetre or two thick. The others make do with an old sari or newspaper. They sleep on headlines. Just savour the bitter irony of that. Stray dogs materialize from the margins and take up residence at their feet, guarding them through the long night – hopeful for a little dal or bread by way of reward the next morning. There is no peace. The horns never stop. The bursts of shouting, the screams of pain – they never stop. But somehow, these kids have acclimatized to the din and the smoke, and they manage to sleep at least partway through the night.

'We cannot give them all a home,' said Geeta. 'But we can give them education and fun and love, and help them to dream.'

Just as we're about to get back into the ambulance, Geeta spots a little girl she's keen to check up on. She is the cutest kid I've ever seen, all smiles and cheek in a torn purple frock with a rather fancy cream crimped neckline. It's like she's off to a party. But it's the middle of the night and she's on her own in this hellish jungle.

GEETA: Rakhi! Where are your friends? Where is Puja?

RAKHI: Puja is over there. (*To me*) She is my best friend.

This girl's name is Rakhi. Even though I have only just met her, she is very keen to impress upon me she does NOT like being absent from school. I sense this information is more to appease Geeta, who is hovering over her, listening to her every word. I think about Geeta's words – *we can help them to dream* – so I ask Rakhi what she wants to be when she grows up. She grins, and tells me she wants to be a doctor. We laugh and she hugs me and I hold her close and I don't want to let her go.

GEETA: You should have gone to sleep. Why are you still awake? Are you not afraid?

Rakhi merely shrugs, almost like she doesn't understand the question.

Rakhi's mum is dead, and she is looked after by her father. He sells buckets and old clothes to get her food.

GEETA: Where is he?
RAKHI: Sleeping.
ME: Right. It's late, you need to sleep. Come on, you need to find Puja . . .

And with that, I walk her down the long pavement, past a thousand bodies, supine in the dust, until I find Puja, hunched over an old transistor radio, singing. I wrap them in their sari and put them to bed.

As I get back into the ambulance, I instinctively take off my squeaky shoes and place them by the roadside. It is time for someone else to have them. I would have done the same with my shirt and my trousers, were it not for the large camera lens in my face. Quite frankly, I don't have the posterior for posterity so it was the best thing for everyone that I kept my clothes on.

We headed back into town. It was now maybe two or three o'clock in the morning, and the place was beginning to settle.

It was then I saw a shape, a single horizontal breaking the horizon. Framed against the yellow smog of the evening was a young boy, maybe ten years old, alone. No fires, no dogs, no junkies. Not one living soul around him.

ME: Who is that?

GEETA: He is one of our children. We visit him. He has HIV.

ME: Doesn't he have any family?

GEETA: No, they are gone.

ME: Is he alone?

GEETA: Yes.

ME: Does no one go to him? Go and touch him? Hold him?

GEETA: No, no one.

I want to get out. I can't. My palm is against the window, pressing hard on the glass. We drive on.

I go back to the hotel, walk through the lobby and feel the cool marble against my soles. The night porter tries not to look alarmed as he sees me, soot-faced and barefoot, heading back to my room. I come in, double-lock my door and turn on the shower. I stand in it for maybe an hour. Lost. I don't even feel the water on my skin – it's like it's going straight through me.

That is how I feel after simply *hearing* about their experiences.

For months after my return, I would dream of Rakhi. I would dream of her lying upstairs in the spare room, next to her mate Puja, their little fingers linked together as they snored. I would dream of them being safe, going to school, moaning about maths and physics and English lessons. I dreamt of making them tea every night – 'It's so plain, Auntie. This food is so boring, Auntie.'

I dreamt I got out of the ambulance. I was under that bridge again, marching through the yellow smog to the distant figure ahead of me. I kept on going until the vague blur on the horizon took form, until the silhouette sharpened, until I could see the bump of that little spine through his vest. And I picked him up and held him, so everyone could see. This boy, with HIV, in my arms. And I walked back, all the way back, through oceans and rivers, through desert and forest, across white cliffs and fresh tarmac until he crossed my threshold and met his two sisters and his second mum and was . . .

. . . safe.

28. A Googly Near the Hooghly

Our diplomatic liaison in Kolkata was a wonderful man called Scott, who was forever torn between his love of the city and the acknowledgement that the pollution in it was turning his kids' lungs into something resembling discarded crisp packets. After two night shoots on the trot, it became clear we needed to get out and do something fun – Bengalis are party people, after all – and we'd be doing the place a great disservice if we simply focused on its darker side.

Scott arranged for us to go to the cricket – a match between local team (and current champions, no less) the Kolkata Knight Riders and their sworn rivals, the Mumbai Indians. 'I'll send a car for you,' he said.

'Gosh,' I said.

At 6 p.m. precisely, a blacked-out, state-of-the-art Range Rover pulled up outside our hotel. I stared at it in disgust. *This is everything that is wrong with the world*, I thought, then got in. *Disgusting.* I sank into the leather seats, soft and cool. *Awful.* I felt my body uncoiling, the stress evaporating. *Oh, God, oh, my God, this is a disgrace . . . This . . . This is so lovely.* We set off, the diplomatic badge glinting in the dust, as we scythed through the traffic, carving through the rickshaws and tuk-tuks.

So this is how the other half live. Or, to be more accurate, this is how the other one per cent live.

Something felt different. It took me a while to realize what it was. Silence. This was my first precious moment of silence in almost a fortnight. Go home and thank God for your silence, for a respite from the onslaught. Yes, there may be the occasional hum of next door's telly. There may be a few kids shouting now and then in the street – but when they get called in for tea, there will be something else. There will be peace. You won't notice it, because doubtless you take it for granted. But it is there. In India, I never experienced quiet, not for a second, until I was in that big, big car.

The match was being held at Eden Gardens – which, if nothing else, was an insult to trade descriptions, being as far from the worlds of Genesis and Ezekiel as you could imagine. For starters, no apples could grow in that smog, I doubt a snake would have the guts to venture out – and I couldn't see Eve hanging around much after dark.

As the car pulled up, I could see thousands upon thousands of locals making their way to the ground, drawn like moths to the floodlights that bled through the rush-hour gloom. Vendors dragged their carts towards the scene, decked with sweets and deep-fried snacks. Kids waving thin yellow banners jumped for joy as they walked through the hallowed gates. It's coming home, it's coming – cricket's coming home.

Hands up, I don't know much about cricket. I know that it has, at least, an air of civility. It speaks of a time gone by, a lost era of gentility, when men made history and women made tea and biscuits. Or so they'd have you believe. This game of Empire has now been co-opted, monetized and made into a national sport by those it sought to control. The Indians took our cultural imperialism and used it as a bat to beat us with. How wonderful.

It turns out that Kolkata was the home of India's very first cricket club, founded in 1792 or thereabouts. Matches started between a European team and a Parsee team, made up of local Zoroastrian talent. (That's not a sentence I've ever written before.) Before long, the Hindus fielded a team – taking part in a match known as the Bombay Triangular. In 1912, the Muslims joined in, making it, you guessed it, a Bombay Quadrangle and, in 1937, it became the Bombay Pentangle, with the arrival of a team called 'the Rest', made up of Jews, Buddhists and Indian Christians. Before it could expand still further, into the realms of the Bombay Heptagon, Nonagon or Enneadecagon, the matches were disbanded, much to the relief of the geometrically challenged.

It was only after the protests of Gandhi, among others, that the religious elements were abandoned, and competitions were played along geographical, rather than religious, lines.

Crowds of supporters, laden with supplies, took their places around us until there wasn't a spare seat in the house. I sat and waited for the inevitable bunch of ruddy-faced gentlemen in white flannels to come on, and readied myself to applaud – more out of duty than enthusiasm. This was a cultural exchange and, as with most cultural exchanges, it needed to be politely endured rather than appreciated.

Sure enough, after a matter of moments, there was movement on the pitch. The crowd erupted: arms started waving, banners were unfurled. Out of nowhere, a group of scantily clad girls started to gyrate to a burst of heavy techno that had exploded from the tannoy. From the clutches of the grey smog came a bunch of burly men in figure-hugging nylon, their outfits topped off with shiny gold helmets and shiny gold shinpads. For a moment I thought, *Oh, that's nice, they're doing some kind of Gay Pride cricketing tribute before the match* – then realized that (a) homosexuality was illegal in India at the time, and (b) this *was* the *actual* team.

'Bloody hell,' said Steve, with a mixture of fear and excitement.

From that moment, I was hooked. From that moment, I became a lifelong supporter of the Kolkata Knight Riders.

Out they came – '*Gambhir! Uthappa! Yadav!*' The announcer was shouting so loudly he had virtually lost his voice by the time he finished reading out the team names.

Then came their opponents – the Mumbai Indians; who'd gone equally big on bling, but with a peacock-blue strip.

'BOOOOO!' I jumped to my feet, screaming. 'BOOOOOO!'

'Bloody hell, Sue,' said Steve, trying to look like he wasn't with me.

'BOOOOOO!'

I'd been watching for a little over thirty seconds and was already over-invested. I'm easily affected by tribal passions and affiliations. You can tell what sort of person I'd be in *Lord of the Flies*. I'd be dancing naked round a flame and hunting little Piggy's specs in a heartbeat.

'C'MON, YOU BEAUTIES!'

There followed one of the most exciting gigs of my life. I say gig, because nothing about the event felt like sport the way I knew it. This felt more like a rock concert, the stadium full of noise, colour and screaming fans. There were none of the gentle, artistic blockings of an afternoon in Somerset – none of the parrying strokes, frantic murmuring and tactical pauses. This was a head-down, pedal-to-the-metal free-for-all. Who has the time to hit or throw a ball for five days on end? Not the Indians, that's for sure. They're too busy creating tech and steel empires to wait that long. The Indian

Premier League has managed to compress the languorous British game into an evening's worth of smashing and bashing, with a drinks interval, techno music and dancing girls. I was IN.

Surely every sport needs the IPL touch? Curling, for instance. Why waste minutes brushing the ice when you can pop on a Chemical Brothers track, get out a flamethrower and turn the whole pitch into a water park in seconds?

Every time a shot hit the boundary, the dancers would spring to life, like shop mannequins in an eighties teen movie. (You know the ones – where a nerdy boy exposes a doll to a special kind of electricity that makes her sexually attracted to him.) Pyrotechnics fired dangerously close to their heads. I tried to dance along, but was consumed with worry that their tan tights would go up in a crisp and take me with them.

Mumbai started briskly, and finished their twenty overs at 168 for 3. By now I'd drunk four pints of beer and several hundred salt lassi, which made me simultaneously dehydrated and desperate for a piss. But I wasn't going anywhere, no, sirree.

An ecstatic cry went up around the stadium and I noticed, on the enormous video screens, that they were cheering the team's owner and all round Bollywood legend, Shah Rukh Khan, or SRK – a man so famous he'd achieved the status of a monogram. That's true star quality, right there. A Google search of my initials, SEP, reveals that I, on the other hand, will always play fourth fiddle to a village in Poland, a type of pension account used in the United States and a police unit in Slovenia.

It was time for the Knight Riders to bat. The dancers whirled and the sirens sounded. By the end of the sixteenth over, I was beside myself. We needed 38 runs from 24 balls. Could it be done?

I became so stressed by the proceedings I couldn't look. I remember Dad used to be the same with the football. He was a Charlton Athletic fan, which is something, Mr Obama, that *truly* defines the audacity of hope. In the days when the team hit the dizzy heights of the Premiership and the matches were televised, he would tape the results rather than watch the game live.

ME: Why is that, Dad?
DAD: Because it stresses me. You know it stresses me to watch it live. There's too much at stake. I like to watch it later, when I feel calmer.

But here's the thing. A normal person – and I use that term advisedly with my family – who gets nervous at watching matches would perhaps calmly look at the score once the game is over. Then, knowing the result, they could sit back without the attendant anxiety and enjoy the highlights.

No. Not my dad. My dad didn't look at the score. He simply watched the match two hours later, in its entirety. *Not knowing the outcome*. In fact, still SUPER STRESSED at the outcome.

God only knows I am no psychologist, but when was merely *delaying* your fears a protocol for stress management?

ME: Doctor, I'm terrified of flying.
DOC: When are you due to take off?
ME: Three o'clock this afternoon.
DOC: OK. Well, why don't you rebook, and get on the five o'clock instead?
ME: Great. Wow. I feel so much better. Goodbye.
(*Leaves.*)

You will notice, in the interests of veracity, that I made that vignette the exact length of an actual GP appointment.

Back at Eden Gardens, two overs later, thanks to some spectacular thwacking from Yadav, we looked confident of taking the match. It was then I noticed a large group of people staring over at us.

Mmm, I thought. *What are they looking at?*

For a brief, narcissistic moment,* I wondered whether news of my skills as Britain's erstwhile premier cake-watcher had made it as far as Mother India.

Much to my chagrin, it appeared nobody in Kolkata had seen any of my oven-based oeuvre. No one was interested in me in the slightest. Instead, their eyes were trained solely on Steve, who was sitting to the left of me.

Now, Steve is not a man who is drawn to the limelight. On the contrary, he loathes it. Steve likes few things in this world and, as detailed previously, those things are family, Wales, surfing, and making intense documentaries about the agrarian poor. In an ideal world, Steve would like these documentaries to remain unseen, so he doesn't have to affiliate himself overtly with the world of television. Television, he thinks, quite rightly, is a mug's game.

People started to talk among themselves and a crowd was gathering.

By now Steve had noticed he was being watched. He started shuffling anxiously. A young kid broke ranks and came up to us.

* They are not that brief. The last phase has been going on since 1987.

KID: (*to Steve*) Hello.
STEVE: Hello.

He sounded suspicious. Steve is suspicious of everything and everyone, unless they are from Cymru and/or a wave.

KID: Selfie?

It was more of a demand than a question.

STEVE: (*uncomfortably*) Sure.

The moment the flash went, the queue for photos doubled. Then tripled. Within moments, Steve was surrounded.

STEVE: Bloody hell . . .

And then the stadium erupted. We must have won, I thought, turning my attention again to the pitch. It was then I saw the video screen. Emblazoned on it was none other than Steve, captured by one of the roving stadium cameras.

ME: What the hell is going on?
STEVE: I don't know.

He was now blinded by flashlights and encircled by fans.

ME: You're on the big screen.
STEVE: Oh, God, it's happening again . . .
ME: What's happening again? Steve? Is this the Rapture? What's going on?

It turned out that Steve bears a strong resemblance to New Zealand captain, and all-round sex-god,* Brendon McCullum. Hence the sudden crowd of super-fans around us.

* Steve requested that in order to use this anecdote I put this bit in.

'We need to get out,' said our minder.

'Oh, bloody hell,' said Steve – approaching full Eeyore.

We pushed through the swell, the floodlights trained on us, video cameras following our every move. We finally made it to the car, and as I turned back, I saw Steve's image fade from the stadium screen and the dancers strike up another techno jamboree.

Fame. She's a fickle mistress.

29. Just Dance

On the way back from the match, as we idled in traffic, a gaggle of women in flawless make-up and killer heels emerged from the diesel haze and began barracking the drivers for money. From a distance, it looked like a gang of Joan Collins lookalikes on the rob.

I was transfixed. I wanted to open the doors and let them in. I wanted to go home with them and learn everything about them. And, most importantly, I wanted to know how on earth they managed to keep their eyeliner so crisp in 90 per cent humidity.

They were fierce, frightening to some, perhaps – but not to me. I recognized their adamantine masks, the armour of noise and colour and jazz-hands that stops the sorrow leaking out. 'Let it out!' I wanted to shout. 'Let it all out! Come on!'

Later, on my return to the city, I got my wish. I finally got to hang with the Hijra, India's transgender community. I wandered down a dusty side-road and there they were, giving much-needed glamour to a drab street corner. I won't lie, they were somewhat easy to spot, in their brightly coloured saris, heavy bling and sixties cat's eye sunglasses.

ME: Hi! *Namaste!*

They stared at me. I ventured the classic English ice-breaker.

ME: Do you want some *chai*?

I gestured towards the *chai wallah*.

WOMAN: No. I don't like tea.

She flashed me a look, her pupils like obsidian. Her disdain had the immediate effect of making me fall in love with her. The woman turned out to be the imperious Aparna, their leader and spokesperson.

The gang appeared to be conducting some kind of covert operation on a corner house, blushed with red pigment, its windows decked with AC units.

ME: (*whispering*) What are you all doing? Are you undercover? This looks like some kind of stake-out . . .
APARNA: Yes, it is. We keep an eye out for births, deaths and marriages. We had word a child had been born in this block of flats, so we are listening out for the cries.

I listened with them. I heard nothing. I wondered if the parents were inside, covering the infant's mouth, somewhat intimidated by the glamorous gang assembled outside their house.

APARNA: No matter – we have another blessing to do. A girl. She is five days old. COME!

I obeyed without question.

We headed down a narrow alleyway, took a sharp left, whereupon a door opened and we stepped into a living room. The host family, led by the father, Mr Roy, welcomed us in with a mixture of fear and joy.

On seeing the baby, the Hijra transformed from a grumpy, back-foot band of spies into a crack team of entertainers. This was a baby shower with a difference. There was no dry Victoria Sponge, no elderly relatives, no awkward standing around the margins of the room making polite conversation. Instead, there was a riotous outburst of dancing, singing and a very loud, slightly offbeat clattering of tambourine as the Bengali fairy godmothers crowded round the new-born. The little one remained resolutely asleep throughout – how, I have no idea, as the din was deafening.

The blessing itself was a rather curious mixture of well-wishing and extortion. It started well enough.

APARNA: May she be happy and healthy!

Amen to that.

APARNA: May she grow up to be a doctor or an engineer!

Could that statement be any more of an Indian cliché? I wondered. And then she ended with the kicker:

APARNA: And may you have another daughter in five years so we can again charge you fifty-one thousand rupees!

Some of you might recoil at the rather blunt fiscal tone of Aparna's benediction. Personally I couldn't help but applaud the fact she had a clear, fixed pricing system so the family could plan ahead and budget.

Then came a bewildering array of instructions, which went as follows:

APARNA: Put these mustard seeds and three basil leaves and a rupee under her pillow for a week, then tap on the baby seven times and on your body seven times. Go to the Ganges and pray to the goddess Shashthu three times, then throw it in the river with your back to the Ganges.

I was now very confused. Throw what in the river? The mustard seeds or the baby? As an exhausted new mother, I would have needed some clarification on that point.

APARNA: And then . . .

We leant in, transfixed.

APARNA: . . . never look back!

She paired this final command with a theatrical flourish and hand gesture. This blessing certainly wasn't short on drama.

I took advantage of a lull in the dancing to ask an out-of-breath Aparna about the business side of the blessings. She was very direct about the need to charge her customers.

APARNA: It's how we earn money.
ME: And do you believe it works?
APARNA: Of course it works! Why would we be asked to give blessings if they did not work?

Because you are mildly terrifying, I thought.

Aparna had been born into a wealthy Kolkatan family, who had rejected her once she began her transition. Now they have no contact. This turned out to be an all-too-familiar story throughout the Hijra community. None of them have families to bless – they will never meet their nieces, their nephews – so they devote their lives to the consecration of other families' little ones.

Of course they believe the blessings work. They have to.

ME: So, if the child thrives, it acts as a calling card to encourage other families to seek out a Hijra blessing?
APARNA: Oh, no. We keep on coming . . .

ME: Really?

APARNA: (*matter-of-factly*) Yes. We have a follow-up system.

And I laugh, because it sounds like something a dental receptionist might say.

ME: And every time you come, they pay?

Aparna nods.

Of course, the prosaic and the profane, the sacred and the secular jog along together very nicely in India – there is no disconnect seen in embracing both the developing capitalist boom and hard-line Hinduism. It's only the Western sensibility that finds this jarring.

The drum starts up again, and with it the singing and arrhythmic tambourine.

As we leave, I can sense the deflation. The Hijra women seem to fold back into themselves.

APARNA: Come! Come to the house!

The Hijra occupy a complex place in society. In ancient times they were revered in palaces as magical beings, but with the arrival of the British, they were, somewhat inevitably, criminalized. Finally, in 2014 the courts gave them legal status as a recognized third gender. However, even though they have the protection of the law, many still despise and fear them.

I can feel a little of this heat as I walk with them. Groups of men stop and stare. Some dart out of the way in fear, or curl their lips in disgust. Others leer and mutter what I assume to be obscenities.

The house itself is not hard to spot: a banana-yellow monstrosity in a dingy narrow street. Inside the door is a room that doubles as their temple – a homage to Trumpian bling, with mirrors, sequins and gold paint in every conceivable crevice. They have gilded their sadness. They have made a shrine to it. They have profited from it. Aparna, after all, refers to herself as Hijra by 'profession'. These women have not retired in shame – they dance in the face of it.

Boy, do they dance.

I thread through the labyrinth of rooms, and out the other side into an open courtyard. There sit a dozen or more women, some in their seventies.

APARNA: Guru!

She points to a beautiful silver-haired woman in the corner.

APARNA: Guru!

She shouts again, pointing at another.

APARNA: Julie Walters!

She gestures vaguely towards the back of the room.

ME: Did you say Julie Walters?
APARNA: Yes, Julie Walters!

She points at a diminutive woman in her sixties wearing a dazzling puce sari.

What the hell is going on in Kolkata? I wonder if Julie Walters has encountered Brooke Shields the Pug.

I kiss the women until there is no one left unkissed. And before I get a chance to say a thing to any one of them, the singing starts up again.

I am whirled around until I am dizzy. Occasionally there is a lull in the festivities – but seconds later one of the Hijra will fill the silence with more songs or percussion. Is this for us, this constant show? Do they really live like this when the camera lens is lowered?

After an hour or two, I start to understand. This community cannot bear to be silent. They cannot bear to be still. When there is time and space, the sadness will creep in unbidden and fill it.

Later that day, I retire upstairs to a room filled with a patchwork of mattresses. Here the women sleep side by side, with barely a centimetre's space between them.

One by one I am joined by the community, some on their own, others in small groups. I ask them about their past, their families, their backstories. Some I don't even have to prompt, they give their lives unbidden. They have come to talk. I listen to them, one after another – different intonation, same outcome. Their stories all begin with Once Upon A Time, for sure – but there are no happy endings here. The princess is not rescued: she is abandoned. The prince is not a prince at all, but a liar and rapist who brings shame and dishonour on her, when, in truth, it is only his to own. It is not just the stepmothers in these tales who are wicked, but the mothers and fathers and brothers and sisters who turn their backs or look away. In the light, I see how tired these women are from the endless carousel of hope, despair and broken promises.

They didn't need a prince to transform them, they transformed themselves – through will, through necessity, through the basic human imperative to live the life they were meant to lead. They are lessons in what we humans will do for love, how far we will cross the lines we make for ourselves in order to feel connected, to be touched, to be truly seen.

I listen to every story in that room. I lean forward and

catch each and every voice as it cracks, as they describe parents, lost. Brothers and sisters, lost. All of it. Lost.

They paint their faces for you. They don jewels and wrap themselves in exquisite cloth for you. For you to love them. For you to honour their fierceness and fragility.

This is the house of the lioness.

The Ganges

THE HIMALAYAS

30. Gangotri

ME: Fred. Tell me the truth. Is it going to be hard?

I am not that fit and, more importantly, I am incredibly lazy.

FRED: It's easy. Honestly. It's around fifteen miles, on the flat.
ME: Really?
FRED: Really.
ME: OK. Well, I can do that. That's easy. No problem.

And, with that, I agreed to undertake a pilgrimage to Gaumukh, the source of that mighty and sacred river, the Ganges.

I will admit, my geography is not what it should be. I have never thrilled to the mention of glaciation, or marvelled at an ox-bow lake. I don't know how precipitation really works, or what a wave-cut platform is. As a teenager, I was taught the subject by the magnificently named Barbara Kokashinska, a voluptuous Pole with an impressive Continental shelf and hair like Farrah Fawcett. I think I might have been in love with her. Anyway, for whatever reason, her high-octane chit-chat about lacustrine plains and metamorphic rocks somewhat passed me by.

It was only once I had arrived in India, once I was there, standing at the foothills of the Himalayas and looking upwards towards its snowy peaks, that I started to question Fred's version of the journey.

FRED: It's easy. Honestly. It's around fifteen miles, on the flat.

On the flat? On the *flat*?

It's the *Himalayas*, Sue. *It's a mountain range, stupid.*

We ended our long drive in the town of Gangotri, in the state of Uttarakhand, some three and a half thousand metres above sea level. We parked in one of its winding streets and took up residence in a nearby café – the familiar reek of fried food, garlic and caramelized sugar drawing us in, like moths to the *E. coli* flame. The menu boasted a dizzying array of local and Western foods. It just goes to show: even in the middle of nowhere, you can't outrun a burger.

Bearing in mind we were starting a long trek up the mountainside, without any recourse to toilet facilities, what did we all choose? Yep, you've got it.

The strawberry milkshake.

We did avoid the chocolate pancakes, however, because we may be stupid, but we don't have a death wish.

The cold sits in your bones here. No matter how many clothes you wear, there is no thaw. We slept the night at a local guesthouse, under matted blankets so heavy I woke up fighting for breath under the sheer weight of compressed horsehair. I was in thermal leggings, a long-sleeved shirt, jumper and bobble hat. I still couldn't get warm. At 5 a.m. the sun reached through the torn pink curtain slung across the window and tugged at my eyelids. It was time.

On the plus side, there was a spa at the hostel, although the menu was a little limited. In fact, there was only one treatment available – their signature experience, if you will – and, boy, was it memorable. Once I'd plucked up the courage to venture a wash, I'd ring a handbell and, out of nowhere, a porter would arrive with a rusty bucket full of boiling water. I'd drag it into the bathroom, stand over the drainage hole next to the makeshift toilet and strip as quickly as I could. Within a second of my skin being exposed, my body would go into shock, my breath coming in gasps as I struggled to cope with the chill. Then, steeling myself, I'd upend the bucket over my head, and let the hot water trace a path to my toes. Plumes of condensation rose like wings from my shoulders. There would be a blissful moment, ten seconds at most, where I felt warm, before the icy wind started nipping again. Then my breath would catch – quick, quick, quick – as I rushed to pat myself dry. Then it was on with the pants, the long johns, three pairs of socks, a thermal vest, long-sleeved shirt and two jumpers. Now, girls, *that*'s pampering.

We set off at first light, a thin yellow spreading between the mountaintops. The donkeys were loaded with kit, thick ropes tied around their bellies. I tried to pet them – they weren't interested. I tried feeding them the apples I'd been stockpiling for this very occasion. They still weren't interested. What did pique their attention, however, were the large chunks of cardboard that littered the entryway to the pass. It turns out those donkeys would do anything for a square meal. Literally. They loved eating boxes, cartons and packets. Anything that had once been a container or packing material and those beasts were on it. As we gathered our belongings, one of them tucked into an *amuse-bouche* of a hessian rice sack, while the rest eyed up their main meal – an old pallet.

The porters milled around us, organizing, checking. Where we were sluggish, they were deft and nimble. It wasn't just the donkeys that were laden, they, too, were lassoed with bags and rucksacks, as they darted here and there, balancing the loads, checking the weights. They wore stained old tracksuits and bobble hats. I noticed their footwear – battered trainers, slip-on plastic shoes. One was in flip-flops. I looked down at my brand new walking boots, the steel D-rings that held my virginal laces glinting in the dawn. I looked at my designer fleeces and 'waterproof shells' and felt even more of a dick than usual.

We set off. Within two hundred metres I feel tired. If this had been a regular walk, I'd have made my excuses, cried off and sat in the pub – but it was supposed to be an epic adventure from the source of a legendary river to its mouth, and if I didn't get to the source, well, there wouldn't be much of an opening to our film. It would be like the Wife of Bath, in Chaucer's *Canterbury Tales*, getting as far as Maidstone before deciding she can't be bothered to carry on with the pilgrimage, and opting for a mooch around the shops instead.

I establish a slow and steady pace, but the energy I have is only sufficient to climb. There is nothing left in the tank with which to attempt to make a television programme. In my head, I was going to reach the summit, my arms gesturing to Gaumukh, the Cow's Mouth, that blue glacier beyond. I would then deliver a piece to camera of such searing wisdom, such extraordinary passion and insight, that it would not only redefine the audience's viewing experience, but the medium of television in general.

The reality is that we are only half an hour into the climb and I have already vomited over my own tits. Thankfully, this is captured on camera, as is the unceremonious attempt to throw me onto the back of a trailing donkey. As I finish another monumental heave, one of the porters shoves his hand between my legs and raises his forearm, lifting me upwards towards the donkey's back. Think biceps curl with a bilious TV presenter as the hand weight. I am so surprised by the motion that I deliver a high-pressure stress fart onto his hand. Serves him right.

Deepak is my guide for this trip. He looks like a Nepalese supermodel and is unbearably jaunty. For him, this walk is like a trip to the supermarket, and he approaches it with a breezy nonchalance that borders on boredom. After some heavy visual cues (collapsing, nosebleeds and copious retching), he notices I am struggling a little, and tries to relieve my distress with some herbal medicine.

DEEPAK: Sue, are you OK?
ME: Assolluulee.
DEEPAK: You sure?
ME: Yess, Deekap, asssolluulee.

As we climb, he breaks off a bud from a shrivelled low-lying shrub called tulsi. He rubs it in his palms, then cups his hands and encourages me to breathe in. It smells like a cross between thyme and the contents of a hoover bag. Local folklore claims that tulsi takes the edge off altitude sickness, easing the pressure on your lungs. It doesn't. I'll tell you what *does* take the edge off it, however – oxygen.

We arrived after a couple of hours at a makeshift staging post. There, we sat on a large stone platform and unwrapped our lunch. I am not sure I have extolled the virtues of Indian food enough – but, my God, I love it. I love it. I love it with a passion.

I unwound the foil to reveal the gooey goodness of a homemade *aloo paratha* – bread stuffed with minced garlic, ginger, potato and spices, then fried. I wolfed it. Then I wolfed another.

We were joined by a couple in their late sixties.

ME: Hi.
WOMAN: Hi!
ME: Have you just come from Gaumukh?

They both stared at me blankly.

ME: Gaumukh? The glacier? The source?

They shook their heads furiously.

MAN: No. Of course not. We cannot go there.
ME: Really? Why not?
WOMAN: The air is bad.
ME: What do you mean, 'bad'?
MAN: There is no oxygen. It is too dangerous.

I notice the man is wheezing and leaning on a walking stick.

WOMAN: It is true. We cannot go any further.

I looked over at Vicky, who was studiously avoiding my gaze.

The donkeys finished off their half-time meal: a bin liner, some packing tape and a few commas of squeaky polystyrene bulker, and felt refreshed enough to continue.

On we went.

31. I Saw a Mouse: Where?

We set off again up the range, towards Bhopasa where we were scheduled to spend the night. The donkeys raced ahead in the expectation of a cardboard-box supper.

My post-*paratha* rush didn't last, and before long I had folded back into myself – silent and focused. Keep walking, Sue. One step. Then another step. Don't talk. Don't stop. Just keep going. I could feel each thump of my heartbeat, every push of blood that lurched through my veins.

Abhra was the first to collapse. He pulled up a couple of miles into the second leg, his breathing shot to pieces. 'My blood pressure,' he said, through gasps. He was flushed and sweating. 'I can't . . .'

The porters rallied around him, shouting in short, sharp sentences. Abhra gave a cry as the porter's forearm pushed between his legs and raised him by his bollocks onto the back of the donkey. *Well, at least that guy is an equal-opportunities crotch-grabber*, I thought. Once he had his passenger onboard, the donkey deftly picked his way over the rocks, heading down the mountainside, taking Abhra back to base, where he was acclimatized and would be able to breathe.

I watched them disappear down the winding track, until all that was left were the motes of dusk hanging in the distant air. This was getting harder. My legs felt heavy, like my skin from foot to groin had been filled with wet sand. Each step forward required every ounce of strength I had. On the journey so far, I'd had Olly in my sights. *Just keep up with Olly*,

I thought. *Olly is strong and fit. Olly will get us there. He always gets us there.*

Only there was something wrong with Olly. Suddenly he wasn't striding ahead, but weaving from side to side, his legs seemingly buckling under his weight.

Altitude sickness doesn't care about your personal stats, you see. It doesn't care how fit you are, how young or old. It doesn't even take into account how you coped in that same situation before. Each time it is different. You will get punished in a multitude of different ways. I knew that Olly suffered at altitude, and tended to get headaches over a certain threshold, but what he was going through now was something altogether more worrying.

'Are you OK?' I shouted ahead. He didn't turn round: he just waved his arm in the air as if to say, 'No, but I'm getting on with it. Let me get on with it.'

We arrived at Bhopasa late afternoon, a creaking timber outpost nestled into the barren mountainside. The sun was sinking behind the peaks and the temperature was plummeting fast. The moment I stopped walking, an unbelievable chill overtook me. My body shook and I couldn't think straight. I tied a yak-hair blanket around me and popped my head-torch on so I could navigate my way around our gloomy billet.

Inside the camp, the walls were thick with mould and the beds wet with damp. As I walked into the bedroom I felt something brush the hem of my trousers. My pulse quickened.

ME: Vicky! Did you feel that?
VICKY: Feel what?
ME: Vicky, are there mice here?
VICKY: No!

She didn't sound at all convinced.

VICKY: I very much doubt it. Are there mice at altitude? I don't think so. I don't think they like heights.

I will always love her for that. What an excuse – mice don't like heights.

Well, it turns out that mice *love* heights. In fact, those little fuckers can't get enough of high-altitude scampering. I felt something at my leg again, and looked down, only to be greeted by dozens of them, darting here, there and everywhere. I have never seen so many rodents in my entire life.

Here's the thing. I am terrified of mice.

It's a common phobia, I know, an evolutionary hangover from the day when our limbic lizard brain held sway over our consciousness, when we needed to react to sudden movement because our lives might depend upon it. But it also stems from childhood, watching Lydia, my grandma, hoist her considerable heft onto a pouffe in full twin set and bellow:

GRANDMA: Christ, Ann! Christ, Ann! Kill it! KILL IT!

I was too young to fully understand what she was talking about, but I vividly remember her rigid, blue-rinsed barnet bouncing in time to her rhythmic screams. Her tonsils waggled like something out of a cartoon. This must be serious, and no mistaking.

I opened my rucksack, drank the best part of a bottle of Rescue Remedy to calm my nerves and headed into the communal room. A large plastic table ringed by plastic chairs took centre stage. Off this room was a small kitchen, every surface blackened by rust and filth. One of the porters lit a gas ring and there was an ominous crackle as the flame ate into the copious dirt surrounding it.

I sat down and, as my eyes began to focus, I noticed that the entire table was covered in rodent droppings. There was one resting on my fork, and a couple in a nearby serving bowl. In fact, on further inspection, there was barely a square inch that hadn't been pebble-dashed with shit.

In desperation, I fired close to an entire bottle of hand sanitizer into my *paratha*, which meant the whole thing tasted like a recently disinfected yoga mat. I didn't care. It was sterile, that was the main thing. *It's all right*, I thought. *I've got loads of energy bars in my pocket. I can live off those, it'll be fine.*

Night had fallen and the wind was up. The porters took to their bed, lying side by side, five or six to a bed, like bobble-hatted sardines. They were in one room, the crew were in another, and Vicky and I had the last room down the corridor.

I went in to say good night to the lads. We all looked shrunken, our lips cracked, our eyes hollowed. Fred was shivering under the blankets, his face cadaverous in the gloom.

ME: You seen the mice, Fred?
FRED: One or two. Sweet, aren't they?

Fred was patently not going to help me with this one. I turned to Luke, the cameraman, in the vain hope he'd volunteer to get up out of bed and Pied Piper the shit out of them down the mountainside.

ME: You seen them, Luke?
LUKE: Yes. Bloody everywhere, aren't they?
ME: Have they been bothering you?

Please say yes. Please get rid of them.

LUKE: No, it's fine.

At which point one ran straight across his luxuriant beard, availing itself of a drive-by crumb as it did so.

Olly was motionless in the corner. He could no longer stand and had not spoken for six hours. We would occasionally go up to him and check he was still breathing. His smart watch was listing his heart rate at around 150 b.p.m. It was clear he was going to have to head back down the pass at first light next morning.

None of us slept a wink. Outside, the porters had erected tents, and the tarpaulin sides billowed and shrank with each one of their cavernous snores. If the noise wasn't enough to keep us awake, then some clever clogs had decided to take all our empty plastic water bottles and burn them outside our window, so a sweet toxic fug filtered through the ill-fitting casements all night long.

Some of the boys had started taking acetazolamide, the altitude-sickness drug. It's a diuretic, which means that you constantly need a piss. That set the routine for the night: the sudden glare of a head-torch, a floorboard creaking, a waterfall of urine, and so on and so forth in a loop.

I tiptoed through the mouse motorway and got into bed. The damp blankets had now frozen stiff in the cold. I downed what was left of the Rescue Remedy and cracked open a new bottle for good measure. Cheers, all. Night night!

Vicky got into bed opposite me, and we turned out our torches.

I've got to be brave, I thought. Everyone must be so sick of my endless cowardice.

I heard the skittering of tiny claws on the wooden planks beneath.

Just breathe. Just breathe. In. Out. In. Out. You can do this.

For hours, I counted sheep, meditated, and did my deep-breathing exercises. Finally, at around four in the morning, my body relaxed enough for me to drift into unconsciousness.

Thirty minutes later I was wide awake again. Vicky had switched on her head-torch – and the beam shone directly into my face.

VICKY: Sorry! I need a wee.
ME: That's OK.
VICKY: How you feeling?
ME: OK. I'm actually feeling a bit calmer about the mouse situation now.

The moment I said that, there was a faint rustle to the left of my ear.

VICKY: That's great.

I detected a slight edge in her voice.

VICKY: Really great.
ME: What?
VICKY: What?
ME: What's that?
VICKY: Nothing!

It remains one of the most unconvincing responses I've ever heard.

VICKY: Don't you worry. It's absolutely nothing . . .

The rustle again, this time louder.

ME: There's something here, isn't there? Here by my head . . .

My heart was racing. I reached for my head-torch and turned it on.

VICKY: Honestly, it's nothing. And anyway – they're fine, they're busy – they're not interested in you.

They're fine. They're busy. Oh, God. Busy doing what?

I turned to my left, and there, silhouetted perfectly in the beam of my torch, was a family of five mice sharing one of the energy bars I had been storing in my jacket.

This was now a worst-case scenario. Not only did I have mice capable of rummaging in my clothes and dragging out food, these were mice that had just eaten an energy-boosting power-ball of nuts, seeds and goji berries. These thieving fuckers were going to be up for *days* . . .

MOUSE 1: Mandy, I don't know what the hell was in that woman's snack bar, but I am buzzing my nut off . . .
MOUSE 2: Tell me about it, Gaz. I am well lit. What even *are* those berries?
MOUSE 1: Goji, innit?
MOUSE 2: Goji?
MOUSE 1: Yeah. From the Amazon and shit.
MOUSE 2: Course. Amazon. Wow, I am buttered, bruv.
MOUSE 1: I feel you, mate. Totally buttered.

I drank the remains of the second bottle of Rescue Remedy, zipped my sleeping bag over my head and began humming random show tunes while rocking gently back and forward.

After all, who needs sleep when you have Barry Manilow's back catalogue?

32. The Summit

The next day, as the donkeys settled down for a straw and bubble-wrap breakfast, the porters began loading the equipment for the final stage of the trek. Olly was helped outside, groin-lifted onto his mount, and sent back down to base camp. His headache was so severe he could barely even talk.

Without Olly, I felt vulnerable – like a storm-stricken vessel without a lighthouse. *You can do this*, I thought. *You're nearly there, just five kilometres left. You have to do this. You have to.*

And yet, within two hundred metres, I was struggling. Seriously struggling. What made it worse was that nothing seemed to help – not tulsi, not oxygen, nothing. I was not going to make it.

Suddenly, out of nowhere, I heard a voice in my ear. Calm and clear.

Take it steady.

No. Not here. No way. You're hallucinating, Sue. Shut up and get on with this walk.

Then again, that voice.

Take it steady.

No. I said, no. You are not going there. You are not. You are going to lock that shit down, right now. You have a contributor to meet. You have a sequence to film. You, quite literally, have a mountain to climb. Get your head together and let's go meet that holy man.

One of the great joys of returning home after a long trip is looking back over the show's 'Bible' and seeing what could have been. The 'Bible' or Editorial Specification Document, to give its fun title – is the extensive scene-by-scene brief given to the channel by the production company. It charts, in detail, all the extraordinary adventures that I am going to have, all the amazing people I am going to meet, and the overall itinerary of the trip.

Casting an eye back over it when I return, of course, lends a different perspective. It becomes a document about all the extraordinary adventures I *could* have had, the amazing people I *could* have met, and the sort of itinerary we *would* have had if we hadn't got sick, got lost or fallen over.

Here's how the Bible saw this next sequence playing out, versus the reality of how it actually went down.

Bible Version

Every day for the past 28 years, Nirmal Baba has dragged ten bags of rocks up from the riverbed as part of his service to the gods. Sue will help Nirmal Baba build his ashram for the day.

Reality

We get to the ashram. Nirmal Baba isn't there. In fact, it turns out Nirmal Baba is five kilometres further up the mountain, chanting by a bonfire and goggle-eyed with weed.

Bible Version

Nirmal Baba has given up sex, as this is a great drain on his energy.

Reality

Nirmal Baba spends the vast majority of our chat together with his hand on my knee and his eyes focused on my jugs. Perhaps that is less exhausting for him than actual sex.

Bible Version

Nirmal Baba will provide some parting words of wisdom that Sue can take with her on her journey.

Reality

Nirmal Baba's farewell gesture is to blow his nose on his sleeve and give the internationally recognized hand gesture of 'Get lost now, you're getting on my nerves.'

But there was no mention in the Bible of a blackbird: a blackbird that had begun following me the moment I took my first faltering steps that morning, a blackbird currently diving in and out of the flames in front of me, desperate for my attention.

I didn't need the Bible to tell me what that was, or what it meant. I already knew.

Don't let it in, Sue. Not now, don't let any of it in. Do you hear me?

I arrived, bent double, at a vast boulder beside the path. In the distance, I could make out the blue tongue of the glacier, jutting forth from the mountain's mouth. This was Gaumukh. Finally, we had reached the source of the Ganges and our film could truly begin.

Fred was now our *de facto* soundman. He pinned the mic to my jacket (now heavily nibbled by mice) and I opened my mouth to start my grand opening piece to camera. I had wanted to say something profound about beginnings, but found I could think only of endings. My eyes filled and my throat seized. I started swallowing heavily.

LUKE: Camera speed.
ME: Sorry, guys. Sorry. I just . . .
VICKY: It's OK. Just take your time.

My throat tightened. Within moments I found myself sobbing uncontrollably, howling on that white rock in a foreign place in the middle of nowhere.

ME: I'm sorry. Guys, I'm so sorry.

And right in front of me, on an outcrop of rocks, that blackbird.

33. The Blackbird

In October 2015 I published my autobiography, *Spectacles*. The final chapter contained these lines:

> *The kitchen door swings open and Dad stands in the doorway. Behind him hangs a grey plastic mask that looks like something out of Halloween. It's a relic of his radiotherapy sessions for yet another bout of cancer – this time in the throat, poor sod. He is looking a little worn, and his voice cracks when he speaks, but amid the agony of recuperation there is an unexpected gain – Dad is joyful again. Finally, after endless dances with death, after sixteen years with the black dog, he wants to live.*

Before publication, around August time, I received the first proofs, and duly sent them to my family to make sure they were happy with everything. All was fine.

In reality, things at home were shifting, getting darker. Mum was increasingly unhappy. She said Dad had changed. On bad days she said she wanted to leave him, though we all knew she wouldn't. On better days, she would cry with guilt at having even thought such a thing. She loved him, you see – and, much as we may avoid it, there is a part of true love that's obligation and graft; a part that's about walking the hard miles.

Dad had taken to falling over, down stairs, across thresholds, even over his own bloody feet. As a result, Mum felt she couldn't leave his side. This made him ratty – he didn't want a bloody carer. This made her ratty – she wanted a semblance of her life and old freedoms back.

I headed down to Cornwall. Increasingly it had been a hard place to visit, a six-hour slog towards sadness. That particular visit, Dad seemed cheery, if a little older and more unsteady than I remembered. I had barely had a chance to take off my coat, before Mum whisked me into the kitchen, put the kettle on and started to talk.

MUM: I think it's Alzheimer's. Do you?

She was stage-whispering over the sound of the boiling water.

ME: Mum, I have just arrived. I have literally just stepped out of the car. I don't know. I don't know any of the specific symptoms. And shut up because he'll be able to hear you.
DAD: I can hear you!
MUM: I think it is.
DAD: Ann!
MUM: I think it's the beginning of dementia.
DAD: Ann! I can still hear you!
MUM: He's different, you know.

No, I think. *Not possible.* Not Dad's brain. There can't be anything wrong with Dad's brain – it's a source of wonder. This is the man who can add long lists of numbers in his head, who polishes off a couple of fiendish Sudokus before breakfast, who stores data better than an IBM mainframe. Yet this, too, is the man who has spent an entire life trapped in his own mind, a mind at war with itself. His brain is a battlefield on which the armies of self-doubt have raged for over seven decades. Now it appears they have won – that he has given up, that he is too tired to mount a challenge.

I took Dad for a stroll around the garden that afternoon. At some point, I became aware that I was holding his hand, supporting him.

Dad is leaning on you. He is leaning on you. He can't walk properly on his own.

I hadn't realized. I hadn't realized it was this bad.

I settled him back down in front of some sport (Dad didn't care what the sport was: as long as the television was full of people hitting things or kicking things he was happy) and I went over to the barn next door to see how Emma and Georgie were getting on.

Emma is one of my oldest mates and, through no fault of my own, I had ended up going on her and Georgie's honeymoon. This would be awkward in and of itself, but I am also Emma's ex-partner. Super-boke. For her and I to be involved in anything of a romantic or sentimental nature, even by proxy, is the stuff of nightmares.

On my way down to Cornwall, they'd given me a call. It turns out that the charming cottage in Somerset that they'd booked to stay in for their post-nuptials had been slightly mis-sold. The front garden did indeed contain a well-stocked array of cottage plants with wooden furniture and barbecue set – but what the owners had failed to disclose was what was in the back garden.

The M5.

Literally. As you sat in the sunlounger you could see the tops of the lorries as they sped towards Taunton.

I dropped in on them on my way down to Mum and Dad. Their instructions were certainly easy to follow – 'Get on the motorway west, come off at J25 and THERE YOU ARE.' I could see them waving as I turned off at the junction.

I won't lie, it was a strange choice for a honeymoon. Not

only was it situated on the slip-road of one of Britain's busiest motorways, but it also appeared to be a disused spa, with many of the ground-floor rooms containing stainless-steel trolleys laden with plastic sheets, waxing equipment and, in one suite, liquid nitrogen. It was a niche market for sure, catering for those lovebirds who fancied a mini-break, a Brazilian and a light freeze for two. After all, nothing says I love you like couples cryonics.

It was settled. I couldn't leave the pair of them in a haunted motorway Champneys, so they came down, thank God they came down, to Cornwall with me.

Our arrival meant that Mum could leave the house – just for an hour or two, she wouldn't want to be gone that long. Just an hour or two where she didn't have the background hum of worry, where she didn't need to keep one eye permanently fixed on Dad's whereabouts.

DAD: I'm fine, I don't need looking after.
MUM: Yes, you do. Will you be all right, Susan?
ME: Yes, we'll be fine. Don't worry. Everything will be fine.
MUM: Don't let him out of your sight.

Dad rolled his eyes, and I laughed. There he is. *There he is.*

As soon as the rumble of the car had faded into the distance, Dad made a bid for freedom.

DAD: I thought we might go for a walk. You know, like we did yesterday. I liked that.
ME: Of course, Dad – you sure you're up to it?

It was a pointless question: he was already getting his boots. Then there was the waterproof coat, scarf and bobble hat. Dad is nothing if not prepared.

He shuffled along to the front gate, his arm hooked in mine. Once onto the track, he started to pick up speed.

ME: Easy there, Dad – we're not in a hurry.

And yet still he sped on, careering sharply.

ME: Dad, you need to slow down – I can't hold you.

My back strained as I tried desperately to support his weight. He was now almost running, his body twisted, head leaning forward.

ME: Dad! STOP!

I couldn't hold him any longer, and at that point Dad swung sharply to the left and dived headlong into the bank alongside the path. As he fell, there was a moment when everything stopped – when the birdsong fell silent, when his boots left the crunch of gravel. All I could hear in the entirety of the universe was a single voice, my voice, which said, simply but clearly: *Your dad is dying.*

Dad tried to raise himself. His forehead was cut and he was bleeding profusely. I desperately tried to pull him up, but he was a dead weight. I ran to get Emma and Georgie, and they came to watch him while I ran back inside and called for an ambulance.

It was then I realized how remote we were, how isolated and cut off. It would take the paramedics forty minutes to get from the main hospital, plus they'd have no idea which unmarked track was ours. In the end, Georgie ran up the lane and waved them down. Emma stayed with Dad, and I monitored the phone.

All of this had happened while I was supposed to be in

charge – in the brief window when I had been made the responsible adult. Dad fell on my watch. It was my fault.

For a long, long time I thought it was all my fault.

Mum had left us happily eating biscuits and watching telly. She returned to a scene of pure chaos. Dad was sitting on a chair in the middle of the dirt track, his face lacquered with blood. Two paramedics stood either side of him, jollying him along while the ambulance made its way along the A30. I couldn't help laughing – the whole thing looked like a tea break on the set of *Holby City*.

The ambulance eventually followed. By this time, Dad was able to stand, so I got in with him and headed to our local A and E. The hospital was one of many savaged by government cuts. As I entered, I got a sense of a building folding in on itself, taking all those who had loved it, and had worked hard for it, along with it.

Dad was wheeled away for some scans, and I paced the darkened corridors for over an hour. I felt strangely calm. I knew exactly what was coming.

I remember the doctor was Scottish. I think he was called Nick. He was kind. That's what I remember most of all. Thank you, Dr Nick. I never got to say thank you for being so kind. Thank you.

He emerged through a doorway hung with industrial plastic strips – like vast tagliatelle. Dad was lying calmly on the hospital bed, his forehead bandaged.

DR NICK: Mr Perkins?
DAD: Hello. Call me Bert, please.
DR NICK: Bert, listen, I'm afraid we've found a mass in your brain.

A slight pause.

DAD: That's OK.

Dad put his hand over the doctor's as if to comfort him. That's the mark of my father, he is the sort of man who comforts the guy who is giving him a death sentence.

Hours later, we return to the house – this house which I have loved from the very first moment I met it. But now everything has changed. The granite isn't beautiful: it is a trip hazard. The walls aren't interesting: they are jagged. The staircase isn't slim and elegant: it is unfit for purpose.

It has been a great house. But I have a feeling it is going to make a terrible hospital.

34. Checkmate

Dad has asked me if he can die here, in the house. I have agreed because although he is saying the word 'die' it does not make any sense and I cannot engage with it as a reality. I have agreed because I don't know any better, and I don't know what is to come. What a savage gift hindsight is.

Dad can't do stairs any more. There is no point in pretending now. There is no plausible deniability from here on in. We decide to make him a bedroom in the lounge, next to the window where he can watch the birds. The carpet is threadbare, so I decide to get a new one – because it will give me something to do. It will give me focus and direction. I head to Penzance, and explain my situation to lovely Lynne, the sales assistant, who is quick to recommend a new eco composite carpet made from corn on the cob.

ME: That sounds good. I like corn on the cob.

LYNNE: The manufacturer lined a rhino's house with it.

ME: Really? I didn't know rhinos were partial to carpets.

LYNNE: A zoo in the States, I think, the rhino enclosure there. They laid the carpet down and just left it. Month later, they came back, removed the stinking carpet and cleaned it.

ME: Did they do any of the rhino's other soft furnishings? The sofa? Curtains? Or was it just the carpet?

LYNNE: (*rightly ignoring me*) They just used hot-water extraction to clean the thing. That was it. And you

> know what? Good as new. No smell or stains. With just water. Amazing, isn't it?

And I wonder, as I reach for my credit card, whether she is saying all this because she thinks there's a chance my dad will end up making as much mess as a rhino.

That afternoon, I ask Dad if he will play chess with me. He says no, he doesn't want to. If he can't play competitively, then what's the point? (He used to play for the county and even once received a prize.) He begins to descend down that familiar rabbit hole – *I'm useless*, he says. *I'm no good to anyone. I should be on the scrapheap. I'm shit. I'm just shit.*

I have grown up watching Dad tell himself he is pointless. Not once has he looked up in those moments and spotted the glaringly obvious: that he was our hero all along.

I press him. 'Dad, please play chess with me. Please.' His reply is the same: he doesn't play for enjoyment. He gets agitated. I have to watch that now: the lump, the meds, they create extreme anxiety. He can shout, cry or even hit himself if pushed too hard.

My body feels heavy with sadness. I wait a while, then return.

> ME: Dad. I know how you feel about it. I understand that. But would you do it for me? Would you do something for me?

He is silent.

Tears prick at my eyeballs. I'm wasting my time. I head to the kitchen and put the kettle on. I open the post and discover that Lynne has sent me some additional information on 'conscious carpeting', including one made from goat-hair and discarded fishing nets.

I bring Dad his tea. It's then I notice he has set up the chessboard and is patiently waiting for me to take my place opposite him.

We begin. I make some early positional posturings with a pawn or two. I try to ignore the fact that his hand shakes uncontrollably as he picks up the pieces. I am not even sure he can see the pieces any more. I notice his thumb running over the contours of the wood as if to confirm what he is holding. He can't distinguish a bishop from a pawn, and when he holds them close to his eyes, I notice they have turned the palest, iciest of blues. A third of the board is entirely invisible to him as the tumour has created a vast blind spot: a wall of darkness to his left. He has taken to seeing things, hallucinating, and twice during the game he bashes away phantoms, the black rats that swarm around him.*

He beats me. He beats me in less than twenty moves.

DAD: Come on, girl, put your back into it. You're not even trying. Concentrate!

So I do. I really do. I focus. I give it my all. And in this, the last game I ever play with him, he beats me in less than ten moves. You see, Dad, I told you but you never listened. You're a hero. You're an utter hero.

It is 11 November, and although I don't know it yet, my dad will be dead in less than four months.

* Dad has Charles Bonnet Syndrome, which can be one of the symptoms of a glioblastoma. Imaginary dark shapes appear from nowhere. They usually take the form of rats, but later he sees shadowy figures walking past him.

35. Mirrors

I am back in London.

Autumn is shaking hands with winter and there's a gloom in the air. I'm starting to feel unwell. When someone you love is dying, you become porous, your body mimicking the symptoms of the person you're so scared of losing.

I had booked in to see my friend, Helen, who is a wonderful human and a fabulous acupuncturist. I've gone to see her throughout the years, never regularly, because my schedule is chaotic – but intermittently, when I can. She will make me laugh by feeling my pulse and saying something like 'Ooh, racing piglets.' Then she will make me cry by sticking a needle in a point that allows me to let loose a little trickle from the river of sadness that flows inside.

I was running early. This never happens. I am never early for anything. I decided to go and grab a snack from the newsagent down the road. I was still a little hung-over from the night before. It had been my book launch, a little party to celebrate my autobiography hitting the shelves, and I had drunk too much out of nerves. I'm not great with hosting parties. I love to go to them, but I hate to host them. The responsibility is too great. What if no one comes? Worst still, what if *everyone* comes? What then?

I went into the shop and made a beeline for the shiny packets – you know the ones, the ones with all the bad stuff inside. It wasn't until I got in the queue to pay that I noticed the row of newspapers in front of me.

Four out of seven of them had my face on the front page. All of them led with variants of '*Bake Off* Star in Brain Tumour Nightmare'.

My first thought was, how could they know about Dad? *No one* knew about Dad. Then it dawned on me that they were talking about *my* brain tumour – my benign little brain tumour. My benign little brain tumour that I had talked about for one whole page in my book.

Genuinely, I think that moment, standing there flanked by Twixes, mobile-phone covers and Doritos extra spicy tortilla chips, was the most painful in my entire life. I don't think I have ever felt such profound sorrow as I stood there, in the middle of a shop, wordless and shaking, trapped between the two iterations of my life: the exterior and the interior, the public and the private.

I was trapped in a Hall of *Mirror*s.

And *Sun*s.

And *Star*s.

And *Express*es.

My hands shook uncontrollably as I handed over the cash. I lowered my head and, as I did so, gravity sent the welling tears splashing onto the counter. I didn't want anyone to see me, I was so ashamed. Look at this headline – this waste of ink, this embarrassment of trees. For me. About me. And all for nothing because I am not dying. I am not unwell.

I don't deserve your headline because this is not news.

The real news, by the way, Mr Dacre, Mr Murdoch, Mr Desmond – the real, seismic news, should you be inclined to print it – is that my DAD IS DYING. That is headline stuff. That is the only news, in fact. You've all been looking the wrong way – because while you've been door-stepping me and waiting outside my ex-boyfriend's house in France for a week my dad is dying.

FROM A FUCKING BRAIN TUMOUR.

I could feel the blood pounding in my temples, my ears hissing as my veins constricted. I was in the midst of a seismic panic attack.

I want to scream at the sharp, awful irony.

Oh, Universe, you sick little fuck.

36. Say It

Love. He wants it, all right. I am sure of that. But he wants it assumed, not spoken. It is almost as if it's too much of a burden for him to have it voiced out loud, to hear the actual words fill the room. I suspect that he doesn't think he is worthy of the sentiment. I am determined that today I am going to tell my dad I love him – even if he can't bear to hear it, even if he says nothing in return.

We are watching *Skyfall*. I am sitting on a rickety stool right next to his bed. I am not even sure that Dad can see where the television is, let alone the pictures dancing across it. He has become so good at dissembling. Even at this late stage he desperately covers how ill he is to spare us pain, though the charade is painful in and of itself.

I laugh at something. He laughs too. I don't know whether he is just copying me, to make me feel less alone. And I do feel so terribly alone here with him in this room.

I ready myself. There is an incredible pressure building in my head and behind my eyes. I wonder if that is where all the unarticulated sentiments of the last forty years have been hiding, and now they are massing, ready to make a break for it.

'I love you very much,' I say, my throat constricting with the excruciating sadness of it all. 'You've been a great dad. I couldn't have wished for a better dad.'

He carries on staring at the TV. After a few beats, he speaks.

DAD: You know, I remember going to Mike Flynn's house for dinner. I was with your mum. We turned up on my motorbike. Anyway, I had a dicky tummy or something – I dunno, something like that – anyway I couldn't finish the spag bol his missus had made. So we had a few whiskies and time ticks on. Eventually, we get up to go and I put my crash helmet on, and guess what? Mike has filled it with all the leftovers. I had pasta and tomato sauce running all the way down my face.

~~~

British Telecom have well and truly messed up. During 'routine' engineering works they have managed to seriously screw the line. There is no phone service, no internet at the house. For three weeks. Mum has no escape: she cannot reach out to her friends, most of whom live in London. Dad cannot Skype his family or pretend he can still play his beloved computer games.

I go mad. I ring every employee of BT. I tweet, I email, I holler to the skies until I have the telephone number of the chairman himself. And *then* it gets sorted. I immediately Skype home, and can see Dad, a blur of thick pixels, crying, with Mum cradling him round his waist.

ME: It's OK, Dad. I can see you. I can see you now. It's OK.

I call in later, just to check everything is working. Dad is cheery again, and we talk about the garden and the weather and the birds. I sign off, as I have been doing since his diagnosis.
~~~

ME: OK, Dad, I've got to go. I love you.

DAD: Love you too.

It is a reflex. He's said it without thinking.

Everything is still and in its place. But I am elsewhere. I am flying through time and space. I collapse on the floor, my head on the cool wood, and I cry more than I have ever cried before because even though I always knew he felt it I have waited forty-six years to hear it confirmed out loud.

37. The Strong One

In the middle of March, I arranged to go down for four days and give Mum a break. I had no idea this would be the last time I had on my own with Dad. The days were long; up at 6 a.m. to start the drugs regimen, then a solid, rolling buffet until 10 p.m. when the final steroid got popped. Dad had developed a slavish fondness for rice cakes, pale Styrofoam discs with the nutritional value of an old youth-hostel mattress, topped with a precarious tower of pre-grated Cheddar. To eat one would have been a tricky task for even the most dextrous of gourmands, but for an eighty-year-old with failing sight and compromised grey matter it was almost an impossibility. As he lifted one from the plate, a shower of waxy, yellow shavings fell to the floor. As he moved it to his mouth another dairy landslide, this time onto his beard. I'm not sure any of it got past his lips. Ever.

He partnered this meal with an orange.

DAD: You know – for colour.

It was imperative I got his drugs right, the daily fistfuls of tablets and capsules. There were anti-depressants, anti-anxiety, steroids, statins, ACE inhibitors and blood thinners, plus an equal number of mitigating pills, which acted to dull the side effects. Each med seemed to have a pharmaceutical twin, a shadow self, that counteracted the worst excesses of the other.

As evening fell, I started doubting myself. I panicked I

was getting it wrong. I double- and triple-checked. I took each pill out of its blister pack and sat up half the night with a magnifying glass checking the tiny manufacturers' marks imprinted on the various capsules and pellets.

Within a few days my horizon had shrunk, until all I knew was the rhythm of care. Rice cakes, with cheese and an orange. Telly. Drugs. Rice cakes, with cheese and an orange. Telly. Drugs. Doesn't want rice cakes. Telly. Drugs. I don't blame you, Dad, they taste like you're licking a quarry. Drugs. You need some food, Dad. Drugs. Have some custard, then. Sleep, awake, sleep. Drugs. What do you mean you don't want custard? You love custard! Drugs. Telly. Sleep. Drugs. Why don't you want custard?

Daddy, please eat.

He lies in the hydraulic bed. I notice his feet are crammed against the bottom board. He never complains, not once. Dusk is falling; time to tuck him in. The bed emits a mechanical yawn as it stretches itself flat again.

ME: Night, night, Dad. I love you.

He is staring at me, really staring at me.

ME: What? What is it?

He is looking right into the soul of me.

DAD: You've always been the strong one, Susan.

I don't know what to say. It is too big a thing to respond to just yet. I can feel the sting of a single tear scoring my cheek. I make my excuses and go and fetch his final steroid of the day, then pretend to busy myself in the kitchen, rattling bottles and clinking glasses for several minutes until I feel composed enough to return.

I approach. His pale blue eyes fix on me again. I offer him some water. He drinks, his eyes never leaving me.

ME: What?

DAD: You've always been the weak one, Susan.

ME: What?

DAD: What?

ME: WHAT? You just said I'm the strong one!

DAD: What are you talking about?

ME: You just said it, like, five minutes ago! You just said I'm the strong one.

DAD: Did I?

ME: Yes! It was a massive moment for me!

DAD: Really?

ME: YES!

DAD: Well, I must have been off my head.

He roars with laughter.

ME: Well . . . Well, which one am I?

DAD: I don't know.

ME: Of course you know. You have to know. Which one is it?

DAD: Well, let's just say you're both. Satisfied?

He is still laughing. And I laugh too because both things are true, and because it is time I learned to get my self-esteem from within, and stop relying on a man with a frontal lobe mass to give it to me.

After that night, Dad doesn't get out of bed again.

38. Fantasy Football

I sit with him in the morning, his hand in mine. He wakes up and turns his head towards me. I wink at him. He puckers his lips and sends me a smacker through the air.

Later, I bend over him and whisper, 'I love you very much, Dad,' and he says, 'And I you.' I can only just hear it through the click and clack of his dry lips.

He is fitted for a morphine syringe driver a few hours later. We are now at the endgame.

His anxiety is worsening. He is gurning and clawing at the bed sheets. Each and every night he is in pain and we call the emergency care line. Each and every night there is another locum doctor trooping out to the middle of nowhere to increase the dosage.

If he were my dog, I would have put him down three days ago. He will live like this for another week.

All of us are gathered around his bed. There is a polarity of late, a gravitational pull that draws us in – as if we are becoming aware the time is nearing and we don't want to be too far away. We circle him. We pretend to make tea or make calls, but we inevitably return, after mere moments, to his side.

Mum is round the other side, Michelle at his head, David stroking his shoulder, and me holding his hand. He is agitated and we are trying to calm him. David pipes up.

DAVID: The England game is on, Dad.

Dad's eyes open a little. I can see they are misty. He is now, I believe, totally blind.

ME: Yes, Dad – it's the match.

His mouth parts in an almost-smile.

DAVID: They're coming onto the pitch now.

We look at David, confused. The telly is off, and the match isn't for another hour or two. It dawns on us what he's doing, and we join in, one by one.

ME: They're looking good.
MICHELLE: Kane looks fit.
ME: And Vardy. Really sharp. They're off!
DAVID: And Vardy's scored! Unbelievable – brilliant bit of poaching at the net.

Dad's eyes are now fully open. He is staring ahead in narcotic wonderment, as if he can see it all being played out in front of him. He raises his hand in a weak fist to cheer the goal, his face widening to a beatific smile. We love seeing him like this so much we want more. And more.

MICHELLE: Terrible tackle from Gomez. That's a red card, Germany down to ten men.
ME: And a speedy run on the wing from Dier. And it's a goal!
DAVID: Unbelievable! I don't believe it! They are breaking again!
MUM: (*keen to be involved*) They are in a diamond formation, Bert!

We snigger for a moment. Mum doesn't know much about football, but she's giving it a good old go.

DAVID: Kane linking up with Alli . . . passing to and fro . . . And . . .
ALL: GOAL!

Dad is open-mouthed, silently cheering.

ME: Incredible dummy from Barkley. REFEREE!
MICHELLE: Definitely a penalty.
DAVID: And it IS a penalty . . . Kane to take it . . . and . . .
ALL: GOAL!!!

For fifteen minutes we stood commentating, around Dad's bed, as he lay there, hallucinating and enraptured.

As it happens, England did indeed win later that night, a mere 3–2 against Germany. But Dad left this world thinking we'd put 42 goals past our old rivals, while they ended the match with only two players on the pitch.

Life is wonderful. And some of its most wonderful moments are shot through with sadness.

39. And I Will Fix You

David, as wise as ever, suggests we make a makeshift lounge in the top room. It will be somewhere where we can get away from it all, but also somewhere where we can begin to recalibrate, as our new family. In our time off, we sit glassy-eyed, watching endless episodes of *Tattoo Fixers* with Mum – who, despite her veneer of prudishness, becomes quite the fan.

MUM: Will that spider's web on his neck ever come off?
ME: No, Mum. It's a tattoo.
MUM: So it doesn't come off.
ME: No. It's permanent. That's what a tattoo is. Permanent.
MICHELLE: Susan's got one.
ME: Shut up!
MUM: Have you?
ME: Yes.
MUM: Will it come off?

We passed days like this. We'd retire to our new room when the carers arrived for their early-evening shift, and make vats of spaghetti with tinned tomato sauce and pre-grated Parmesan. The sort of food we ate when we were kids. We'd eat it and try not to focus on the sounds of Dad screaming as he was turned and changed.

MUM: (*glued to the screen*) What's that on his side? That tattoo there . . .

ME: It's a penis.

MICHELLE: It's a cock and balls, Mum.

MUM: Why would you do that?

ME: They were on holiday.

MUM: When I go on holiday I go and see if there's a concert on at the local church, I don't have a penis engraved on my ribs.

DAVID: Well, you should live a little.

MUM: And what's that?

ME: That's the new design – the one that's going to cover it. It's a foot-long 3D rip-effect space robot emerging from his chest cavity.

MUM: Oh. It's horrid, isn't it? I think I'd have stuck with the penis myself.

We start taking shifts throughout the night, though none of us, in truth, sleeps a wink. I like the 3–5 a.m. slot, when the still cold air, as yet untouched by sunrise, starts to eat into your bones, when the trees begin to emerge from the blackness, silhouetted by a fresh blue canvas.

I remember the silence, the molasses sky, the ash trees silhouetted against the retreating silver. The baby owl screaming in the tree, the noise driving clean through the quiet. But I also remember a time before this. I remember the heavy exhalation of gas in the oven before it caught alight. The clink of glasses over dinner. The memory of two excitable beagles ploughing through the dog-flap at dusk.

Home. This place used to be my home.

It is now just a repository of loss, bounded by walls, with a roof over its head.

I hold Dad's heavy hand in mine, and with the other, I jab at my iPad.

I have taken to reading endless internet articles about death. A quick search of my browser history reads:

– *How do you know when someone is dying?*
– *What happens in the final stages of dying?*
– *How do I know when someone is close to death?*
– *How can you stop someone hurting?*

I know he is dying. I need to know when. WHEN. I am human. I cannot bear the not knowing. Nothing, not even death, is worse than the not knowing. I need a schedule. A timeframe. I need to understand. When is it going to happen? When?

I need to know. I need to prepare.

In retrospect, it was all so stupid. No amount of preparation can steel you for your new life – the one where the table is missing a leg, the car has three wheels, the sat-nav voice is indistinct.

This pain. This is the price. This is the reckoning. This is what you get to feel when love is replaced, pound for pound, with loss.

Dad would wake, every thirty minutes or so, through the fog of midazolam and morphine, and scream. I'd console him, whisper in his ear, stroke his hand, then he'd succumb to the darkness once more.

As five o'clock came, I would feel my back stiffen, and I'd sink my forehead onto his chest. Whereupon I'd feel a light tap on my shoulder and turn to see David, or Michelle, or Mum standing there, ready to take my place.

It's 27 March. It is Easter Sunday.

Dad is out of midazolam. We ring the local pharmacy. They are out of stock. We ring another. Same story. We ring several more, but no one has it available. Midazolam is a common palliative-care drug. It's routinely used as part of a package of pharmaceuticals to alleviate agitation, stress and anxiety. Dad is anxious. He is twitching and calling out, and he needs this drug. Now.

Michelle and I set out in the car. We will not return until we have these meds.

The sun is shining. We pass villages, their slate roofs gleaming in the spring light. We can hear church bells. We go to Hayle. Nothing. We try Camborne, Pool, Redruth – nothing. Michelle is frantically calling pharmacy after pharmacy, while I drive, the sound of my dad screaming in my ears.

An hour later, and we finally find a chemist who has the drug in stock.

'You're lucky, it's the last packet,' said the sales girl. She had no idea what she had just waded into.

'We're not lucky,' said Michelle, her voice rising.

There are fourteen people dying this weekend in West Cornwall. All of them need this drug. None of this is about luck.

40. It Pays to Go Premium

The day begins with sun, which we weren't expecting. I have developed a lump in my throat and I can't swallow. We don't know it yet, but this is the day that Dad is going to die.

We started to gravitate to his bed. No one left the room for more than a few minutes. I noticed his feet were turning purple, and his nose was icy to the touch. Death was creeping over him, gently stealing him away from us, inch by inch.

Now I understood what all those articles meant. Now I understood the timeline.

The freeze spread across his face. His body motionless. Michelle stood at his head, her hands in the thatch of his hair – the hair that had withstood age and the endless, toxic carousel of chemo and radiotherapy . . .

Mum had his right hand in hers. David was to his left, hand in hand – stroking him. I was sitting at his shoulder, the side of my head lying on his chest. I could hear his heart beating just millimetres from my ear: two lives separated by a thin sheet of skin.

You can go now, Bert.

It's OK, Dad – you can go now.

Still Bert's brilliant metronome beat on. You can ravage his body, Cancer, but let me tell you, no one will ever taint this man's beautiful heart.

'Apparently your hearing is the last thing to go,' one of us said. I can't remember who.

Michelle reaches for her iPad, and searches on Spotify for

the three tracks Dad loves best. We want him to hear them one last time.

She presses play. First comes the third movement of Bruch's Violin Concerto, all sprightly and vigorous. Next, there is 'Danny Boy'. We all bow our heads and try to sob as quietly as we can.

Then, suddenly, a woman's voice starts bellowing:

VOICEOVER: DO YOU HAVE DRY CRACKED SKIN? DO YOU WANT TO TURN BACK TIME AND GET A FRESHER, ROSIER LOOK?

Michelle is stabbing at the screen, trying to make it stop.

VOICEOVER: THEN TRY OUR REVOLUTIONARY SKIN CARE SYSTEM, WHICH WILL LEAVE YOU REJUVENATED AND FEELING GOOD AS NEW.

MUM: What's going on?

MICHELLE: It's just Spotify, Mum.

ME: What? You couldn't pay for Premium? You tight bastard.

DAVID: Susan, now is not the time.

Michelle is punching the screen, trying to make the adverts stop.

VOICEOVER: WHEN LIFE SEEMS TOUGH . . .

And then we laugh. All of us. We roar, like we're going to burst – a collective eruption that cuts through the pain.

Finally, his third chosen track kicks in, the theme tune to *Star Trek: Voyager*. We fall silent again. It's silly, all of this. It's so impossibly silly that Dad is dying and we are listening to the sounds of the *Starship Enterprise*. It's all so silly, you see?

Suddenly, the morphine driver starts beeping, Dad is now out of drugs. His heart races a little in response.

'He reacted. He can hear,' I said. 'He can hear everything.'

I love you, Daddy.

I love you, Bert.

We love you.

We love you.

And then, just then, I felt his heart slow a little, like a feather falling to earth.

One . . .

Two . . .

Three . . .

Then his chest fell silent.

'He's gone,' I said. But they all knew anyway.

The morphine driver beeped again.

'Good to the last drop,' said David. And we laughed and cried at the same time.

My dad saw me take my very first breath.

I had my head to his heart when he took his last.

~

That final time I was on my own with dad, those few days I got to spend alone with him, I remember asking him if he thought there was an afterlife.

ME: If there's anything behind the curtain, Dad, will you make sure you come and tell me?

Dad was staring out of the window at the blur of trees beyond.

DAD: Absolutely. Of course I will. I'll come back. I'll come back as a blackbird, and then you'll know for sure.

41. Blackbird (Redux)

Six months later, four thousand metres skywards, and six and a half thousand kilometres east, I saw, in the haze of a puja fire, a blackbird diving in and out of the ash. And I remembered.

I'll come back as a blackbird, and then you'll know for sure.

And it's crazy. And it doesn't make sense. And that's just fine with me.

My little donkey is picking her way through the sharp grey stones, fresh from the constant landslides. '*Chulla! Chulla!*' roar the porters. 'Hurry up! Hurry!' They rush at her, slapping and cajoling. 'Leave her alone,' I hiss. 'She knows what she is doing.' She alone can be trusted to bring me down this mountain.

You don't notice much on the way up. You're so shot with tiredness, so absorbed by the fight for breath that you don't notice what's disappearing as you climb. It's only when you catch your breath at the top that you realize the world has gone white and cold around you.

When you descend, the beauty of the natural world reappears, unfolding piece by piece. There is a re-emergence of life, of bloom and colour, with each step you take. First comes the sound, the dry percussion of wind on leaves. Then the thin lines of trunk and branch decked in green. Finally there is an explosion of orange and red, as the acers emerge once more. I was on that donkey's back for four hours, as it picked its way along the thin scar of a track. To my left, mere centimetres of rubble between us and the edge of the ravine. You could see the drop, thousands of feet down towards the clean green twist of water. I thought about my dad. I thought about the unspeakable beauty of this place – and how he could never have seen it with his own eyes. How circumstance and finance and fear would have put paid to even the thought of a trip like this – and how lucky I was, how boundlessly fortunate to see this place, with this clarity, on this day.

Varanasi

42. Coincidence

The universe is strange. We seek order in the chaos, and sometimes we are lucky enough to find patterns, which console or enlighten us. Coincidences, those concurrences of events without obvious causal connection, are the cat's eyes on the road – helping us to believe we're in the right lane.

Whether or not these events are meaningful in and of themselves is no matter. We perceive them as important in relation to other experiences we have had. We take comfort in the apparent impression of a universal order. Or, at least, I do.

Our next trip was to Varanasi, also known as Benares, the City of Light. A fortnight before I was due to fly, I started to have extreme pains down the left side of my stomach. This became so unrelenting that I decided to get it checked out before leaving the country, just to be on the safe side.

The problem with scans is that they always find *something*. Tucked among the organs, arteries and visceral fat will be a bulge or a lump or a speck. Then, suddenly, to add to all your worries about the outside world you'll be gifted with a whole new arena of concern – your bloody insides.

I have had a million and one scans before, but there was something unbearably sad about being in that tube that day. I felt the presence of Dad, who had lain in these things countless times, the dull chime of magnets around his head, dye coursing through his veins. I thought of him as the blocks were placed either side of my head, as my torso was strapped and my legs bound.

How sad that I should find communion with him in this sterile tube. I want to think of him when I am walking in the forest, or tickling the dog, or eating fish and chips on the harbour wall. I don't want to think of him here, in a place like this. It is too much.

When you have an MRI scan, you have to sign a release form before the procedure, part of which takes the form of a questionnaire.

Q: Do you have any metal implants?

That one is easy.

A: No. Next.

Q: Do you have a pacemaker or a heart replacement valve?

Also easy.

A: No

Then comes the kicker.

Q: Have you ever been treated for metal in your eyes?

Ah.

Every time – EVERY TIME – I read this question, I think back to the time when I was eighteen and pressed down too hard on a piece of paper with a propelling pencil. A shard of lead pinged into my eye and briefly got embedded in my cornea.

The next question does not help quell my rising fear levels.

Q: Is there *any possibility* of metal/metal pieces in your eyes?

I think about that, and every time – EVERY TIME – I ask the consultant if:

1. It is going to be OK (even though the lead was removed over twenty years ago)
2. Lead is even a metal

And even though he says it's all going to be fine, I panic nonetheless – panic that this forgotten chunk of pencil is going to rip through my eye tissue, fire upwards out of my skull towards the magnets and destroy hundreds of thousands of pounds of state-of-the-art NHS equipment while shredding my peeper in the process.

This time, there was an even greater reason for concern. While stripping down to my underwear in order to pop on some rather fetching blue scrubs, I noticed that there appeared to be some gold filament woven into my knickers. They were posh pants that Anna had bought for me, and I hadn't thought twice about wearing them until now. I stared down at them, woefully. Then came the familiar argument between The Two Susans.

MAD SUSAN: Christ. These pants are gold. They are actual gold. They have gold in them. Gold is a metal, isn't it? That means that once that machine gets going, my pants are going to take off from my pelvis, slice through these surgical trousers and jam the magnet.

SENSIBLE SUSAN: Sorry, but who puts real gold in knickers? You think Anna has bought you eighteen-carat high-waisters? Who the fuck do you think you are? Tutankhamen?

MAD SUSAN: You won't be saying that when my gusset is responsible for taking down a £1.2 million piece of medical equipment.

SENSIBLE SUSAN: Oh, piss off, Cyberman pants . . .

CLINICIAN: Ms Perkins? We're ready for you now.

I had to make a choice – should I go with Sensible Susan, or Mad Susan? Well, put it this way, I ended up throwing my pants in the medical waste bin and going commando for the scan. I am nothing if not my mother's equally paranoid daughter.

The scan took ages. Gosh, they are being thorough, I thought. After it was all done, after the metallic bangs and crashes had subsided, the radiographer came out of his ante-room, walked across the shiny hospital floor and shook my hand. It turned out he was Mel's cousin.

Coincidence.

I went through the results with the consultant urologist, a man roughly my age with an immediately warm and engaging manner. I was relieved to find out that nothing serious was wrong – I merely have an odd ureter and a slightly clubbed kidney. Who knew?*

ME: Am I OK to travel?

CONSULTANT: Of course you are. Where are you off to this time?

ME: Varanasi.

CONSULTANT: How wonderful. My family are Hindus. For us that is a special place – a very special place. To die there is to achieve *moksha*.

ME: *Moksha*?

CONSULTANT: Freedom, a liberation from the endless cycle of life and death. That's what we believe.

We talked for a while. I told him about my dad. He told me that his father was also dying, from kidney cancer – from the very disease his son was spending his life trying to cure.

* NOW THEY ALL KNOW, YOU OVERSHARING NUTTER.

That twisting irony again. As I was leaving, I turned back to him on a whim.

> ME: I'll say a prayer for him, at the ghat. I will say a prayer there, I promise. Goodbye.

Then I carried on walking, without turning round, for fear I had said the wrong thing. I so didn't want to say the wrong thing. And I cried all the way home.

43. The Magnet Boys

It was seven thirty in the morning, and the sun was already making a nuisance of itself. We parked up by the vast Raj Ghat Malviya Bridge, and the boys got out to set up. There was the sudden and violent cacophony of car horns, dog barks and telephone ringtones, then the doors slammed shut and I was returned to peace again.

I love this moment of the day, first light, mouth still thick with sleep and brain just coming to, feeling mildly fretful about what is to come. We park up in a strange new place, with strange new people, and for ten minutes I'm left alone in the car to gather my thoughts away from the noise and the smog.

It's the same routine wherever I am – forest or jungle, city or village. I flip down the passenger side visor and slide the plastic tab across to reveal a tiny mirror, smeared with grease. It measures no more than 7 x 15 centimetres. I say this, in part, as justification for the lack of personal grooming displayed on camera. No resources, you see?

Wherever I am, however, I will gamely try to put on a little slap. Standards.

I get out my make-up bag. I say bag – bag is a rather grandiose title for the worn little pochette I carry around with me. Even the sight of it is enough to send Anna into a tailspin back home. *Why don't you wash it? Why wouldn't you wash it? Oh, God! What the hell is on that brush? Is it skin? Is that face skin, Sue?*

My routine is always the same. First, a good slathering of Factor 50 sunscreen. Everywhere. It's white and oily, and sits on my skin like goose fat. Once that's blocking my pores, good and proper, it's time for more Factor 50, this time mixed with a little tinted moisturizer. Now, not only am I greasy but faintly orange. I swirl my trusty, crusty brush into a pot of black eyeliner and paint around my peepers. I've never been taught how to do it, but I figure it's OK to just go all the way round in a circle. There's a hint of Shakespears Sister, but not too much. Finally, I blot it all down with powder from the dusty compact. I am not sure how much of it is really mineral powder any more, and how much of it is just accumulated dust. Anyway, whatever those particles are, they do the job and soak up some of the sunscreen ooze.

There's a gentle tap on the window. It's Olly, dangling a microphone cable provocatively.

I'm box fresh. I'm good to go. I am ready for my close up, Mr de Mille.

A large group of boys had congregated round the car. I noticed they had slicked their hair back with coconut oil. Sharp. They looked more photogenic than I ever could.

I rolled off the front seat, and was immediately hit by the forty-five-degree heat. I could feel the moisturizer slipping down my face, leaving the sunscreen underneath to harden and turn yellow in the heat. By late morning, it looked like I'd been potted, like a Victorian shrimp.

The kids tumbled down the riverbank, slapping and kicking one another. Oh, to have surplus energy again. I say 'again' – I don't think I've ever had it. I've only ever had the exact amount of energy necessary to do the things I love: reading, talking, playing music and laughing. My cardiovascular needs are therefore somewhat modest.

They flew, laughing, onto their boat, a thin rickety thing that looked like it had been fashioned from outsized lolly sticks. The craft barely registered their weight as they tumbled on board. We headed off to the centre of the river, between the two banks and a hundred metres downstream of the mighty bridge.

These boys are the sons of fishermen, and would no doubt have followed in their fathers' footsteps, were it not for the fact that this stretch of the river is clinically dead. Nothing lives in these waters any more. Yet still the kids come here, day after endless day, and drop their nets into the water, not in the vain hope of catching carp or mullet but of harvesting something far more dazzling.

Cash.

The Raj Ghat Malviya is a monstrous feat of engineering. It's essentially a double-decker bridge, the upper level for cars, the lower for trains. It's the trains we're waiting for, crammed full of pilgrims en route to the city, desperate for a sign of Ma Ganga. It's tradition that when they see her, snaking beneath them, they'll throw whatever change they have into the river by way of an offering.

We drop anchor in the middle of the river, fifty metres or so downstream of the bridge, and wait. After a few minutes I can hear the rumble of an approaching train and look to the boys – only to find they have turned their backs to the bridge, and bowed their heads, like they're extras in a waterborne *Blair Witch*. As the rolling stock rumbles into view, one of them makes a dash towards me, grabs an umbrella and opens it above my head.

ME: What are you doing?
BOY: Don't talk!
ALL: Don't talk! Mouth shut!

I can hear the train rumbling above.

ME: What the hell is this umbrella for?

I wondered if they had spotted a raincloud ahead. Then came a forceful splat, which hit the spokes and showered outwards. It certainly felt like rain.

The boys laughed.

ME: (*laughing*) What? What is it?

One of them points to his groin, another to his bum.

I look down and realize with horror that the spots of moisture on my skin and clothes aren't rain, but human piss – a tinkle-sprinkle raining down from the locomotive toilets above. It transpires I'd got lucky – it wasn't a solids day.

Once the train was out of view, the boys began their day's work. First, they unfurled their nets into the water, the edges weighted and fringed with black magnets they'd taken from old refrigerator doors and the like. (Nothing is wasted in India – everything is repurposed and recycled.)

Once the nets were fully submerged, we waited for the current to do its work, drawing the shiny coins towards us. As the kids waited they held diving competitions, hurling their skinny bodies this way and that off the end of the prow. Then, when the time was right – and they seemed to just know when the time *was* right – they pulled the soaked rigging from the depths, and with it the shiny offertory. Praise be.

I held that net. I held it for five seconds and then I couldn't hold it any more. These boys single-handedly reeled it in time and time again. I looked at their little arms, like pistons. There was no muscle. But then it wasn't muscle-power fuelling them, it was something far stronger – necessity.

The eldest boy back-flipped into the murk and returned a minute later with a coin.

'What's it like in there?' I asked. Later, a scientist would tell me the water contains dizzyingly high levels of faecal coliform bacteria. It's no exaggeration to say that swimming in this part of the Ganges is akin to swimming in raw sewage.

BOY: It is good. But I am used to it.

ME: What was it like to start with? Do you remember the first time you dived?

BOY: It was scary. I was frightened.

ME: How come?

BOY: The bodies. You see the bodies. I am used to it now. I am strong. I dive in so the younger ones don't have to see the dead people.

ME: Are they bodies from the ghats?

He nodded. I imagined swimming through the filthy water, its dimness punctuated by pale bloated faces, half-burnt mouths open, as if screaming through the deep.

He gestured upwards, towards the bridge.

ME: They come from there too? Suicides?

He nodded again, his eyes lowering, as if trying to remove the images from his head.

The others were unconcerned, busying themselves with counting out the cash. I wondered if they felt bad about taking the pilgrims' money. It would be like me standing in the middle of Rome's Trevi Fountain and catching the coins as people threw them over their shoulders.

ME: Do you feel bad? Those coins are meant as offerings . . .

He held a tower of coins between his thumb and forefinger, smiling. 'Ganga provides,' he replied.

An hour later and it was time to head back to the bank. There was more human piss on my shoulders, and something resembling phlegm on my waistband. I tried not to think about it. I got off the boat and waded through the mud and shit and plastic bags to get to the ghat and the street above. I hadn't been back long when a shout went up.

In the distance, I could see our crew boat coming in, with people waving to us from onboard.

A crowd started to gather. All men. There was a lot of jostling and chatter. Several got out their phones. The crowd grew. I could feel hands in the small of my back and hot breath on my neck. There is no such thing as personal space in India.

Another shout went up, this time nearer – and the crowd parted. In rushed one of our Indian crew carrying a young woman, soaking wet and screaming. He laid her down on one of the market stagings, a raised concrete plinth in the centre of the street. The crowd moved to surround her. I could see she was writhing and clutching her stomach. Her eyes were full of blood. Her hand moved to her head to replace the veil that had fallen to one side. Even in agony, she felt the need to conform.

Immediately Lucy, the producer, and Vicky were on hand, moving her gently into the recovery position, talking to her, reassuring her. I started asking around for a paramedic. We three women bustled around, desperately trying to help, in the middle of a crowd of a hundred or more men who did nothing other than stare.

Behind me I could hear someone explaining in English how two people had just thrown themselves from the bridge, and how they had managed to retrieve only one. The other was seemingly lost to the water. I imagined that boy diving for coins and finding the body, skimming past the puffed face and twisted limbs.

The crowd around me chattered and started taking photos. They behaved as if this was a routine occurrence, and nothing special.

'Is somebody going to do something?' I asked, pushing back at the throng around me. *'Is anybody going to do something?'*

Then came the familiar rumble of Abhra's 4x4 – an ancient black gas-guzzler with gaudy gold trim. His baby. His pride and joy. His team fought through the throng, lifted the screaming woman into the back seat and drove away.

The next day, Abhra showed us the morning papers. The story had made the news. The girl had survived, thank God. She was sixteen, and came from a Muslim family in rural Uttar Pradesh. She had wanted to marry a Hindu boy and her parents had refused to sanction the match. She was just a little kid who had fallen in love, and then, in heartbreak, fallen through the sky to a certain fate. But she had not counted on the power of the river.

Ganga will provide.

44. The City of Light/The Heart of Darkness

Varanasi is one of the world's oldest continually inhabited cities – as old as or older than Jerusalem, Athens and Beijing. It's been a centre of culture and learning for over three thousand years, and is regarded as the spiritual capital of India.

It's an unusual city: although it's built around a waterway, only one of its banks is inhabited, framed by the eighty or so 'ghats', or stone-stepped embankments, which line its edges. The opposite side is little more than a mud flat, which gets completely flooded during monsoon season.

We take a wooden boat out at dusk and putter along the river towards the main ghat. We are accompanied by a dead cow, belly up and bloated like a bovine space hopper, which drifts on the current alongside us. Around it, children swim and play. *Sadhus*, covered head to toe with human ash, chant on the banks, stoned out of their brains.

We pass an ancient temple, partially submerged and so stooped it makes the Leaning Tower of Pisa look positively upright. It is a fool's errand to look for right angles, for order of any kind, in this place. The whole city, despite its UNESCO heritage status, feels like it is inexorably surrendering to the deep. Everything is crumbling here, slumped and wonky. It looks like a scene from a generic disaster movie, where an extinction event has decimated a once beautiful and pristine city. Think *Independence Day* and you'll get the general gist.

But Varanasi isn't about the visuals, as I was to learn. For the millions of pilgrims who come here each year, it's about something far more profound.

Most ghats are for bathing, or for puja, a religious ritual performed by Hindus where offerings are made to the gods. One of the riverside platforms, however, appeared to be staging some kind of women-only dance spectacular. As we floated past we were blasted by music from the tannoy, and could make out the odd limb whirling, the occasional glint of jewelled sari in the moonlight. Occasionally the women would whip themselves up into a frenzy, screaming and clawing at their necks, before throwing themselves into the river, then clambering out to start the whole process over again.

ME: What's that? What's going on?

GUIDE: They are prostitutes – sex workers. This is their offering to the gods. They are asking that they die now and get reborn into another life where they are not prostitutes.

ME: Where have they come from?

GUIDE: All over. They come from all over India.

I can appreciate the dancing, the music, the sense of a beat driving you into madness – these are the familiar markers of a celebration. It's harder, however, to understand a party where the end goal is death, where you convene in order to beg for your life to end, where you pray that your next turn around the block won't involve selling your body for cash.

It is a hard mental gap to bridge, and next to impossible for a visiting Westerner.

ME: This party looks so expensive.

GUIDE: Yes, very expensive.

ME: Would they have paid for it?

GUIDE: Oh, yes.

ME: But wouldn't it be better if they saved that money and used it to escape sex work?

My guide fell silent. I didn't know if he was stunned by my ignorance, or offended by the question. Either way, I didn't persist.

I can appreciate the value of faith. Of course. I understand it provides solace, lifting you in times of need. I find it harder to appreciate a system rooted in the belief that your circumstances will change in the *next* life, keeping the most disadvantaged locked into an acceptance of the status quo. If you believe an easier life is waiting, then it gives you, perhaps, less or little incentive to engineer a better outcome in this one.

I think of that boy with HIV under the bridge in Kolkata and my heart breaks because that is not a snapshot of his life – that *is* his life, in perpetuity. Without change, without mitigation, without hope.

That night, the moon hung in the thinnest, sharpest crescent I'd ever seen. Like you could pick it from the sky and carve up the dark with it.

I'd finished the last shot of the day, and wandered down one of the ghats in an attempt to grab a few snapshots of it. As I descended, one of the steps crumbled beneath me. I lost my footing, and stumbled downwards head first, my arms outstretched. As my hands reached out to break my fall, they plunged into something soft at the bottom of the steps, which cushioned my landing.

As I landed, I instinctively knew what that soft substance was. My nostrils quickly provided the proof, should proof have been needed.

Shit. Human shit. I had fallen in human shit.

I knew it was bad. My elbow felt broken, and I could feel blood trickling down my arm and fingers. My jeans were ripped at both knees, which were bleeding too.

I was in the middle of one of the most unsanitary places on earth with human shit running into the open cuts on my hand. I shuffled onto my side, removed my belt and tourniqueted my arm. Then I reached into my pocket, pulled out a bottle of my old friend, hand sanitizer, and poured the entire contents over the wound.

I heard a noise, incredibly close, yet unfamiliar. It was a deep bellow, like a cow in labour. It took me a while to realize the sound was coming out of my own mouth. The alcohol had hit the exposed skin and mingled with my blood. The pain was so sharp, it felt like I'd been electrocuted.

I got up, and claret started filling my shoe.

I staggered back up the steps. Some five minutes later I got to the top, hunched and limping. The crew were there to greet me.

VICKY: Sue? You OK? What's happened?

ME: Fallen. Shit. Shit. Fallen in shit.

I was babbling.

Matt raised the lens.

VICKY: You OK?

Vicky is an incredibly kind, decent and empathetic person. However, she is also the director on this shoot, which means all of those values are surplus to her job description.

VICKY: How are you feeling?

Now, when a director says 'How are you feeling?', what they really mean, is 'Do you want to tell us on camera how you're feeling?'

In fact, now might be the perfect time to give you a quick Director's Phrase Translator:

DIRECTOR: How was that for you?
Translation: I need you to do it again.
DIRECTOR: Yeah. That was great!
Translation: I need you to do it again.
DIRECTOR: Can we try it another way?
Translation: Can we try it MY way?
DIRECTOR: How would you feel about . . . ?
Translation: Your answer is irrelevant. This is what we're going to do, regardless of how you feel.
DIRECTOR: We're nearly done.
Translation: Give me another hour.
DIRECTOR: We'll only be another hour.
Translation: We'll be another two.
DIRECTOR: The edit's coming along nicely.
Translation: I don't think we have a film. Why did I ever work with you?
DIRECTOR: You've got a lie-in tomorrow.
Translation: See you at 7.30 a.m. sharp.

So, back to Vicky:

VICKY: How are you feeling?

I made the translation in my head.

VICKY: Do you want to tell us on camera how you are feeling?
ME: Vic. I don't want to talk about it. I'm not in the mood.

I growled at her. Deep down, however, I knew that the wound on my hand was going to need bandaging, and that the sudden appearance of that bandage on screen was going to require an explanation. She was right.

ME: OK, fine. Let's just get it done.

I was properly grumpy.

Matt swung round, ever-ready.

MATT: Good to go. *Speed.*

I started talking. Actually, not talking – raging. I barely paused for breath as I described how I felt.

There was a pause. *Yep*, I thought. Nailed it. *That was some righteous chat, right there.*

VICKY: Great.

Oh, shit. Let's remember the translation:

DIRECTOR: Great.
Translation: I need you to do that again.

I began once more, describing the accident, how I felt – the smell, the chaos, the grinding poverty. I came to a stop after several minutes. Well, that's sorted that.

VICKY: Great.

Oh, God. Not again.

VICKY: Just one more thing. Could we make it a little less edgy?
ME: (*howling*) What?
VICKY: We need it more mainstream – you know, a bit more BBC1 . . .

'HOW DO YOU MAKE FALLING IN HUMAN SHIT MORE BBC1?' I raged. How can a headlong tumble into steaming ordure be made more fucking mainstream? What alternative phraseology for 'I am covered in cack and bleeding like a stuck pig' would be more acceptable to the primary channel of our nation's public broadcaster?

I took a deep breath, channelled the ancient gods of Dimbleby, and yes, I made it all a little more BBC1.

Then I went home, poured iodine on every pore of my body, bandaged my arm, slept for three hours and got up again, determined to give Varanasi another crack of the whip.

~

The next morning, I had the wonderful Navneet as my guide around this labyrinthine city. He wove effortlessly through its snaking tunnels, his white kurta flapping as he led me through the endless clay-coloured streets. I followed him, the tacky soles of my flip-flops sticking to the baking cobbles.

The narrow passageways are full of dead-eyed men, begging for food. Grandmas hold parasols in one hand and a limp, dying cobra in the other. They grab it by the throat and hold it up. *Picture? You want picture?*

No, no picture. No picture. Just let it go. Please, just let it go.

Cows wander in and out of shops; bikes and motorbikes weave through the shit. There is never-ending noise and bustle. Young dogs give birth in the gutter, whilst the older ones look on, scarred, battle worn – eyeless, limbless. Everything suffers here – nothing, no one is exempt.

A dentist sits in the gutter. His eleven o'clock appointment has arrived. His patient crouches in the road and opens her mouth wide. He fills a gum shield with what looks like pink expandable foam and pushes it onto her upper jaw. Moments later, he removes it, places it on the pavement and waits for the impression to dry. He picks up a rusty tool and starts work fashioning some dentures.

A young woman comes towards me, holding a new-born babe in her arms. He is fast asleep. She looks at me and chants, 'Milk, milk, MILK.' She raises her thumb to her mouth to indicate drinking from a bottle. 'Milk, milk, MILK.' The thin little baby doesn't stir. I can't watch it any more. I put my hand into my pocket and move towards them.

'Don't,' says Navneet. '*Don't.*'

I learn later that this woman works as part of a gang in a coordinated scam. The women scout the slums for new mothers, then rent their babies from them for a few rupees a day. Let that sink in. They rent babies. *They rent babies.* They then bring the babies to the city, drug them so they don't cry and interrupt business, and start working the streets, begging. But these women don't ask for money – they are way too smart for that. They ask for milk. This way they look like credible mothers to us naive tourists.

If you fall for it, they will refuse to take your money. That's the second way they gain your trust. In an effort to prove how honest they are in their request, they will walk you to a shop that sells milk. You buy the milk and give it to the 'mother'. She is grateful, so grateful. You walk away feeling swollen with a sense of a good deed done in a shitty world.

As soon as you are out of sight, the 'mother' walks back into the shop, returns the formula to the shelf and gets the money, minus the shopkeeper's cut. They're all in it together.

'Don't,' says Navneet.

I can't breathe. That child. That child locked in an opiate daze. Prey – from the very get-go, from the moment it draws breath. A prop. A money-earner. A mewling cash prize.

I can't breathe.

Don't.

I feel I am in the very Heart of Darkness. What was it Conrad said? 'He hated all this, and somehow he couldn't get away.' I am here for two weeks. Day and night. The horror – the horror.

I am trying to drink it in. I am trying to be a journalist and be objective, almost dispassionate about my surroundings, while proffering a personal opinion when and where relevant.

But the truth is, I am descending into madness. The heat and the stink are burning out my nostrils. My ears ring constantly from the incessant shouting. I feel jumbled, disoriented, but most of all – vulnerable.

~~~

Perhaps the most famous destination for visitors to Varanasi is the Manikarnika ghat: the cremation site where Indians from all over the country bring their loved ones to be burnt by the waters of Ma Ganga, thereby achieving *moksha*, or freedom from the material world. The fires burn twenty-four hours a day, every single day of the year; some fifty to sixty million trees a year are felled to keep these pyres alight. Everything here takes place in a heat haze, faces and limbs distorted by the raging flames that encircle you. This place
~~~

is Bosch, directed by David Lynch with art direction by Syd Mead.

The sandalwood used at the cremation ghat is expensive, and not everyone can afford it. Some bodies don't make it as far as the official burning site, some are just doused in paraffin further downstream and tipped in, partially burnt. As we floated past we saw a dog carrying a human arm. After that I stopped looking at the banks.

In town, through the narrow, cobbled lanes, bodies wrapped in gold, orange and pink satin, decked with flowers, are transported on bamboo biers. Bells are rung. There are drums. The mourners follow.

Most tourists charter boats and float past the Manikarnika, but we got close to the cremation area itself. The heat was unlike anything I'd ever experienced and I could barely breathe in the smoke. I could hear the anguished sobs of mourners processing round the bodies. Ash rained down from the sky in an unrelenting grey. Mad dogs, not content with the heat of the midday sun, decided to get a little more cosy by lying right next to the flaming pyres, on a bed of smouldering ash and bone.

ME: Why are the dogs so close to the bodies?
GUIDE: You see, you will see.

I turned to Olly, who has been round the globe at least twice.

ME: Is this the worst place in the world?
OLLY: No.
ME: OK.
OLLY: It's the second worst. Kigali narrowly trumps it.

I start talking to camera again. Behind me, a mourner

smashes the skull of his dead auntie, with a thick stick, to free her spirit. As visceral as this place is, at least the relatives get to engage with their grief. In the West, we put our loved ones in a box, then wonder why we can never move on with our grief. Here they watch the flesh decay, and witness the spirit released. The mourners arrive weeping; they leave believing their relative has achieved eternal freedom. As I talk, ash whirls around my face, and grit lands on my lips. Human grit. Human grit in my mouth and in my eyes.

I am mid-sentence when a black ball is thrown from the pyre towards me. It lands at my feet. A dog launches itself on it, biting into it and releasing an odour unlike anything I have ever encountered. If pressed, I would describe it as a cross between molten Époisses, cat piss and vomit.

I gagged. Olly gagged, the boom swaying in his hands.

OLLY: Oh, God, I'd heard about this.
ME: Jesus. What is it? What is that smell?
OLLY: Oh, God, it's awful. It's . . . it's . . .

It's the central nervous system of a human being. It doesn't fully disintegrate in the heat. Instead it retracts, like a network of reeking rubber bands, into a tight ball. And guess what? Dogs, the filthy fuckers, love it.

OLLY: I take it back.
ME: What?
OLLY: This is the worst place on earth.

We manage to finish up, and I walk past the smoking corpses to the water's edge. To my right, a man is cleaning his teeth with a twig and some Colgate, before scooping a handful of river-water into his mouth to swill it all out. I thought about the pollution levels in the river, clinically dead and full of raw sewage. Cleaning your teeth in it seems the oral equivalent of having a bath, then rolling in fox shit.

There was something I wanted to do before I left. I shut my eyes. There was the crackle and pop of flesh behind me. I tried to tune into the ebb and flow of the river. I cleared my head of any thoughts, bar one.

I thought of the kind urologist, and I thought of his dad. I wasn't sure whether he was dead or alive. But I asked the river, and the sky and the birds and whatever else in the universe was listening to me in that moment to grant him peace and *moksha* by proxy. I didn't even know if it was possible for a non-believer to ask for such a thing. But I asked for it anyway, and I truly meant it.

As we headed off, away from the smoke and the stink, I noticed a large gap in one of the bridges crossing the river. I'm not sure whether it was mid-construction, or whether the central part had worn away over time. That's the thing about India: the weathering and degradation caused by heat and humidity means it's impossible to tell whether something is just beginning or slowly coming to its end. I stared at this gap, this space between two certainties, this passage of light and air between the strutting steel.

And I thought, *That's it. That's Varanasi.* This is not a city simply based on what is concrete and present. This is a city based on belief. It is part construct, a portal to another world that cannot be captured in an iPhoto or a travel book. To truly inhabit Varanasi requires faith, the leap into the void that lends this place its extra dimension.

For those of us without that faith – it jars. It is chaotic, infuriating and oppressive. For me, it was hell. But to those who believe, who can see beyond the temporal, rest assured, it is nothing short of paradise.

The Final Push

45. Return to Rakhi

Vicky had been teasing me for months, little hints here and there, that there might be a surprise in store for me on my return to Kolkata. Once in the city, with the pressures of filming upon us, it became impossible for her to keep the secret any longer. The team had arranged for me to catch up with Geeta at the Hope Foundation, and with little Rakhi, the pesky, brilliant street kid I'd fallen in love with some three years earlier.

ME: How is she? Tell me! Tell me!
VICKY: (*beaming*) You'll have to wait and see . . .

That sounded good. Everything sounded good. I was trilling with excitement. What was she doing? Was she off the streets? In school, perhaps? Would she remember that night when we played in the streets all that time ago?

We parked up in a familiar street. Olly went on ahead to mike up Rakhi. I stayed behind, waiting excitedly. I could just make out the silhouette of Geeta further up the road and started grinning from ear to ear. It took all my energy not to run up the road to them and smother them all in a giant hug.

Twenty minutes later Olly returned.

ME: How is she? Is she well? Does she look good? What news?
OLLY: Yeah. Yeah . . .

His voice trailed away.

ME: What?

OLLY: Yeah, she's . . . she's different.

A warning bell sounds – faint but audible.

It was time to go. 'Speed,' said Matt, walking backwards, taking yet another personal leap of faith as his trainers skirted a turd.

I wandered towards the group. Two girls were standing, one side on, the other looking away. Both were in regulation navy school uniform. I felt a strange anxiety as I approached. Geeta waved. The girl standing side on waved. The girl with her back to me didn't turn around.

That girl was Rakhi.

Geeta and I hugged. Rakhi looked down at the ground.

I wanted to grab her and hold her close, but my hands fell limp at my side, superfluous.

ME: Hey, Rakhi.

She turned to face me. It was then I knew. Her eyes, which had held the sparkle of polished glass, were now dull and unfocused. It was like she was looking through us, all of us, in an effort to see something or somewhere else.

The other little girl was Rekha, Rakhi's sister who I hadn't had the chance to meet on my last trip. She was happy and full of chat, which made the difference between them all the more painful.

We headed into a café and ordered tea. Rakhi seemed disturbed by the hiss of the water boiling. When we sat down, I noticed that she would constantly look around her. Every sound, every sudden movement, would prompt a glance backwards or a frightened shift in her seat.

I know what this is. I know it all too well. This is a stress response. This is the behaviour of someone who has been bent out of shape by fear. I wander outside and grab a moment with Geeta. It doesn't take a genius to work out that Rakhi is a very different girl from the one I met three years ago.

GEETA: There are some boys, calling for her at night. And that scared her. She now understands that she has to protect her body. And that reality is hitting her hard. So that is reflected in her face.

I feel like a fool. I know Rakhi for moments. I see her in snapshots, framed by sentiment, without context. Without the grinding reality that is bringing her down. What a fool I am to think she would be untouched. You cannot live on the street and not be eaten alive by it.

I can feel a pressure building in my head. I want to burst. Now is not the time. Rakhi is rocking from side to side, one foot to another. Her head swivelling round and round. She taps her chin rhythmically with her index finger. This is a symptom of PTSD.

ME: Does your sister take good care of you?

A beat.

ME: Do you think anybody can take care of you?

Nothing. Just rocking.

And then, finally, she speaks. Geeta translates:

RAKHI: I just want a good sleep in a safe place at night.

Think of the simplicity of that request as it falls on Western ears – a good sleep in a safe place. It is a request verging on the banal where we come from. Here, on the streets, it is a virtual impossibility. It is nothing but a vague dream, held in the out-of-reach place.

But that's OK, I thought. I can fix that. I can sort her somewhere. I have money. I will give her family money. It seems like an easy solution, and to suggest it exposes my ignorance – because easy doesn't exist in her world. The truth is that both girls could have a place in a boarding school, but Rakhi is too scared to go.

REKHA: She's frightened of a ghost because a man died by the school.

Only Rakhi can overcome this fear. Money can't do it. My insistence that there are no ghosts can't do it.

There's another reason she doesn't want to go away to school – she doesn't want to leave her dad. Her dad is a kind, sweet man who has brought up his children alone. He earns pennies selling buckets on the streets. It's an impossible decision for the girls. Do they go to school, pursue their dream of becoming doctors, or be around their only surviving parent and help him, like he has tried to help them?

Rakhi is stuck in a prison of limitations, both physical and mental that is so complex it's painful to watch.

What was I expecting? Fun? A fun sequence? Fun doesn't feature when you're an adolescent kid sleeping on the street. Danger does. That kid I met three years ago doesn't exist any more. She's been whittled down by poverty and fear. The camera rolled, and I cried because of all the potential wasted, the trajectory thwarted. And I raged because of how angry I felt at those predatory boys, possibly victims themselves, who had no idea how a look or a word could transform a young woman's world.

And then, almost inevitably, Steve asked for a version in

which I wasn't crying as much, or swearing as much, and I said, 'Go fuck yourself, Steve.' And he nodded, because he got that sometimes rage and expletives and tears are the only, and perfectly natural, human response to this God-awful situation.

Real help is hard to give. Things must happen slowly. And that's the most difficult understanding of all. There is no quick fix.

But it's OK, because I have time. I have time, Rakhi – and I am not going anywhere.

46. The Sundarbans

I head further south. The wind gets up and the air begins to clear as the river widens to greet the sea. I am in the Sunderbans, a cluster of low-lying islands in the Bay of Bengal famed for its unique mangrove forests. Not only is this delta a haven for many rare and endangered species, it's also home to over four and a half million people.

It is hard to imagine a more delicately balanced ecosystem than this one, and yet it's under constant threat. Land reclamation, logging and shrimp farming all contribute to an erosion of the landscape, which, if continued unchecked, could prove nothing short of calamitous to the region. The mud flats and vast tangle of mangrove roots that stretch along the coastline of India and Bangladesh, where land meets sea, where freshwater meets seawater, are Nature's own shield, providing protection from cyclones to the dense population surrounding it. To destroy the mangroves is to offer the earth up, unchecked, to the raging elements.

Life is precarious on the Sundarbans, its residents living on a sliver of land barely above sea level. The fishermen feel this pinch more than most. The river is no longer yielding the catches it used to so now they gamble with their lives, venturing beyond the licensed fishing areas into the protected forests of the Bengal tiger reserve. The rewards are great: vast hauls of crab and snakes. The potential risks, however, are horrendous.

To highlight the hazardous existence of the Sundarban people, we had arranged to meet a widow whose husband had been killed while venturing into the tiger reserve. I am not quite sure how it happened, but due to some awful mistake in the translation process, it became clear on our arrival that this woman was still very much in the whirlwind of shock. It turned out she had not lost her husband six months ago, as we'd been led to believe, but just a few weeks previously. She was still reeling with the trauma, and faintly rocking forwards and back, as if her core was so shattered by grief she could be buffeted by every gust of wind that hit her frame.

There was no way we were going to interview her. I ended up just holding her. She leant into my shoulder, almost burying her head in my armpit, and I put my arms around her and rocked her as she sobbed. I held her and held her until her body stopped vibrating and the sun fell and her daughters called her in for her evening meal.

We took a boat out to the reserve to see where the fishermen felt desperate enough to stray. Our boat, however, wasn't a tiny wooden vessel like theirs, low to the water and susceptible to a tiger attack: ours was a larger, sturdier affair.

I travelled out with a crew of government agents tasked with maintaining the perimeter fence of the tiger sanctuary. On first glance, they looked like something out of *Dad's Army*, with their tin helmets and knackered batons. I stared across to the mud flat and wondered what my chances would be.

I didn't need to wonder for long: their leader made it abundantly clear.

ME: What would happen if you walked across that mud flat?

LEADER: You would get eaten. Three seconds.

He looked me up and down.

LEADER: You? Maybe two.

There was relish in his voice. I wondered if he made a habit of calculating the exact time it would take a predator to bring down a tourist – and if, indeed, he had put a clock on his own mortality. Everyone needs a hobby, I guess.

The brigade left the safety of the boat and hopped onto the bank. They were wearing safari shorts and wellies. The wet earth sucked at their feet, plunging them deep into the mud, each boot buried a good twelve inches deep. You couldn't run here, even if you tried. You would just sink into the clutches of the sandy soil and await the inevitable.

The men seemed remarkably unfazed, all things considered – going about their work with minimum fuss. One produced an old rifle with a chipped wooden butt and trained it on an area of perimeter fencing. He began shouting at his co-workers. His crew pottered round the fence, checking it for holes, and shouted back when they found one.

ME: Listen, I know I'm not an animal expert, but is that a good idea? The shouting?

Their captain merely shrugged his shoulders.

ME: Only . . . might it alert the tigers?

My voice was drowned out by more shouting and some laughter, as one of the men went inside the reservation to check the camera traps. I guess his mate with the rifle was supposed to protect him, but he was too busy screaming at a co-worker, the muzzle pointing, rather unhelpfully, skywards.

I can only assume that the tigers were full and simply

couldn't be bothered to venture out for another kill. But I stayed put on the boat, just in case.

~~~

Ganga Sagar is the largest of the Sundarban Sagar islands and, mercifully, tiger-free. It is a place of Hindu pilgrimage, and home, on 14 January each year, to one of the largest human gatherings on the planet.

On this day, over two million Hindus come to the water's edge to take a dip at the confluence of the Ganges and the Bay of Bengal in a festival known as the Ganga Sagar Mela. The year we visited, it was designated a Green Mela, an eco-initiative attempting to curb the devastating littering of the site which occurs when the pilgrims descend. It was a great idea but, having witnessed it first hand, I am not sure it achieved what those in advertising like to call 'brand penetration'.

There were plenty of signs up, for sure. It was just that no one seemed to read them. There were thousands of Portaloos too, with men and women in high-vis jackets explaining to the rural visitors how to use one. No one wanted to, preferring to use Mother Nature as their bathroom. The tannoys, slung from every pole on the island, blared forth environmental messages, but no one was listening.

There's a reason Hindu visitors disregard all attempts to clean up the river. It's not a case of stupidity – far from it. It's a case of faith. Hindus believe that the Ganges is their mother – Ma Ganga. The mother will provide, the mother is strong, and you cannot hurt the mother because she lives for
~~~

ever. When we drop a plastic bottle into the ocean, we know the consequences. When a devout Hindu does the same, even if he or she is fully cognizant of the environmental catastrophe the planet is facing, there is the unflinching belief that nothing, *nothing*, can ever damage the eternal parent. To even suggest such a thing could cause offence.

Boatloads of pilgrims arrived on the island from all over India, but mainly, it seemed, Gujarat. Extended families gathered together and shared food from the vast vats of dal and rice cooking over open fires. Above them sat large vinyl signs saying, 'No Fires', and a diagram of a flame with a cross over it. Nope, they're still not listening. As dusk fell and the temperature dropped, over two million people huddled under their saris and shivered in their kurtas, waiting for the sun to rise and give them some much-needed warmth.

We were staying in a government block in the middle of the throng, a single-storey concrete cube with overhead strip-lighting that took you, with the flick of a switch, from darkness to the full Wembley Stadium. Even the cockroaches stopped in their tracks when the fluoros reached full capacity, so dazzling were the lumens on display.

We had been told that the most auspicious time to enter the water was 05:17 a.m. However, being tourists, we assumed we knew better, and decided we'd start filming around 07:30 a.m. I got into bed around 1 a.m. and turned the bedroom floodlight off.

At that point, just as my head hit the pillow, the tannoys kicked in again. Every few minutes there would be the whine of feedback and another muffled bellow emerging from the speakers that surrounded us. I lay there for an hour, vainly trying to kip, before turning the lights back on again. Catherine, our fabulous producer, was wide awake, as were the entire crew. We might as well put our pants on and get out there.

Outside, on the main drag, it was like a grungy Glastonbury – balls of beige street food bounced around in vats of oil, trinkets were for sale, families were singing. We turned left and followed the strong stench of marijuana until we came across a row of *naga sadhus*, naked men in little huts, covered with ash and ganja'd out of their minds.

Each priest sat there, proudly displaying his dusty junk. It was a veritable boulevard of bollocks, a sack smorgasbord. In one hand they held some peacock feathers, which they would smash down over your head by way of a blessing. Their other hand was open and extended in that classic religious gesture – *give me money*.

We wandered all night, greeting strangers, sharing food with families. By the time we made it to the beach it was just after 5 a.m. and dawn was about to break. Next to me were thousands upon thousands of pilgrims, all barefoot. Some came with their grandparents, some held little children, and a surprising number had even brought their cows all the way here for a blessing.

I took off my shoes and socks and walked towards the water with them. A gentle lap, meniscus deep, started to spread over the cold sand.

I hadn't known what to expect. Frankly, I get twitchy when someone puts a windbreak down within a hundred metres of me so I'd been a little anxious at the thought of sharing a beach with such a vast throng. But I didn't feel claustrophobic. I felt strangely clear. Free. Elated. And ready for a dip.

I began to experience a strange sensation, almost out of body. I looked at my watch. It was exactly 5.17 a.m. The sky was a baby pink. To my left, low on the horizon, was the sun, and to my right, in perfect alignment with it, a full moon. They cast a direct line across the sky, with all of us as the central point. It was the first time I had truly inhabited what the word 'auspicious' meant. How lucky I am. How truly lucky.

It was time for me to give my final piece to camera. As always, I hadn't planned what to say, but something came out that seemed to wrap things up. What was more important to me was what I didn't say: the understanding that this place had given me over the course of this pilgrimage – an understanding that was just for me, and not for television.

Grief doesn't have a narrative arc. It doesn't fit the media storyboard. I didn't arrive on a mountain, devastated and shocked, and then move to a place of resolution, by an ocean, some four months later. The truth is, I didn't get over my dad dying. You don't. Your heart keeps its own clock. It doesn't care for hours and minutes; for the fake lines of measurement, which the outside life uses to calculate success, age or achievement.

The heart has a tempo all of its own, curious and unique. It isn't linear, it loops back and forth – it can inhabit multiple spaces, all at once. In my heart, it is always 3.30 p.m. on the final day of March. My hand is on your chest and I can feel that final, gentle pulse under my palm. It is always the summer of 1975 and I have mumps and you are making up a bedtime story about a hyperactive squirrel, which doesn't quite make sense. In my heart, you are always happy and sad, well and ill, alive and dead. You are all things, in all times and places, good and bad, in my heart for ever. My beloved dad.

You don't get beyond this place. Ever. This is your place now.

Grief has no final piece to camera. There is no pithy

up-sum. It doesn't come as a realization or a learning. It is just there, as black is there, and you learn to accommodate it. One day, you may even take its hand and acknowledge you are no longer strangers. Then you'll go on. Different. Damaged.

But you go on.

~

I am home. My suitcase wheels turn for the last time and find rest in the thick hall carpet.

I walk upstairs to the bathroom. The heated tiles warm my bare feet. I lean my face against the flat, smooth plaster and switch on the light. I switch it off again. And on. And off. I stare at the cleanliness of it all. The order. I know it is quiet, but I can't make out the silence yet. My ears are still full of India.

Anna comes and finds me – finds a mad woman, with hair that smells of planes, standing there switching the lights on and off.

ANNA: What the hell are you doing, Bug?

She calls me Bug.

ME: Look at it. Isn't it wonderful?

Isn't all of this just wonderful?

Acknowledgements

Since these are the acknowledgments, I have waived my natural aversion to lists.

Thanks and love to:

Ann Perkins, Croydon's very own prepper. Thanks for making us apocalypse-ready, Mum.

David, who can rustle up a twelve-course buffet with less than five minutes' notice.

Michelle, who has had to take on the role of eldest child since the *actual* oldest child is an incompetent oaf.

My in-laws, Pete and Lynne, for wine and song.

And my incredible nieces, Ellie and Anna.

I love you all. You're nuts, but I love you.

My darling chums, you know who you are – I'm so lucky to have you.

The Giedroyc family.

Emma and Georgie, for being there where it really mattered. I'm sorry I've repaid you by routinely whipping your arses at poker.

Kate Barsby, for characteristic brilliance with the cover artwork.

Debi Allen, my friend and agent, who saw me shouting in a hot room in Edinburgh in 2006 and decided to take a chance on me.

My US manager, Marcia McManus, for her resolute belief that, despite the fact that I am a myopic forty-nine-year-old woman, with a paunch, I will one day crack America.

Charlene McManus, Jess Molloy, Emily Harris, Linda Kay and Jessica Lax. Without you, I would never know where to go, when to go and how on earth to get there. Please never leave me. I've forgotten how to do life when you're not around.

Louise Moore, for her faith and persistence. I'm sorry I don't understand the nature of a deadline.

Rowland White, for deft stewardship and lengthy lunches. Now *that's* the way I like to work.

All the Michael Joseph team; especially Bea, Ariel, and Hazel for making sure everything was porepr;y speelchecked and in its place.

Thanks to Roy McMillan, the audiobook producer, for his sweetness and his sensitivity; and for enduring four days in a locked box with me, listening to my stomach gurgle.

Charlotte Moore, for opening the doors on a whole new world.

Clare Paterson and Lucy Carter for their wisdom and care.

Steve, Vicky, Matt and Olly and all who worked on the shows at Indus and Folk. I hope I have done our fantastic adventures justice.

The families of the Mekong and the Ganges who let me into their homes and their lives.

The staff of the NHS who work so tirelessly, and in such straightened circumstances, to help us when we need it most. Special thanks to Dr Jones, the palliative care gang at West Cornwall and Mr Talbot and his team at Treliske.

Tig, for reminding me that joy comes when you least expect it.

The Richardson family, and in particular their magnificent daughter,

Anna, whom I love.

How to help:

If you'd like to sponsor a child in Kolkata, visit:
https://www.thehopefoundation.org.uk

You can donate to the wonderful book boat in Laos here: http://www.communitylearninginternational.org/projects/the-book-boat/

x

Discover the woman behind the spectacles in Sue Perkins' memoir...

Available now